How to Change
Someone You Love

How to Change Someone You Love

FOUR STEPS TO HELP

YOU HELP THEM

BRAD LAMM

ST. MARTIN'S PRESS ⁄M NEW YORK

www.stmartins.com

Book design by Jessica Shatan Heslin/Studio Shatan, Inc.

ISBN 978-0-312-59082-6

First Edition: January 2010

10   9   8   7   6   5   4   3   2   1

Author's Note

The names and identifying characteristics of many of the individuals in this book have been changed. Many of the case studies represent composites in order to better illustrate common problems and their resolutions.

In loving memory of Leona Lamm—
my grandma in every sense of the word

Contents

PART III

OVERCOMING COMMON BARRIERS TO CHANGE

PART IV

PRACTICAL APPLICATIONS:

COPE WITH THE PEOPLE IN YOUR LIFE AND

RESTORE YOUR RELATIONSHIPS

Acknowledgments

To my family and friends, you have my love. To the many I have touched through my work, you have my gratitude. Thank you for letting me share my hope as we work on getting better together.

To Maggie Greenwood-Robinson, my heartfelt thanks. You helped me make it all read right. To Todd Shuster, my thanks, as you made me write right. Drew, Paul, Steven, and Brian, my thanks for the creative help.

To Jennifer Enderlin and all at St. Martin's Press, thanks for the opportunity to bring my change message to many more people. My publisher, Sally Richardson, thank you; thank you for inviting me in.

There are so many fingerprints on my recovered hide. Thanks to each; you know who you are. Jerry. Scott. Mark. Kelly. Bryant. Cathay. Corey. Jeremy. Alfredo. Fabio. Jonathan. John. Chet. Jeanette. Freddy.

And my great Scott—here's to our family and all the love.

To all of you who want to change someone in your life: Lead with love and purpose, and you cannot mess it up!

Change Begins

Let me ask you: Are there people in your life who need to clean up their act? Kick bad habits? Get their lives back on track?

If you're tired of watching your spouse, child, relative, or best friend go downhill, dragging you with them, I will help you turn their lives around. You don't have to endure behavior that is unhealthy, abusive, and possibly deadly, and that threatens to unravel relationships. You can change it.

Many books will tell you that you can't change anyone. They advise you to not even try. The problem is, they ignore the tremendous power you actually have to change people. This book is different. You have the power to change your spouse, your children, your relatives, your in-laws, your coworkers, and your friends; but most of us don't know how to tap into it. Every page of this book will give you the faith to act and turn your hopes into reality.

While most books about change are written for the addict or troubled person, *How to Change Someone You Love* reaches out to the loved ones of that person—loved ones who know that change is critical and urgent. On these pages, I offer you a one-of-a-kind set of tools to help you put aside so much of the conventional psychobabble about not intervening, not seeking to control the "Universe," and not creating a codependent relationship.

Instead, I will help you make thoughtful, coolheaded, loving, lifesaving decisions to intervene and initiate change. Put another way: *This is not just a self-help program; this is a help-you-act program.*

It *will* help you act too: Stop your husband from drinking himself to death. Keep your brother from losing it all to gambling. Get your kid off drugs. Motivate your best friend to lose weight. Make your spendthrift brother-in-law stop maxing out his credit cards. Get your sister out of an abusive relationship. Erase the anger in your coworker.

I will show you how to eliminate people's negative behavior, even when they repeatedly resist getting help—and put them on a path of healing. You can trigger lasting change—and do it with compassion, acceptance, family strength, and most of all, love. As a former addict who has devoted my life to helping others, I know firsthand what it takes to break the cycle of negative and self-defeating patterns of various types and degrees.

But how? You've tried everything. Or have you?

Maybe not. You're about to discover some techniques *you've never tried before*. They don't involve nitpick nagging, pleading, begging, arguing, bribing, protecting, reprimanding, punishing, manipulating, or ambush-type interventions, but rather a loving, truthful method of changing others for the better—and changing your life in the process.

I'll show you an effective four-step process that gets a person to accept help so change can begin. Yes, it is an "intervention," but not the type you've heard about or have seen on TV. Most interventions are confrontational, a stressful surprise attack on a person that can end in damaged relationships, hard feelings, and a deep sense of betrayal and alienation. By contrast, my method invites the troubled person to participate from the beginning. There's no secrecy, no ambush, no ganging up on someone— just a loving, courageous process carried out by concerned family and friends.

My program helps you support a friend or loved one in conquering all sorts of troublesome behavior: weight gain, eating disorders, addictions, credit and debt problems, compulsive shopping, sexual issues, moodiness, abuse, anxiety, Internet obsessions, poor schoolwork, noncompliance with medical treatments, and more.

In *How to Change Someone You Love*, I'll show you how to:

▶ *Determine whether the problem that's getting on your nerves is an uncomplicated one, likely to clear up with time, or something more serious that requires action.*

▶ *Use my simple, effective four-step program to create lasting, often lifesaving change.*

▶ *Take on and beat your own fears and reluctance to step up to the problem.*

▶ *Remove and overcome the external dynamics and obstacles that stand in the way of your motivating necessary change.*

▶ *Discover your number-one source of power—and plug into it—to help others change for good.*

My message is one of hope and encouragement. It will help you claim your power, keep you from looking at someone's resistance as final, and let you see that you can help restore a loved one to his or her full potential. My belief is that when you tap into your personal and family strengths, any set of circumstances, from the off-putting to the addictive, can be turned around, with lives changed forever.

So before you divorce your husband, fire your employee, or write off your best friend, take a good, long deep breath and read this book. Whether they drink it, smoke it, touch it, sniff it, spend it, gamble it, eat it, Google it, obsess over it, cry about it, or drive you up a wall with it, I will help you get your loved ones to stop doing whatever it is that's destroying them. Change is about to begin—from the troublesome to the addictive and everything in between. With this book as your guide, I'll help you find the answers you seek, the answers you deserve, and the understanding you must have to help people become the best they can be. It's not just about changing someone else's life either. It's also about changing yours.

PART I

At the End of

Your Rope Is Hope

ONE

You've Got the Power!

If anyone needed to change, it was me.

From the time I was a teenager, I had a preoccupation with catching a buzz. The son of a preacher, I grew up in a drug- and alcohol-free home in Eugene, Oregon. Our house, situated on an acre of land, was a neat, modest wood-frame home on Kirkwood Street, a road away from my father's church. Our house was surrounded by azaleas, rosebushes, towering oak trees, and a large lawn that I and my three brothers mowed regularly. There was a garden in our backyard where we grew a lot of our own food, and we were able to can a season's worth of fruit and vegetables. Folks from the church, many of them farmers and fishermen, would stop by with beef, lamb, salmon, and crab to fill our two large freezers. There were sidewalks, neighbors waving from their porches, and schools within walking distance of my house. Life in Eugene was largely predictable and tranquil.

But mine was not. I was born with a birth defect: abnormal breast tissue. In other words, I had boobs. I looked like I needed a bra. I refused to take a shower at school, and my secret was something I tried to keep. But in fifth grade, I was exposed by a coach who took delight in making sure I was always a "skin"—that is, assigned to the team that had to take their shirts off to play ball. "Look at Lamm's tits!" the coach would yell. It was cruel.

To be laughed at. To be different. To be in fear of discovery. It just hurt way too much. I decided one day that I should kill myself—and confessed my intention to my parents. They were shocked: "We never brought it up because we didn't want you to be even more self-conscious," they said.

My emotional crisis forced a decision on their part—to correct my deformity as soon as possible. At age fifteen, I had surgery, and voila, the outside had changed. Yes, the physical was improved, fixed. But the birth deformity, although corrected, left me feeling damaged emotionally; the psychological scars of being laughed at and mocked as a kid still remained. For most of my life, I felt like I didn't belong, like I could never belong, like every room I walked into was an unwelcome one.

The same year I had the surgery, I attended a Christmas party at a retirement home where I played the piano on Sunday mornings for the old folks' church service. When no one was looking, I snuck a bottle of champagne, locked myself in a bathroom, and chugged it down. My first experience with alcohol equalized all the unease with which I lived. Gradually, alcohol became something I felt I needed desperately, in order to remove my insecurities, make me feel like I fit in, and provide relief from my feelings. The more alcohol something had, the better, and I conscientiously read the bottle labels to make sure I was getting the highest proof available.

My drinking escalated. At the beginning of my freshman year in college, I'd get drunk before classes, then snort cocaine to boot myself out the door. As time went on, drugs of all types became a fixation, especially cocaine. It was an obsession, lord and master over my life, all I ever thought about.

I decided to leave college at age nineteen. My life at that point had become an endless series of flirtations with recovery from drugs and alcohol, yet I always ended up right back where I started: in the drugs, the alcohol, and the nicotine. I was self-medicating with everything that could release me from the pain I felt. My grandma Lamm called my pain "a bag of dead chickens." "Why do you insist on carrying it around everywhere you go?" she'd say.

Of course, she was right. I needed to drop the bag to get better. But I couldn't. To do so would mean I would have to do something about my addiction; I would have to face the dreaded *c* word: *change*. I was not ready for that. The thought of living without my crutch was too frightening.

I decided to "find myself" and settled in Kamakura, Japan, an ancient seaside city, where I lived in a picturesque hillside home near the beach. I taught piano and English, studied Japanese and Buddhism, and wrote music. I bought fresh fish from the local fishermen. I cooked healthy foods, tried to live a healthy lifestyle, and worked to fix the pain I felt through spiritual exploration and dedicated self-discovery.

I wasn't doing hard drugs, but I was doing alcohol, mainly beer and wine, and sometimes to the point of blacking out. The beer was making me fat. I smoked to control my appetite and keep the weight off. I binged and even purged when I had eaten too much. If it wasn't one thing, it was another! I hated my lack of self-control. I prayed daily for strength. "Please God, relieve me from this!" But I felt my prayers went unheard and unanswered, or maybe I just wasn't worth being listened to. Maybe I was too damaged by my past—that sack of dead, rotting chickens I kept lugging around. I wondered, too, if maybe God had turned his back on me.

One Saturday afternoon, while browsing in a little office supply shop, I slipped a book of Shinto prayers in my pocket. I rationalized that it was okay to reward myself by stealing something, since I hadn't drunk anything for five days. I deserved to get something for nothing. Not for nothing, as it turned out. A security guard pulled me aside, and within minutes I was surrounded by guards, speaking a hundred miles an hour in a language I barely understood. They threatened to call the police, but in the end I cried my way out of it and charmed my way back to my moped. I went straight home and drank until I passed out.

After I awoke, I read a prayer in I Corinthians 10:13 and claimed it: *No temptation has seized you except what is common to man. And God is faithful; he will not let you be tempted beyond what you can bear. But when you are tempted, he will also provide a way out so that you can stand up under it.*

But to no avail.

My way out always led back to another unanswered prayer. Was I not praying hard enough? Or was I maybe a hopeless case, as I feared? I always ended up back where I'd begun, which was nowhere—fast.

Then one day a solution came to mind—the notion that if I moved to

New York City (the center of the universe in my mind), I could make the connection, find the answers I lacked, and moderate what I had been unable to control. Within a week, I was packed up, ready to go. I would make a fresh new start of it! I took boxes of a life that I'd cobbled together to the post office and mailed them to New York. I kissed my friends good-bye, and closed the latest broken chapter of my life, promising myself that the future would be better.

This was a fantasy, and the reality was far from it. Within a short time of arriving stateside, I landed a job as doorman at the world-renowned Limelight nightclub. I was in heaven or hell, depending on your view. Drug dealers slipped me drugs each night if I would let them in. Alcohol and cocaine were always a handshake away.

A chance meeting, while I was working the Limelight door, led to a job hosting an entertainment show that aired in six cities. Turned out I was pretty good in front of a TV camera. A man named Conrad Shadlin, the top agent for weather anchors on television at the time, took notice. He wrote me a letter and wanted to take me on as a client. He promised he'd train me on how to be an on-air personality and teach me how to do the weather. I signed on. Maybe he would lead to my prayers being answered.

My first gig as a weather guy was in Boise, Idaho. The year was 1996. My parents and brother Scott lived there too, and I was happy to be reunited with them. Life in Boise would be a fresh start. I promised myself (again) that I was done with drinking. I swore that I would never do drugs again. I wore a nicotine patch on my shoulder. This would be the time everything clicked for me! I loaded my car and headed for Boise. But by the time I was through New Jersey, I had ripped off the patch and lit a cigarette. I resumed drinking within a week. I tried to stop, and was in and out of 12-step meetings in Boise.

I reported the weather on the morning show three hours a day live, Monday through Friday. I threw myself into my work and became something of a local celebrity about town. I loved what I did and who I was becoming—a son, a brother, a friend, a local star! Yet alcohol was still my constant companion and first love.

I'd get home from work, start drinking, and not stop until I passed out. The alarm would ring at 3 A.M. I'd shower, get coffee'd up, and be back on the job. During this time, I struggled like never before with bulimia, purging to control the weight I was gaining from alcohol and food binges. I was desperate to stay thin and avoid those "ten pounds" they say being on television adds on you. To heal, I tried prayer. I tried fasting. I tried begging for change from a higher power, and yet there I would land, alone in my house with my dogs, a pack of smokes, and a glass of something that would take me away.

In 2000, my agent got me a better job in Washington, D.C., doing weather in one of the top ten markets in the country. This was my dream job. I had arrived. But within weeks of landing in D.C., I was snorting cocaine again, in addition to everything else. I had inexplicably drifted deeper into addiction. When push came to shove, the addiction always won.

Coke and alcohol made me feel safe. I felt completely sure of myself. Drugs took away all my fears. They did that socially, distancing me from other people, making me feel less vulnerable. They did that professionally, drugging me through the stresses of work. The Xanax I gulped by the handful made my job as a TV weather guy easier and lighter—and the weather, well, better.

Once, while delivering the weather on the noon broadcast, I started sweating, even though it was sixty-five degrees in the studio—a result of all the drugs I was taking, along with the bile gurgling up in my throat. It was like the scene from the movie *Broadcast News* where Albert Brooks's character, a newscaster, starts sweating and never stops. I explained it away with excuses and lies: "I have a fever. . . ." or "My blood sugar must have gotten too low. . . ."

I eventually replaced cocaine with crystal meth, a sniffable form of speed, to control my weight. My first experiences with it were so pleasurable that I didn't think there could be anything else that exhilarating. The drug had cracked open a door, letting in a paranoia that was malevolent and insane. Late one night, I tried to pry a molar out of my jaw with pliers, convinced that someone was listening in to my conversations through an implant in the tooth.

My life took on a deeply fragmented quality, with different personas emerging and becoming more distinct but also more false. At work, I was the composed weather anchor; after work, I was the addict, throwing back double vodkas and sniffing crystal meth with abandon. I didn't know who I was, severed from the thread that led to the real me.

In the mornings, I'd look in the mirror and think, "What happened?" I had the résumé of a model citizen, not a common drunk. Hometown: Eugene, Oregon. Occupation: weather anchor. Parents: beloved minister and devoted mother, both of whom raised me in an alcohol-free home with lots of love.

In other words, nice person, from a decent middle-class family. Why couldn't I beat my addictions? Of course, there is no simple answer. Trying to describe the process of becoming an addict is like trying to describe space. It's too big and mysterious and pervasive to be defined. All you know is that you can't live without the escape.

I went through countless detoxes to get cleaned up. But I didn't keep the post-detox promises. Active addicts try, and active addicts fail. That's how it works. I made the promises, and I really did try to keep them. But I kept rationalizing the third drink or the fourth or fifth. "Just today." "Bad day." "I deserve a reward," I told myself. "I'll stop tomorrow."

I was existing in a state of self-imposed chaos, lying and hiding and keeping secrets and feeling trapped, absolutely trapped, in the whole mess. Sickened, drained, unable to feel—it was perpetual numbness. No sadness, no happiness, no highs, no lows. Nothing. This is why an addiction like mine was so difficult to kick. My pleasure receptors were so fried that my brain no longer had the ability to feel any pleasure on its own. When you're this addicted, you're so depressed that you want to get high, again and again. By turns, I wanted to die, or be delivered.

All told, I spent twenty years living in active addiction. Then scary realities began to intrude on my life, ultimately triggering my change away from drugs. At age thirty-five, I started to notice that tiny blood vessels had begun to burst all along my nose and cheeks. My doctor told me my liver was in bad shape. A tremor in my hands developed, then grew worse, then persisted for longer periods, all day sometimes. Active addiction is heartbreaking and cruel. It took me to a place of desperation and loneliness, of unrelenting pain and humiliation.

One day, during a brief moment of lucidity, terrifying realities dawned on me: It might just be a matter of time before I drove home drunk one night and ran someone down or ended up in jail or lost my job. I really might kill myself if I kept living the way I was living.

Then along came my friend and business associate, Paul. Six months earlier, Paul and a group of three guy friends had been instrumental in getting me to resume therapy to tackle my alcohol and drug use. I had stopped the crystal meth, but finally failed at moderating the alcohol consumption. My drinking was off the charts. Ironically, by that point, I didn't even enjoy drinking. The fun had stopped more than a decade earlier. But the patterns of behavior had become so ingrained, so enmeshed in my brain chemistry, that getting between me and my addiction was like prying apart two pieces of metal that have been welded together.

But Paul, bless his heart, had not given up on me. He called me at noon one day. Six times. "Call me back," he said on the voice mail. "Okay, this is the fifth call . . . call me back, Brad." I could barely get out of bed to finally pick up the phone. I was sick—sick from being up all night drinking. I wasn't sure what had transpired the night before but I sensed it hadn't been anything good. I didn't even know how I got home. Paul wanted to meet for a late lunch.

I knew I was a mess and I knew I didn't want to die. Because I was afraid of losing my livelihood, and because I was afraid of losing my relationship with him, I showered, dressed, and headed to meet him. Paul urged me again to get help. He told me what he had seen, which is what I advise friends and family to do today: "We made a deal six months ago that you'd moderate— that you'd slow it down, or stop if that's what was needed. But you didn't. You're a very sick, chronic addict, and I believe you're going to die out there unless you go away and get help right away."

I respected Paul; his voice mattered to me. But I wanted to scream, "But you don't understand. I'm a preacher's kid. I play the piano at church. I was on TV." I knew he was right. I was thirty-five and desperate and was sick, sick, sick. And I needed help.

I was so beaten down and so tired that when I met with him, I said yes to help. I said, "I will do what you tell me to do." I knew he cared for me. I knew he had love for me as a friend. If you'd asked me that day if I was "done" with the addictions, I would have said that I needed to learn how to drink less. Honestly, I didn't consider giving up drugs altogether.

Not that I liked any of it—the smoking, the drinking, the drugs. It's just that the bar was so low to what I thought was possible that I didn't believe I could actually ever stop and stay stopped.

I was like a boat adrift at sea, and Paul had been the wind filling my sails and carrying me in a direction I had no real say in. I allowed myself to be navigated, and so began my own journey of change and restoration.

My therapist suggested a treatment center in Minnesota called Hazelden. But stubbornly, I went online to research another one that looked like a spa. I remember clearly thinking that if I could just get away for a bit— get off the merry-go-round of my life and get some good therapy—that perhaps I could fix what ailed me.

That next morning, with bags packed, I headed to the airport, boarded a plane, and admitted myself to treatment in Laguna Beach, California. I had not raised a white flag and surrendered in my heart. I did not consider myself "done." But I had said yes to help, and that was a start.

The last time I had a drink was on that plane on the fourth day of February 2003. I ordered two double Bloody Marys. As I was drinking the second double, the little boy sitting next to me jabbed me with his finger and made a sign with four of his fingers. He had counted the four little empty blue bottles of SKYY vodka sitting on my tray table. "That's a lot!" he said. He didn't know the half of it.

With my head hung low (and $10,000 in cash in a FedEx envelope in case of emergency—remember, I was really not thinking clearly), I checked myself into treatment. The rehab provided a safe, therapeutic environment in which addicted folks like myself could get through their physical withdrawal (the detox part), then work on themselves and learn to navigate a drug- and alcohol-saturated world (the treatment part). I was not locked down, I could walk out anytime. From my bedroom window at rehab I could see a liquor store just across the street to remind me that the world was just ready and waiting to welcome me back into my addiction.

We had individual treatment plans designed to help us work through the guilt and shame that are part of addiction. Educational groups. Process groups. Groups. Groups! Groups!!! I was given a key that first day in just the schedule—what you've got to do, you are unlikely to do on your own.

Many addicts have underlying issues, such as depression, anxiety, childhood trauma, or sexual or domestic abuse. Many suffer from severe eating disorders or chronic pain, real or imagined. Others have lost people, places, and things that serve as daily reminders of what was—and push them toward a drink or drug or other harmful behavior. All of these are potential triggers to active addiction and need to be addressed to achieve a sustainable recovery. To stop and stay stopped is tough, dusty work, but change does begin—and so it did for me.

On day three at treatment, my counselor, Carol Coleman, looked me dead in the eyes, and told me I needed to crack open if I wanted to get well. "Brad, you're only as sick as your secrets . . . and until you start getting honest, you won't make it." Something clicked. I cried and cried like a dam had opened. The tears came out like something *had* cracked open inside me.

Recovery was rough, tough going. I spent hours tracing my relapse history and building a timeline of progression, identifying many of the feelings and thoughts that led to each setback. I had believed that my addiction marked me as a morally deficient individual. I believed that if I'd just tried a little harder, I could have handled it, and myself, better. But the reality was that by the time I got to the inpatient program, I began to understand that in the end, I had to come to terms with my disease. I really got it that I was sick—not a bad person—and I went from feeling like a mistake to feeling like a human being. In my heart, I knew my true recovery had begun.

My journey on the road to becoming whole, healed, and full of hope has been complicated, to say the least. That first year of radical change was the most difficult of my entire life. After all, I had spent decades building these patterns of behavior that codified and fed my addictions. Peeling those away from my life took consistent, hard work. I made many, many mistakes! The only mistake I didn't make was that I didn't pick up a drink or a drug. I learned to pick up the phone and talk with other people instead. My feet proved smarter than my head at many points. My feet led me to a 12-step meeting or other help when my brain said, "Go get loaded."

But then came a crisis point. At day 106 of my new life, I didn't believe I could make it without drugs or alcohol. I hit a wall big time. I had lost a lot following my return from rehab. Many things had changed.

I returned to work and found the locks had been changed—and a legal battle for compensation ensued. My relationship that I thought was the love to last a lifetime was in tatters and freefalling in a quick, painful spiral. Plus, I had worn myself down. Not enough food, sleep, or support. I was not thinking clearly on that springtime day, and the options seemed out of frame. Hopelessness had profoundly replaced the hope I was feeling. A drink suddenly seemed like a good idea.

I was in the midst of painful, self-revealing work in recovery that caused many feelings, faults, and frightening realities to become terribly evident. I was looking in the mirror like never before, and what I saw hurt like hell. I hurt more than I'd ever hurt before, with nothing to deaden the pain.

My mind hurt. My body ached and my spirit cried out, literally. I yelled into the air in my living room, "I CANNOT TAKE THIS ANYMORE!!!" I thought I could not make it without a drink or drug—and given that per-ceived reality, I decided it would be best that I killed myself. "At least I will die sober," I thought.

I sat down, calm and clear, but stretched spiritually so thin that I was like a thread just waiting to snap. I resolved to end my life.

Even as I write this now, tears fill my eyes, because the reality of that painful moment in time comes flooding back. I thought, "I will not pick up a drink or drugs—but there is no way I can live through this pain without them, so I must take my life."

Feelings are not facts, but at that very moment in time, I was unclear on that point, and the resolve I felt to take my life felt like victory in the face of inevitable relapse. I believed there was no way I could not drink and make it through this.

I wrote letters to seven people that early morning in a desperate scrawl. I sobbed and sobbed, alone and afraid but resolute. This is the way. I will not pick up a drink or a drug.

A hunting knife that had belonged to my grandpa Lamm was the object that I would use, I decided. He was an old farmer who hadn't much liked folks like me I reasoned; his knife seemed the right answer to a botched life like mine.

I paused to pray. When I paused, doubt crept in. I asked the question and was unsure of the answer. Would I go to Hell if I took my life? Would I be forgiven?

With that question in the front of my mind, sobbing, knife in pocket, letters in the other pocket, I climbed in my Jeep and drove to my church.

I had rejoined the church two years earlier in an attempt to set right my life. I thought if I reconnected with God, then maybe I'd have a chance. Pastor Candace and Pastor Phil welcomed me in, and I had a spiritual awakening of sorts. With the church's 500 members, I felt surrounded by love and a God who loved me. I donated more money than ever before, thinking perhaps that's what I'd done wrong in the past—been too materialistic. Give more away to get something more back?

That fateful day—day 106—I arrived late, wearing sunglasses to hide myself, and sat in the back row alone. Over the past two years, I had occasionally shown up at church in a similar disguise because I was still high on meth from the night before but still looking for answers.

Pastor Candace asked if anyone might come forward to pray with her. She asked, "Who here is in pain?" I stood up and headed forward. As she placed her hands on my shoulders, the entire congregation behind me, I wailed and cried and hurt. She asked me to bow my head, and she prayed to God in a soft, soothing voice. Her prayers on my behalf calmed my spirit.

I asked her, "I've decided to kill myself. It's the only way. Will I go to Hell if I take my life? I just cannot live without a drink." I was sobbing hard.

Pastor Candace led me to her office after service and talked with me for a while. I gave her the knife, and I never saw that thing again. She called my 12-step friend, Mark, who drove to the church and picked me up.

Paster Candace helped me in my struggle with addiction, and that day, I know, she saved my life. She is one of many who, along the way, helped me. I have not, could not, become well by myself.

The rest of that fateful day 106, a group of supportive friends surrounded me. I was fed, physically and spiritually, and that desperate moment passed. Today, as I write these words, more than 2,400 sober days have come and gone, in pain, joy, sorrow, gratitude, crisis, and dancing.

Make no mistake—I believe myself recovered. But I can unrecover, or lapse back in a moment. So it is important for me to take things one day at a time, maintaining a healthy respect for this disease.

Each day, I wake up with a choice, and by choosing not to drink, just for that day, I am a better son, friend, husband, and person. I choose to enjoy the gifts that come from a recovered life, a loving relationship with my family, the ability to help others through my work, and a strong faith.

Many years of sobriety have now accumulated; many small efforts have resulted in a family that loves me, a community that understands me, and professional acclaim. None of this has required me to go it alone without guidance or support from others. Admitting error and need has not been fatal. It added to the emotional fabric of my life and connected me to others. I became motivated to help people, and I believed there was a way to do that. So I took a leap of faith and became trained as an interventionist, to help family, friends, and others change someone they love.

Looking back, Paul and those three guy friends had done much to initiate change in my life. And that's the point of the work I do today. There is strength in numbers, and power in the love we have for the people in our lives.

And so in my work, I use a unique program crafted in love, one that anyone can use to get a person to change, no matter how many times attempts have failed in the past. Some of the very same techniques that led to my own change—a concerned friend giving "eyewitness" observations of my behavior, a heartfelt invitation to change, and a prearranged plan for help—are integral parts of the change process I use today. This method works, and is near-miraculous in its effectiveness.

PEOPLE CAN CHANGE

I understand that you may be a little skeptical right now. We tend to assume that people change rarely, slowly, with great difficulty, or not at all. We've been told that we're "hardwired" to think, feel, and act certain ways, that it's all set in stone at an early age. It's just the way we are.

In early studies, childhood psychologists often pegged the age of final jelling as early as five and as late as thirty. In other words, adults past their twenties should just forget about making meaningful changes.

Well, good news. This assumption is wrong, dead wrong. The truth is that people can change easily and, quite often, instantly. An irresponsible person can become a responsible one. A volatile, angry person can begin to be kind. A gossiper can become more discreet. A substance abuser can get sober. A spender can become a saver. I don't care what it is, every bad personality trait or unhealthy behavior can be turned around. People really can change and make their life (and yours) better.

All they need is a little help to shift their attitude, behavior, and spirit.

That's the key: *People need help to change,* particularly if they're engaged in self-destructive behaviors, they're emotionally unstable, they have huge mood swings, or they exhibit extreme combativeness or other corrosive behaviors that threaten to undo or destroy relationships. The most effective catalyst for changing another person is *you.* You may not see yourself as an influence on others, but that doesn't alter the fact that you are!

You see, people change, for better or worse, through their relationships with other people. Proof of this is everywhere. Take an example that made headlines not long ago: the phenomenon of obesity and thinness spreading through social networks. A landmark study published in *The New England Journal of Medicine* found that one person's obesity can significantly increase the chance that his or her friends, siblings, and spouse will also become heavy. And if a person slims down, the people around him or her also may lose weight. Both obesity and thinness are "socially contagious," concluded the study's authors. At the heart of the matter is the sharing of acceptable norms for weight, not just sharing the same eating-and-exercise habits. If someone you care about gains weight, your notion of an acceptable body size may change. You may decide it's okay to go up a couple of sizes. And surprisingly, the researchers found weight was not affected by geographic distance. If you have a close friend or a sibling who lives a mile or a thousand miles away, that person's weight gain or loss can have the same effect on your weight. In addition to gaining weight, behaviors like drinking and smoking can spread in social networks.

The same researchers have studied other aspects of change in which social networks exert their influence. One study, published in 2008 in the

British Journal of Medicine, showed that happiness is catching, rippling through social networks to up to three degrees of separation. Knowing someone who is happy makes you 15.3 percent more likely to be happy yourself, the study found. A happy friend of a friend increases your odds of happiness by 9.8 percent, and even your neighbor's sister's friend can give you a 5.6 percent boost. Researchers defined happiness as a perfect score on the questions "I feel hopeful about the future," "I am happy," "I enjoy life," and "I feel that I am just as good as other people." To spread a little happiness around, be upbeat yourself. Or if you know someone who's naturally happy and you're not, hang on to that person and hang out with that person as much as possible. This same research also found that bad moods are contagious too! Each unhappy connection you have (for example, a grumpy friend, relative, or acquaintance) increases your chances of being unhappy—by 7 percent.

All of this research backs up many previous studies showing that close relationships are extremely influential in how we act and what we do. In many ways, we are who we hang with.

Think about the validity of this for a moment: You learned nearly everything you know from others—how to talk, how to dress, what to eat, how to act in society, and how to have intimate relationships. Who you are, what you know, how you act—these parts of yourself were all formed through interactions with your parents, relatives, friends, employers, and teachers. People in our lives affect us in a big way. So why not harness this positive principle to motivate a loved one to change?

In programs like Alcoholics Anonymous or Narcotics Anonymous, addicts help addicts stay sober. In such 12-step programs, you are encouraged to get a "sponsor." A sponsor is someone who has been in the program long enough to help the new member understand the particular recovery program and how it works. When I help someone who is recovering from an alcohol or drug addiction, I know that the more regularly I am in contact with that person, the more effective I can be. If I hope to change someone for the better, I would want to be with that person on a regular basis because I would have more opportunity for influence and more connectedness. Seeing him or her almost daily would be ideal. This type of contact builds a healing bond that leads to change.

Who has that type of contact? You do! You have more power to change a friend or loved one than a therapist does because you have far more contact with that person, hands down, than anyone else. So often we're looking for the expert or the know-it-all to come in, sweep the problem away, and save the day. But it's you who has the power and the influence. You're going to see me introduce a lot of radical concepts in this book, and one of them is this: Family members and friends are better than therapists, especially in initiating change and supporting change so that it sticks. My change program is built on the natural bond and influence that exist in families of origin and friendships.

If you know someone who desperately needs to change—maybe they're deep into some kind of self-destructive behavior or they're just making life intolerable for others because of a troubling, recurring set of behaviors—you can make change begin. Your efforts won't involve the usual stuff like nagging, prodding, manipulation, or threats—none of that. Sure, some of this might work, but it will have only minimal, temporary impact. The more you try to scheme or coerce your depressed boyfriend to get in therapy, your chubby mom to lose weight, or your lazy kid to get a job, the more they will resist. They'll argue. They'll fight. They'll deny they even have a problem. In fact, they'll ignore you, cheat, sneak around behind your back, or do any number of things they can think of to get you to back off. The more you push, the more they push back. You demand change. They dig in their heels. Deception and lies separate you. Now it's a power struggle where one of you has to lose. And of course, no one likes to lose.

It's simply human nature to resist being coerced or told what do, especially when people think they've got a good thing going and don't want to leave their comfort zone. But it's also human nature that someone will change when offered a loving plan, encouragement, respect, acceptance, compassion, trust, and support. So give up the fight. Wave the white flag of surrender. De-escalate the power struggle. Turn down the heat of anger and turn up the dial of love. Push pause on fear and step into hope. What happens may surprise you.

Sarah Durham: Clicking the Habit

From what I learned, it wasn't unusual for forty-three-year-old Sarah Durham to spend eighteen hours a day online. She'd wake up early, grab her laptop, and steal away to the attic of her home, not bothering to change out of the old, oversized Florida State T-shirt she liked to sleep in. The attic space was cramped by boxes of Christmas tree ornaments, old cans of paint, and dusty suitcases. There were no windows. The only illumination was a single lightbulb dangling from a wood beam.

Sarah would turn on her computer, and chat on Internet dating sites and instant-messaging programs. Her day was spent cyber-chatting with a catalog of men in Los Angeles who had responded to her online profile. She would emerge from her attic for only brief intervals at a stretch.

Two years earlier, Sarah had posted her profile on a popular dating site. Her profile described a single, fun-loving woman who enjoyed the outdoors, dancing, and all types of music. Photographs of an attractive, blond, shapely Sarah adorned her profile. Sarah in a bikini. Sarah in a low-cut evening dress. Sarah in form-fitting jeans. It worked. Within the first week, she received nearly one hundred e-mails and fifty-two "winks" (the online equivalent of flirting). She winked back. Before long, winking became hot-listing, and hot-listing became e-mailing, and e-mailing became online courtships. Soon she was skipping meals and staying up late at night to chat with newfound male friends. There was no need to leave her house, change her clothes, fix her hair, or put on makeup for a date. With a few finger strokes of keys, Sarah had within the walls of her home flirtation, romance, and the ability to test sexual boundaries without face-to-face consequences. Every day the same scene played itself out, all behind the screen of a computer. Her household bills piled up, along with the dishes and dirty laundry. In two years' time, she had detached herself from the outside world and forsaken any semblance of a normal life.

Got the picture? Okay, what if I told you that Sarah was a married, stay-at-home mom from Jacksonville, Florida? That she became estranged from her husband and children as she obsessively tapped away, day after day? That Sarah, a redhead whose waist protruded over her belt, wasn't even using her own pictures to lure her cyber-lovers?

All true, *then*.

Today, Sarah has fully broken with this past life.

Her change began when her husband, Rick, called me about this crisis. Rick was a thirty-nine-year-old active-duty air force pilot, devoted family man, and elder at their church, who was away from home approximately 150 days a year. Several times, while home on leave, he noticed that Sarah seemed to be sleeping less and would become agitated if she couldn't sign on to her computer. Growing suspicious, Rick would tiptoe into the attic and see his wife staring at the computer screen and would often catch a glimpse of an image. Later on it all made sense: He realized that his wife was forming romantic attachments online, and placed "snooping" software on her computer to prove it.

For some people like Sarah, the crutch is not alcohol or food, but an equally potent and self-destructive dependency on the "high" they get from nabbing an online bargain, gambling, or just spending hours surfing the net, posting to blogs, instant messaging, online dating, taking part in video games, or looking at porn. In the United States, specialists at the Internet/Computer Addiction Services, a therapy clinic in Redmond, Washington, estimate that between 6 and 10 percent of the country's 189 million Internet users have a destructive relationship with the Web of the kind that alcoholics share with the bottle. Sarah was one of them.

Desperate to return his family to a normal life, Rick called me for help. I was moved when I realized that he was still prepared to forgive Sarah, though his marriage was being torn to shreds by her obsession. "I still love her. I thought we'd grow old together, and I can't bear to see this happening to our family."

I knew Rick was heartbroken, and I reassured him that he and other members of his family could indeed put the pieces back together. As he listened intently, I explained to Rick the four components of my change system, and how we should proceed. I asked Rick who should be invited to a meeting to help make change happen. I asked him to spell out what sort of change he thought was needed. I explained to Rick that if he followed a few simple principles, which I would help him with, he would save himself a lot of time, tears—and the precious relationship he had with his wife.

Rick was encouraged, and hopeful. Following through on what we had discussed, Rick invited her to a gathering of family members. "We want our Sarah back," they said tenderly but firmly, huddled around her in the warmth of her living room. "We want to get you healthy. We've made some calls. We've found the best help." That message got through. She cried, hugged them, and accepted the airplane ticket they had purchased for her. Six days later, she boarded a plane for a place in Arizona where she could get help and connect with others who had become hooked on the Internet. After two months, she was back home, taking care of her family, and staying out of chat rooms. She still had a computer at home; but with software installed to limit certain applications, she used it in safe ways.

Sarah's emotional transformation started as quickly as it took you to read the previous paragraph. Change began! As Sarah and her family discovered, genuine renewal is possible, and it can begin now.

As we begin this journey together, I want to equip you with a few empowering thoughts about change to get you started. Here goes.

YOU ARE NOT ALONE

As isolated as you may feel while coping with your loved one's behavior, the fact is, you are not alone. At this very moment, millions of families are going through what you are going through; millions of others have survived the storm and are willing to help, guide, and encourage you. Although knowing that others suffer certainly doesn't lessen your pain or anxiety, you can draw hope from knowing that many have solved their problems, experienced change, and learned to live more satisfying lives. You can too—thanks to the help offered by support groups. There are more than 500,000 support groups in the United States (that's a conservative estimate), serving upwards of 20 million people. This figure includes branches and chapters of national organizations, as well as strictly local groups.

Among support groups are two broad categories. First, there are support groups for the addicted or afflicted person. Name any handicap, medical condition, or other life-disrupting problem, and you'll probably find a support group ready to help.

Second, there are support groups for people like you—the family and friends of those who need to change. Al-Anon, for instance, is a support group for families of alcoholics, and also provides aid to families of persons addicted to mood-altering drugs. Adult Children of Alcoholics (ACOA), National Alliance of Mental Illness (NAMI), and Celebrate Recovery are other examples. You can also find support groups on my Web site, www.BradLamm.com.

Both types of support groups exist in a variety of forms. Some are highly structured. Others are informal. Some groups meet on a regular basis—once a week, once a month—sometimes in the homes of members. There are even some support groups in which you can attend meetings online; Al-Anon is one. Some groups work closely with health and psychology professionals; others go it alone. However they differ in their structure, self-help groups share a common goal of bringing together people with similar experiences who, by sharing, can gain strength and support from one another.

If you get involved in a support group for family members, you'll feel less isolated knowing others share similar problems. You can also exchange ideas and effective ways to cope with problems and gain a new sense of control over your life. No matter the group or method of organizing, their underlying message is "You are not alone in this."

Support groups have been integral to my own recovery. People there welcomed me. My goal was to live. Survival, basically. They told me that if I eventually helped other people, I would receive and be helped myself. A wonderful thing happened. I got better. In two or three months I was in better shape than I had been for twenty years. I needed a miracle and got it.

Support groups are hardly a novel concept either. In fact, they may have first been spawned millions of years ago, according to some anthropologists. Early humans learned that survival of the clan, village, or colony depended on support, with everyone working cooperatively to provide food and protection against common enemies. Through the centuries, support of this nature was provided by a variety of organizations, such as the guilds of medieval times, the "Friendly Societies" that developed out of the Industrial Revolution in England, the grange movement of rural America, and churches. Of course, the modern support movement began in the

United States in the 1930s with one group that still ranks among the largest: Alcoholics Anonymous.

Support groups remain a powerful and constructive means of helping people help themselves and others. If you're interested in joining or forming a support group, first determine if there is a self-help clearinghouse in your area or state. Clearinghouses provide directories of existing groups, publish newsletters and books, hold workshops, and help people find an appropriate group or get a group started. The phone book or Internet is a good place to start. A local hospital or social service agency will probably be able to help. Meetings of support groups are often listed in the community bulletin board sections of local newspapers. There are two national clearinghouse organizations—the National Self-Help Clearinghouse Department and the Self-Help Center—that can also provide information about local groups, as well as books and pamphlets that tell what to look for in a group before joining and suggestions on how to start new groups. (See Appendix I for other resources.)

Don't keep the problem to yourself and don't run from it. Circle the wagons. Ask for support. It's a good thing. We humans are communal beings. We like the buddy system. We thrive best when we work together and share our experiences and our abilities. To enhance the quality of your life and help your loved one, turn to the people who love you and turn to the people who have learned to deal with similar problems. Ask for support, accept support, and count your blessings, because life will get better.

YOUR LOVE HAS INFLUENCE

Quite frankly, there's nothing more influential than love. It has long been sung that "you're nobody 'til somebody loves you," and by the time that we become teens, it's likely that all of us have experienced at least some degree of the influence of love. We find out early that it makes you do things that you wouldn't normally do. We realize that love makes you say things that you wouldn't normally say. And we know that it makes you feel things that you wouldn't normally feel.

I've seen rather radical changes in friends who were in love. Cyndie, who used to be a pack-a-day smoker, spent the early months of a relationship hiding her habit from her marathon-runner boyfriend, Jeremy. When he caught her sneaking a smoke one too many times, he issued an ultimatum: the cigarettes or me. Cyndie loved him very much. She told me that some things were more important than the kick she got from smoking. She's since given up the habit and now she runs marathons with Jeremy, who now also happens to be her husband.

I also have some newlywed friends, the Ramseys, who started their marriage out on rocky footing after the wife realized that her husband was drowning in debt, mostly due to maxing out his credit cards. She told him, "I love you very much, but I don't love this credit situation. You've got to do something." That very day, he called the credit card companies and worked out payment plans that fit his budget and would ultimately free him from debt. The motivating factor? Love.

When I was younger, I certainly didn't want to change for anyone. Or so I believed, until I realized that many of my talents had been motivated by relationships. I went from being an eat-beans-out-of-a-can guy to becoming a gourmet cook because of someone I liked at the time and wanted to impress. I learned to play killer cards because of another relationship. The relationships may be over and done, but many of my accomplishments testify to the influence of love in my life.

Nothing influences people more toward change than love, from romantic love to love between parent and child to love between siblings to loving friendships. The loving bond of spouses, lovers, close family members, friends, and others is more influential than any other factor in persuading people to take life-altering action. As you'll find out, an intervention, and indeed the entire change process, can be a profound demonstration of that love.

So yes, love is a great change agent. But how exactly do you express life-changing love? As I say in my Change Seminars, love is not always an emotion or a mushy feeling. *Love is action*. It's how you treat people.

When we're frustrated or stressed by someone's behavior or bad habits, we may say things we do not really mean or intend to say, all blown out of proportion to reality. Or we may become sullen, communicating through moody silence. All these behaviors do is engender hurt feelings, create emotional wounds, and strain relationships. That's not love or loving. What *is* loving is to hold back from saying the unkind or negative thing, even when you're frustrated, provoked, or fatigued. Not to say the unkind or critical thing is love in action.

Love is also listening to someone, not only with your ears but also with your heart. When we are communicating with another person, we need to give them our full attention, to be completely present, without censoring, criticizing, lecturing, or comparing. True listening is very active. It takes courage and patience. Until your loved one feels that you are listening, he or she may not be open to your influence.

Love assumes (and looks for) the best in others. When you believe that others want to be their best, you exert a powerful influence that can bring out the best in them. Most people have much potential, often obvious, but often dormant. And they tend to respond to how we treat them and what we believe about them. The German writer Goethe put it: "Treat a man as he appears to be, and you make him worse. But treat a man as if he were what he potentially could be, and you make him what he should be."

Finally, as I tell my clients, do not give up and do not give in. It is unloving and harmful to shelter people from the consequences of their own behavior. In doing so, we teach them they are flawed and weak. When we give in to irresponsible behavior, we condone and unwittingly foster that behavior. And, if we give up—by turning our backs on them—we zap their motivation to try. My approach of *do not give up* and *do not give in*, crafted in love, requires responsibility and action on your part. Otherwise, you head down the path of least resistance, giving in when you really care or giving up when you don't. When real love is the motivator, change begins.

BE OPEN TO MESSENGERS OF HOPE

When I recently asked a mom, Shannon, if it hurt doing nothing while her son was drowning in drug addiction, she was clear that she was in pain, though she wanted things to get better. But she was stuck. Her "normal" had become so used to the hurt, pain, drama, disappointment, and fear that it proved a real challenge for her to shift focus, and gain a truer perspective. Being stuck is bad, but you can pry yourself loose. You just need a tool called hope.

That's how Shannon pried herself loose. The prying was possible, however, because she was open to messengers of hope—people who demonstrate that there is hopefulness in what looks utterly hopeless. While I was working with Shannon, I urged her to join a support group for families of drug-addicted kids (Nar-Anon.com). At first, she was reluctant to discuss the problem with anyone because she was embarrassed. She was also scared to contact a social service agency because she was a single mother and feared her two other children could be taken from her. She was so angry at her son and ashamed of herself, even though it made no sense to think she was to blame. Still, I kept after her to connect with a group. Finally, Shannon did take my advice. Joining a support group, where people took the time to let her vent her feelings and told her she was not alone, made all the difference. Shannon met other parents whose kids had gotten off drugs. The support group enabled her hope.

What exactly do I mean by hope? Don't confuse it with optimism. Optimism, which is a great attitude to have, is based on directional signs that things are going well. The medicine worked. The economy is getting better. Your kid is getting better grades this semester. Optimism assumes that the present course will continue and bring positive results. Optimism arises from a perceived pattern of success. Hope does not. It springs into being amid the worst kind of gloom. It's believing in spite of the circumstances, and then watching the circumstances change for the better.

The late minister and author Norman Vincent Peale once offered this poignant insight:

> *Have you ever stopped to wonder what it is that keeps you going from one day to another? What lies behind your ability to fight your way through periods of discouragement or depression? What makes you believe that sooner or later bad times will get better? It's a little, four-letter word that has enormous power in it. Power to bring failures back to success. Power to bring the sick back to health. Power to bring the weak back to strength. It's hope.*

We have the option of being full of despair or hopeful, tragic or triumphant, victims or victors. Hope is a powerful attitude that opens doors where despair slams them shut. A hopeful attitude helps us see the best, work for the best, and, ultimately, experience the best in life.

Shannon chose hope over despair. Hope inspired her to action. It was her fuel, the fire that enabled her to stand up, invite folks in to help her, and begin change for her son. Parents move mountains. So do brothers and sisters, and loved ones each and every day. As she did, you can choose hope over despair and do-nothingness.

Helping a loved one in trouble is not only fully possible, it's often urgently important. The attitude we take is key: choosing support, action, love, and hope over anything else. You are your loved one's most powerful force for change. You can give that person a fresh start—and you may even save a life. There is strength in numbers. Together we can accomplish what we cannot do alone. Fall into hope and action! You can and must do it!

TWO

Old Dogs, Leopards—and Scorpions Too: Debunking the 5 Myths of Change

Our cultural mythology states that you can't change someone else, you can only change yourself. We've all heard that mantra, right? But as I told you right from the start, you can change not just someone, but anyone, and I mean, anyone.

But if you turn your back on this fundamental belief, you'll miss a great deal, because you are buying into one of several deeply ingrained cultural myths about change. I call them myths because they are untrue and they silence discussion about the power you have to change another human being. If believed and acted upon, these myths can do a lot of harm, because they get in the way of helping you and someone you love live a truly quality life. And you don't want to do that, so let's start debunking some of the more popular myths that have sprung up around change.

Myth #1: People Never Change

There's a silly little fable about a scorpion and a turtle at the riverbank, and each had to get to the other side of the river. The scorpion couldn't swim, so it asked the turtle to ferry it across. The turtle agreed to carry the scorpion on its back, reasoning that the scorpion would be foolish to endanger itself by hurting the turtle. After all, they both would drown. But halfway across the river, the scorpion stung the turtle in its neck. As both were dying—the turtle from the scorpion sting and the scorpion from drowning—the turtle asked, "Why did you sting me?" The scorpion replied, "Because it's my nature. It's what I do."

This fable is right up there with the proverb "A leopard can't change its spots," or switching the analogy from the feline to the canine, "You can't teach an old dog new tricks." All three imply that you cannot make people change their established patterns of opinion and behavior, because these are their "nature."

To which I can only politely reply, "Hooey." My experience as an interventionist and Change Seminar leader has been that people who don't want to change will quote these worn-out clichés as an excuse to continue as they always have. If they were totally honest, what they really mean is: "I am too set in my ways to change now." All too often, they have gotten stuck in a routine, habit, or frame of mind that is comfortable, and nothing and nobody can change them, or so they claim.

But is this true? Can he stop overeating when he knows it's bad for him? Can she overcome old lessons and ingrained childhood habits? Would he walk away from a bad situation he's gotten himself into?

Think about it. It's not so unusual to hear or speak phrases like: "This sermon changed my life," "You're not the same person you were when I married you," or "I didn't know any better when I was your age, but I'm different now."

Look back over your own life. Is there anything about it that was the way it was when you were fifteen? Twenty-five? Thirty-five? Had you deliberately tried to keep things status quo, how successful do you think your life would be today? Do you feel you have grown, developed, matured in any significant ways? Of course you have. See my point? The bottom line is that neither personality nor behavior is fixed. You and everyone else can change.

Technically, a leopard can't change its spots, but it can run up a different hill every now and then. As for dogs, it's quite possible to teach an old dog, or in this case, a person, new "tricks," new behaviors. Most researchers believe that while some parts of personality tend to be inherent and relatively fixed, humans adapt to new circumstances and contingencies more easily and successfully than any other species. We can and do change constantly.

Until quite recently, medical science held that the all-controlling brain, when fully developed, was a done deal. Then they discovered something called the brain's "plasticity." This means our gray matter is flexible and adaptable; the brain is not a fixed, limited system. It can generate new neurons, and more brain regions can be recruited, brought into play, to help us change our behavior, and indeed, our entire way of being in the world.

Most of this insight has been gained from studying older people, who are often viewed as the least changeable in our society. The truth is, older people are great learners and change artists because they have broader knowledge to begin with, a better experience-based vocabulary, and more perspective than younger people. In fact, the aged brain has a remarkable and enduring capacity to make new connections, absorb new data, and thus acquire new skills.

In a nutshell: No one is ever too old (or too young) to make a dramatic change in one's life. Grandma Moses didn't begin painting until she was seventy-eight. At eighty, George Burns received his first Academy Award. Ronald Reagan was sixty-nine when he became the oldest person ever elected president of the United States. Golda Meir was seventy-one when she became prime minister of Israel. With a little more than his $105 Social Security check and a great recipe for fried chicken, Harland Sanders, a high school dropout, founded the Kentucky Fried Chicken franchise at age sixty-two. So the next time you hear the phrase "You can't teach an old dog new tricks," remember this: Lots of old dogs become artists, start businesses, run countries, and learn all sorts of new skills and behaviors. We can all learn how to sit, stay, roll over—and change!

As for the scorpion's argument, "It's just my nature," let's pick this apart. Because it may be the scorpion's nature to sting does not mean that you should abandon your desire to change someone you love and stop them from squandering this treasure called life. Human nature is a bundle of qualities and traits, including ways of thinking, feeling, and acting shared by all humans. All of these things are subject to change. Why? Because inherent in human nature is the capacity for choice. Our ability to make choices is a large part of what makes us human. Choices can work for us or against us. We've all acted in ways that we wouldn't want broadcast on the evening news. We make mistakes, and some people make big or even criminal mistakes. The choices we make can lead us down a road where we don't necessarily want to go. To change someone you love and keep them from going down that road, you've got to give them love, support, and information to make the best choices. The change process you'll learn here will show you how.

My Quaker upbringing also taught me something I have observed from my day-to-day work to be absolutely and fundamentally true, whether you are religious or not: that we are all redeemable. Anyone can experience personal transformation in spite of what appear to be insurmountable limitations and obstacles. Human beings are capable of change! Stay true to the best of what exists inside of you, and you can be a force in changing someone you love.

Myth #2: You're Powerless

The second myth of change is that you're powerless to change another human being. This is such a widely accepted belief that many people won't even dispute it. It has roots in Al-Anon, whose creed states that you are powerless to control a person's desire to drink alcohol, take drugs, or engage in destructive behavior. Let me say up front that this is not an anti-Al-Anon paragraph; Al-Anon is a great support organization that has helped millions of people, and I recommend it to my clients. But like any other large organization, it has issues that could use some revisiting.

There has been too much of a shift in our culture from the view of the robust, independent person, capable of great individual achievements, to the notion of the fragile, powerless victim. The idea that we really are powerless, that we should just watch and wait until someone hits bottom, is dangerous. You watch and wait and pray and hope and you end up with a dead spouse, or kids with asthma because someone is smoking in the house, or a family that's bankrupt because Mom gambled away the life savings. The bottom we identify and act on may be your own. Tell yourself: "I will sink no deeper and will begin change now."

Saying that someone's self-destructive habit has really gotten out of control doesn't mean that you are powerless to help them. It just means that someone's habit has gotten out of control and this person needs to change. Sure, change can be extremely difficult and often painful, but that doesn't mean that it's impossible, that someone can't do it, or that you're powerless to help them.

If you care about someone who has a self-destructive problem, I know you find their behavior frustrating, maddening, or confusing. Sometimes it's all you can do to keep from pulling your hair out. You agonize over what to do, or what not to do. You think, "If he loved me, he wouldn't do this!" So there's no question that something has to change. Your loved one's abuse, absenteeism, or money problems are ruining your life too—which is why you must help that person change his or her destructive behavior.

Where most people go wrong is in their manner of approach. The human brain behaves like a two-year-old: Tell it what to do and it automatically pushes back. You can tell your boyfriend umpteen times to stop abusing credit cards or to manage his money better, but if you nag or finger-wag, nothing will change. So what should you use? In chapter 4, you'll learn some techniques, but here's a little preview of coming attractions: One way to do this is to describe what you've observed while your friend or loved one is in the throes of bad behavior. You don't demand, nag, bribe, threaten, or yell. You just hold up a figurative mirror, giving the clearest information you can because you care. Describe what you're seeing; point to specific events, and how they affect you and others. Always be as clear as you can. I call this an eyewitness account. Going through this is easier than you might think, especially when you care about someone. And as you'll learn, getting help and support from others is vital. But if you can give an eyewitness account, the person may see clearly enough to enter a process that will make a real difference. Ultimately, if you patiently invest the time to go through my change process, your efforts will be rewarded with a happier future—for you and your loved one. Please don't ever give up; transformation can and will happen.

Myth #3: People Can Change on Their Own

If someone could change on their own, they would do it in a heartbeat. After all, who wants to live a life that has spun out of control? Who wants to be fat? Who wants to be drunk or strung out on drugs all the time? Who wants to lie awake nights, terrified of winding up on the streets? Who wants to be stressed out, scared, or uncertain about the future?

Most people do not change entirely on their own. Allow me to use myself as an example again. I had been smoking since 1982, drinking since 1982, and doing cocaine and other drugs since 1984. By the time I attended my first 12-step meeting back in 1991, I had nearly a decade of disordered behavior behind me. I went to meetings, tail tucked between my legs, ashamed to be there. I attended meetings like this off and on for two years, and even once picked up a "one-year coin," to celebrate one uninterrupted year of sobriety. Only trouble was, I had not been sober that year. I was living a lie. Back then, I went to many meetings, yet never spoke to another soul. I kept my head down, while expecting that some kind of recovery osmosis would occur just from showing up on occasion. I was worn down, worn out, and brittle.

Then, toward the end of my drinking and drugging career, I chose to leave my dream job as a TV anchor because it was interfering with my drinking. My friends were shocked at my decision to walk away. My agent was ticked off. I switched careers anyway.

I was in such deep denial about my addiction that I actually went into the bar business. Can you believe it: the bar business, of all things! I was so successful at it that I opened a nightclub in short order, then a lounge. In reality, my new career was yet another excuse to drink and drug with impunity.

Looking back over that period in my life, it became clear to me that if someone had stepped in and talked to me, had done some form of intervention earlier, I would have accepted help. I would have gone to treatment, and I would have stopped using drugs. But instead I was living in denial, thinking that I would be able to quit drugs on my own. "I'll quit tomorrow," I would say to myself. But tomorrow didn't come until much later.

A great deal had to happen before I could change. You would think that blacking out almost every day from alcohol would do that, but in my case it did not. And so it went. I lied and deflected blame, and the hole I dug for myself got deeper and deeper. Denial—first of drinking, then of the self—stretched to include more and more bits of reality, and after a while, I literally could not see the truth, could not see who I was or what I needed. If I could have stopped, I would have.

Quitting was simply not possible without help, even in the face of severe consequences. When my friend Paul insisted I get help without negotiation or delay, I took the next step. For me, change began. Another person reached out, and I took his hand, finally.

Change begins when you extend a hand to someone who needs help. And that person doesn't even have to be ready. That's the next myth I'll blow out of the water.

Myth #4: You Can't Help Someone Until They're Ready

What another pile of hooey! "We can't help her until she's ready. . . ." I have heard that thousands of times from the families I work with. It's a myth with a capital M! In fact, what we do through the change process is *help them get ready.*

In my opinion, this myth has its origins partly in a construct called the Stages of Change Model, or SCM for short. It holds that when it comes to making a change, most people pass through a series of predictable phases. It was formulated by psychologists at the University of Rhode Island after they studied how smokers were able to give up their habits. The model has been applied to a broad range of behaviors including weight loss, injury prevention, overcoming alcohol, and drug problems, among others. It is used successfully by many treatment centers throughout the United States.

The idea behind SCM is that behavior change does not happen in a single step. Rather, people tend to progress through different stages on their way to successful change. These stages include *precontemplation*, when someone can't (or won't) deal with their habit or behavior right now; *contemplation*, someone wants to change but isn't quite ready to act; *preparation*, he or she is ready to take a step; and *action*, the person decides it's time to make a move. Further, SCM holds that people progress through the stages at their own rate. So expecting behavior change by simply telling someone, for example, who is still in the precontemplation stage that he or she must get help supposedly won't work because that person is not ready to change. Each person is supposed to decide for himself or herself when a stage is completed and when it is time to move on to the next stage.

I'll concede that some people may go through stages toward change, but their progression (or lack of) toward change doesn't help you one bit. Right now, you may be dealing with a friend or loved one who is mired in some sort of difficult, dangerous, or deadly behavior. It's not only compromising his or her life, it's ruining yours—and probably has been for a long time. Or maybe the situation is more benign; you're dealing with someone who is just plain annoying or a pain in the neck. Even so, these folks can cause significant stress if they don't get help and start changing. There are other drawbacks too. It's tough for people who are physically and psychologically addicted to something, for example, to move through stages of change. Addicts, in particular, benefit from intervention to get well, regardless of what stage they may be in.

Bottom line: If it's a personal relationship that's bringing more stress than joy, or a loved one in the throes of addiction, I don't think you can sit on your hands, waiting for someone to contemplate or prepare. You can't wait until they're ready to change, or even until they've "hit bottom" on their own, typically by getting arrested or killing someone or getting divorced or losing their job before they will accept help. You've got to take action to save your sanity and give your loved one a shot at a fresh start. If you don't, you'll continue to be sucked dry.

The SCM also asserts that a person's decision must come from within, because long-term change supposedly can't be externally imposed. A study called "Invitational Intervention: The ARISE Model," published in 2008 in *Alcoholism Treatment Quarterly*, refutes this. It looked into factors that successfully keep someone healthy and abstinent at the one-year mark. Take a look at the findings:

▶ *People mandated by the court to enter a treatment program were the most successful at staying abstinent.*

▶ *People who entered a treatment program after an intervention were the second-most successful at staying abstinent.*

▶ *People who admitted themselves to treatment were the least successful.*

Externally imposed change—the court mandate and intervention—was the most successful route to change. In my own work, people who seek help after an intervention are highly successful in making powerful changes in their lives—and staying changed. Again, I can't say it enough, or in too many ways: You are the force for changing someone you love.

Here's the deal: Many people are never "ready" to begin change—they need help to get ready—and a lot of people never even move through predictable stages. In fact, I've seen some people quit bad stuff like cigarettes and alcohol in minutes and remain abstinent forever. But for the most part, people in crisis are broke, broken down, and often not thinking right. They will not raise any white flags of surrender. So why would you hold them to a standard that requires straight thinking and healthy processing skills? You wouldn't, nor should you. So don't buy in to this tired old myth. Throw it out with the theory of the Flat Earth.

Please consider this truth: With your love, help, and support, change begins; and you have as many tries as you wish to take. As you apply my techniques, take heart when things go well, but do not be overly discouraged when they don't. The next word, the next day, the next interaction gives you another chance to make a positive impact.

Myth #5: Fear Is the Best Motivator for Change

My sister's fat. My husband smokes. Uncle Joe drinks too much. My dad doesn't exercise enough. People are killing themselves, and they know it.

And yet they carry on by overeating, lighting up, or slumping in front of the television and throwing back another beer.

Consider: Doctors at Washington University School of Medicine in St. Louis found that among a group of smokers who had had surgery to remove early-stage lung cancer, most started smoking again within two months. In another study by researchers at Johns Hopkins University, nine out of ten patients who'd recently had coronary bypass surgery failed to take steps to improve their nutrition, exercise more, and reduce stress. And despite intensive public-education campaigns, more than 23 percent of Americans still smoke, 15 percent binge drink (21 percent of women ages eighteen to twenty-five), and one-third don't always wear their seat belts.

We humans sometimes seem to be perversely resistant to doing what we know is good for us, or to not doing things that are clearly bad for us. Yet the ways being used to try to change people, such as scaring people about the health risks, are ineffective ways to motivate behavior change, according to studies into what works—and what does not—in getting people to live healthier lives. As a motivator for personal change, fear is right up there with nagging. Neither works very well.

People slip further into denial when told all the bad things that will happen to them, and they never hear words of love and encouragement. No one wants to change when they're being told that what they are doing is wrong. Your friend or loved one already knows you disapprove of his choices; so lectures, reasoning, and scare tactics won't bring about change. When you try to "help" this way, reminding someone of only bad repercussions, they do what we all do—they tune you out, tell you what you want to hear, or retaliate in some way. They'll often go on the defensive and they won't be motivated to change. Don't expect them to say, "Gee, thanks for pointing that out *again*." And the more you lecture, the crazier you'll get. Although it's perfectly fine to communicate your fears to someone, using fear-based admonitions to the exclusion of other techniques doesn't work well at all.

If you want someone you love to change, you're going to have to do something different from what you have been doing. Researchers at Brandeis University in Waltham, Massachusetts, asked forty-four married partners what they did to get their spouses to eat right, exercise, and make other healthy changes. Husbands, as well as wives, said that these approaches were the most effective:

▶ *Do it together. Invite him to join you on a walk or bike ride; sign up for low-fat cooking classes.*

▶ *Lend a hand. Buy her a gym membership or a series of personal training sessions; pack him a low-fat lunch.*

▶ *Be supportive. Praise is far more likely to change behavior. Praise him when he skips desserts; be patient when he's cranky during cigarette withdrawal.*

Why are these strategies successful? They make the recipient feel good because they're seen as motivated by the partner's love and concern, not by a desire to control.

Just as "it is easier to attract flies with honey than with vinegar," it is easier to get your loved one to listen to your loving words than your criticism. So choose the honey alternative to nagging and threatening, and help your loved one by talking about what you do like about him or her and what positive changes please you. While you do not want to nag, you do need to voice your concerns in a loving way. You might mention that you want to have him in your life for a very long time. Let her know how important she is to you. Tell him you value him in your life. Take every opportunity you can to let her know how you feel about having her as your spouse, partner, friend, or relative. Talk about the things you would like to do in the future, or as you grow old together. The joy of living is a more powerful motivator than the fear of dying, so that's where the emphasis should be to "sell" change.

Compelling, positive visions of the future are a strong inspiration for change, and you'll learn how to create these in chapter 4. People will always choose love over fear as a motivator for seeking help. Love is the most powerful dimension of the human imagination, and it unleashes powerful forces for change.

Many people go through life accepting these myths that we've all heard forever, holding on to them because we've been taught to do so, or because they seem to be somehow absolute. Yet change cannot happen until you unlearn and let go of these myths. So say good-bye to leopards, scorpions, and old dogs. Once you do that—and I know you can—you'll be ready to take action in ways that will make a profound and lasting difference in the lives of people you love.

THREE

When to Step In

Many of us have a loved one, a family member, or a close friend who finds himself or herself in trouble and needs help. Allow me to share with you some proof of this, gathered from government data, addiction centers, national surveys, and health organizations:

▶ *1 in 6 Americans report that they "drink too much," while 1 in 20 say they have problems with extreme drinking.*

▶ *1 in 38 Americans have an eating disorder. One out of 10 are men; 9 out of 10 are women.*

▶ *1 in 43 Americans have a gambling problem.*

▶ *1 in 15 Americans regularly use illicit substances.*

▶ *1 in 20 Americans are currently dealing with depression.*

▶ *1 in 5 American adults smoke cigarettes.*

▶ *1 in 13 Americans suffer from an unhealthy Internet dependency.*

Looking over these startling statistics makes you wonder: Why do people do things that they know are harmful, or deadly? The next time you see someone who is toting an oxygen bottle with the tubes going into her nostrils at the same time she is smoking a cigarette, stop and think. Why is she doing something that she knows has wrecked her breathing and quite possibly has shortened her life? It doesn't make sense, does it? She would probably advise you never to smoke, while at the same time being unable to stop her own problem.

Have you ever gone to a restaurant buffet with some overweight friends and watched them go back for seconds or thirds or more? You scratch your head and wonder what is going on. Maybe they just don't care. Aren't they full? Where is the on/off button? Let's explore.

There are numerous reasons why people do harmful things to themselves, including peer pressure, stress, boredom, thrill seeking, depression, adolescent rebellion, family breakups, economic stress, crime, relief from emotional or physical pain, and being out of touch with one's own spiritual balance and inner harmony. And if a drug like alcohol, cocaine, or tobacco is involved, and you ask people why they do it, they will give you different answers. "I enjoy it." "It perks me up." "It calms me down." And so on. Be it conscious or unconscious, dangerous or not, people do what they do for reasons.

The most difficult question for us is: Should we step in or step aside? It's normal to be hesitant when trying to help friends or family members engaged in troublesome or destructive behavior. You don't want to intrude, but you want to do what's in their best interest, especially when people are seen as hurting themselves or others.

A Life Saved by Stepping In

Lauren Conley, a twenty-nine-year-old elementary school teacher, has grappled with these questions. Her closest friend, Bette, was suicidal a few years ago. I met Lauren when she was part of a family intervention to help a younger sister get into treatment for anorexia. Lauren told me about Bette, who had been depressed—a depression Lauren attributed to a busted romance. They would talk almost every night, long distance. Lauren lived in Chicago, Bette in Denver.

"I'm going to kill myself," Bette had been saying in a sad, half-joking way.

"Why?" Lauren asked.

"Why not?"

"How are you going to do it?" Lauren asked. Then Bette would describe different methods, and Lauren would tell her why they wouldn't work. Jump off a balcony? You'll ruin your nose job. Slit your wrists? It messes up the bathroom. Overdose on pills? Suppose you don't take enough? Lauren tried to make Bette laugh. After all, she reasoned, people who laugh don't kill themselves, right?

But Lauren got scared. She had heard all too often that threats of suicide should be taken seriously. Afraid of waiting too long or not reaching out at all, she called Bette's brother, who took it seriously too. He drove over to Bette's and found her despondent and depressed. A makeshift noose, formed from an electrical cable found in the bathroom, showed that she had been thinking of hanging herself. Bette admitted she wanted to hurt herself but fortunately agreed to go to the hospital for a mental health evaluation. She was admitted into a treatment program right away, as a result of that evaluation. Long story short, Bette's life was saved because people who loved her took action.

How do we bring ourselves to intervene? Maybe we should, maybe we shouldn't. These are tortuous questions. If you are waiting for someone to make a change on their own and you are wondering how long to wait, stop right now and get out your mental calculator. The deciding factor will be adding up the costs of that person's behavior—the costs to that person and their friends and family, including you.

DO THE MATH

Self-destructive behavior always hurts, and may eventually kill. Note some jarring statistics from the Centers for Disease Control (CDC): It costs each smoker in the U.S. nearly $4,000 dollars a year to smoke. In years of life, it costs adult male and female smokers an average of 13.2 and 14.5 years of life, respectively, because they smoked. Tobacco use is responsible for approximately 438,000 deaths each year. Then there's obesity.

Recent data estimate that about 400,000 deaths are associated with obesity each year in the United States. The Centers for Disease Control has released a study citing that the cost to treat obesity-related diseases has soared—to a mile-high $147 billion, double that of the cost just ten years before. Amazing and troubling, but true. Fat kills.

As for domestic violence, each year, nearly 1,500 women and 500 men are killed by an intimate partner. More than 31,000 people complete suicide each year in the United States, and approximately 1.4 million attempt suicide. On average, 89 people take their own lives every day. Most people who complete suicide suffer from depression, addiction, or other diagnosable mental illnesses, but two-thirds of those who die by suicide *are not receiving help for that illness* at the time of their death.

The cost of my own addiction was nearly a million dollars. I estimate that over the twenty years of active addiction, I spent, on average, $40,000 a year. Between the alcohol, the pills, the coke and the crystal, the cigarettes and the nonsense, it was buckets and buckets of dough. That's just the dollar cost and doesn't count lost wages, productivity, dreams, schemes, or what-ifs.

Any way you sort the data, the numbers are alarming. But the problems don't really hit home until you associate them with the loved one, employee, or relative in your own life—and see that they will eventually self-destruct before your own eyes. The costs of waiting until something awful happens are just too great.

WEIGH THE PERSONAL COSTS

Beyond those costs, there are personal costs to you. Think about it: What is this person's behavior doing to your life? Your peace of mind? Your health? Your finances? Your relationship? What is it costing you? Trust me, there are costs to you—huge costs. Let's talk about them.

Emotional Costs

If your loved one has an addiction or suffers other serious problems, you and everyone else in the family will be affected at some level. Members of a family, for example, often experience loneliness, frustration, fear, anger, and shame. They may occasionally feel anger and resentment toward the whole situation and then feel terribly guilty for having these feelings. They may also feel a sense of hopelessness about the situation. Some family members may also use alcohol, drugs, or gambling themselves as a way of coping with the problems in their family and to neutralize the emotional pain.

Problems like addiction or abuse create an unstable family environment. Children may feel insecure or unloved. They may also be more likely to show antisocial behavior and have problems such as skipping school, aggressiveness, hyperactivity, and eating disorders. In households dominated by addictions or ruled by any sort of chaos, the children's safety—as well as their psychological and emotional development—may be at risk.

You've got to ask yourself: How much pain are you experiencing over this situation? Do you wonder how you're holding yourself together? What is it doing to your kids? Emotional pain comes in many forms—depression, anxiety, or feeling neglected, misunderstood, sad, trapped, vulnerable, hopeless, or just plain wrung out.

You've absolutely got to take your emotional temperature and recognize that you're hurting. The emotional pain just isn't worth it. When you get this, I believe you'll be strengthened and motivated to move your loved one in the direction of meaningful change.

Health Costs

Normally, close relationships are wellsprings of health-enhancing support. But inject persistent domestic conflict or strain, interpersonal problems, an addiction, or any destructive behavior into the mix, and you've got trouble. Accumulating evidence indicates that these problems and conflicts deal a blow to *your* body—and especially the heart. In one study, researchers found that British adults who were in adverse close relationships were 34 percent more likely to suffer heart problems, ranging from chest pain to deadly heart attacks, than those who weren't. Numerous American studies have produced similar findings. For example, a long-term analysis of more than 1,000 marriages found that strained matrimonies take a clear toll on physical health over time.

Negativity-plagued relationships are damaging in part because of the effects of chronic stress. In addition to damaging the heart, ongoing stress can deplete the immune system—creating openings for colds, cancers, and other maladies—and also lead to depression and risky coping behaviors like excessive drinking.

What is your particular situation doing to your health? What could it do? Is it worth it? Decide to take action based on your answers.

Financial Costs

There are financial costs, of course. Maybe you didn't get that promotion you wanted because you've been distracted by your spouse's self-destructive behavior. Or because of her drinking, she lost her job, and now there's a severe strain on family finances. Or you're strapped financially because of his gambling debts.

Here's one maybe you haven't thought about: Suppose you're a supervisor at work, and all of a sudden you find yourself dealing with one of the fastest-growing business problems in the country: employee Internet abuse. According to a Gallup Organization report, the average employee uses office computers for nonwork activity about 75 minutes per day. At $20 per hour, that works out to annual lost productivity of about $6,250 per employee.

Okay, that may not hit you where you live, but for people in management who are responsible for productivity, there are costs—personal and professional. Employees who play online games, chat with online friends, or look at online pornography during work hours not only cut into corporate productivity but also diminish profits and create enormous personal stress for supervisors.

Many supervisors and managers don't yet realize that problematic online use can easily turn into a psychological addiction, one that's a legitimate clinical disorder. If you're an employer these days, you can't just fire employees summarily for online misuse. Fired workers have actually sued their former employers for wrongful termination, claiming that they suffer from a mental disorder and holding the company responsible for providing access to the "computer drug." Sure, lawsuits like these may seem frivolous and even dumb, but more cases are being seen in court each year—all the more reason to step in. Ultimately, employers have to create better policies regarding what employers expect from employees' use of the Internet at work.

No matter what form they take, the costs of whatever crisis you're in are enormous. You've got to step in, not only for the person in trouble but to stop the deterioration of your life—and everybody else in it.

Here's the deal: Anything that happens to one person has consequences for the people around him. For example, when a family member becomes depressed, addicted, obese, or whatever, the effect of that behavior is not localized within the depressed person, but rather ripples through the family to affect all its members. The collateral effects are real, and they are serious.

AWARENESS LEADS TO ACTION!

Pay attention to the behavior you observe in your loved one, partner, employee, or relative. Maybe it has recently changed for the worse. He has started abusing drugs or alcohol, become moody or aloof, or begun picking fights with you. Maybe he's irritable or angry all the time, and the smallest thing sets him off. Or she's started having trouble getting along with bosses, colleagues, family, or friends. Perhaps you've picked up on feelings of hopelessness, worthlessness, or guilt, or noticed changes in sleep patterns, low energy or motivation, or fatigue. Has black and white become a whole lot of gray? Has her weight fluctuated? Has he lost interest in activities previously enjoyed? Does she frequently withdraw from other people? Does he appear confused or have poor concentration?

Maybe he is neglecting some major area of his life that needs attention or refuses to take care of his health, look for a better job, manage his finances, or work on his relationship with you. Has she jeopardized or lost a significant relationship, job, or educational or career opportunity because of a habit? Has he borrowed money from friends, family, even strangers to pay off catastrophic debts? Has she lied about the amount of time or money spent on the habit? Has he committed a crime to get money to pay for the problem?

Then ask yourself: What is this behavior doing to you? Are you depressed, anxious, sad, or otherwise a basket case? Do you experience errors in judgment, accidents, and poor physical and mental health? Is it your sense that events are out of control and potentially dangerous? Are you having money problems? Are you satisfied with the way things are? Ask, then answer these questions.

Once you think through these questions, you need to do some writing. Writing is a way of clarifying what you already know against the inner voices of indecision and avoidance. When you write things down, everything starts to add up. You'll access your own opinion about what to do next.

To help you, I've created eight brief questionnaires. Choose the questionnaire or questionnaires that apply to you. If you think your loved one is dealing with depression issues, then you'll want to answer the questionnaire that deals with emotional issues, for example. With each question, all you have to do is answer yes or no. If an answer is yes, then spend some time listing the costs to your loved one and to you. As you consider each question, ask yourself:

▶ *What is this person's behavior doing to him or her? To you and your family?*

▶ *How is it interfering in any way with your peace of mind or quality of life?*

▶ *Does it make you feel depressed or anxious a good deal of the time?*

▶ *What has it cost your relationship?*

▶ *Have you had health problems because of it? What are they?*

▶ *What are the financial costs?*

▶ *Who else in your family or circle of friends is being adversely affected, and how?*

Are you ready? Grab a pen and jot down what this situation has robbed from you. This exercise is not to paint you into the victim's corner. Just the opposite. If you desire to really get honest (and you must if you wish to take action), then listing the real costs is an invaluable step in seeing where you really are in all this.

Let's go.

ALCOHOL ISSUES

1. *Do you feel your loved one drinks more than other people?*

Yes ☐ No ☐
If yes, how is this affecting him or her? How is it affecting you?

_____

_____

_____

2. *Do you worry or complain about your loved one's drinking?*

Yes ☐ No ☐
If yes, how is this affecting you?

_____

_____

_____

3. *Has your loved one ever tried to stop drinking but been unable to do so?*

Yes ☐ No ☐
If yes, how is this affecting him or her? How is it affecting you?

_____

_____

_____

4. *Has his or her drinking ever created problems between you?*

Yes ☐ No ☐
If yes, what are the problems? How are they affecting you and your relationship?

_____

_____

_____

5. *Has your loved one ever gotten in trouble at work because of drinking?*

Yes ☐ No ☐
If yes, how is this affecting him or her? How is it affecting you?

_____

_____

_____

6. *Has your loved one ever neglected obligations, family, or work for two or more days in a row because of drinking?*

Yes ☐ No ☐
If yes, how is this affecting him or her? How is it affecting you?

_____

_____

_____

7. *Has your loved one ever been arrested or ticketed for drunk driving (DUI or DWI) or driving after drinking?*

Yes ☐ No ☐
If yes, how is this affecting him or her? How is it affecting you?

_____

_____

_____

8. *Has he or she ever gotten in trouble at work because of drinking?*

Yes ☐ No ☐
If yes, how is this affecting him or her? How is it affecting you?

_____

_____

_____

9. *Has he or she ever lost friends because of drinking?*

Yes ☐ No ☐
If yes, how is this affecting him or her? How is it affecting you?

_____

_____

_____

10. *Has your loved one ever been hospitalized because of drinking?*

Yes ☐ No ☐
If yes, how is this affecting him or her? How is it affecting you?

_____

_____

_____

DRUG ISSUES

1. *Has your loved one ever used drugs other than those required for medical reasons?*

Yes ☐ No ☐
If yes, how is that affecting him or her? How is it affecting you?

_____

_____

_____

2. *Does he or she use drugs more than once a week?*

Yes ☐ No ☐
If yes, how is this affecting him or her? How is it affecting you?

_____

_____

_____

3. *Has your loved one tried to stop using drugs but been unable to do so?*

Yes ☐ No ☐
If yes, how is this affecting him or her? How is it affecting you?

_____

_____

_____

4. *Are you worried about your loved one's drug use?*

Yes ☐ No ☐
If yes, how is this affecting you?

_____

_____

_____

5. *Has your loved one's drug abuse ever created problems between you?*

Yes ☐ No ☐
If yes, what are the problems? How are they affecting you?

_____

_____

_____

6. *Has he or she lost friends because of drug use?*

Yes ☐ No ☐
If yes, how is this affecting him or her? How is it affecting you?

_____

_____

_____

7. *Has your loved one ever neglected obligations, family, or work because of drug use?*

Yes ☐ No ☐
If yes, how is this affecting him or her? How is it affecting you?

_____

_____

_____

8. *Has your loved ever gotten in trouble at work because of drug use?*

Yes ☐ No ☐
If yes, how is this affecting him or her? How is it affecting you?

_____

_____

_____

9. *Has he or she ever lost a job because of drug use?*

Yes ☐ No ☐
If yes, how is this affecting him or her? How is it affecting you?

_____

_____

_____

10. *Has he or she ever engaged in illegal or dangerous activities in order to obtain drugs?*

Yes ☐ No ☐

If yes, how is this affecting him or her? How is it affecting you?

_____

_____

_____

INTERNET OR COMPUTER OBSESSIONS

1. *Has he or she begun to use the Internet more often and for increasingly longer sessions?*

Yes ☐ No ☐

If yes, how is this affecting him or her? How is it affecting you?

_____

_____

_____

2. *Has your loved one ever tried to control, cut back, or stop his or her Internet use, but been unable to do so?*

Yes ☐ No ☐

If yes, how is this affecting him or her? How is it affecting you?

_____

_____

_____

3. *Does he or she seem to feel restless, moody, depressed, or irritable when not using the Internet?*

Yes ☐ No ☐

If yes, how does this behavior affect you?

_____

_____

_____

4. *Has your loved one's Internet use ever affected your family relationships?*

Yes ☐ No ☐
If yes, how? What effect are strained family relationships having on you?

_____

_____

_____

5. *Has your loved one ever lied to cover up his or her amount or type of Internet use?*

Yes ☐ No ☐
If yes, how is this affecting him or her? How is it affecting you?

_____

_____

_____

6. *Has your loved one had problems at work or school because of Internet use?*

Yes ☐ No ☐
If yes, what are the problems? How are they affecting you?

_____

_____

_____

7. *Has your loved one had problems with family or friends because of excessive Internet use?*

Yes ☐ No ☐
If yes, what are the problems? How are they affecting you?

_____

_____

_____

8. *Has your loved one been preoccupied on the computer, with ever-longer sessions online, and withdrawal symptoms like anger and craving when prevented from logging on?*

Yes ☐ No ☐
If yes, how is this affecting you?

_____

_____

_____

9. *Does your loved one ever experience high levels of anxiety, stress, or insecurity whenever a computer is unavailable?*

Yes ☐ No ☐
If yes, how does this behavior affect you?

_____

_____

_____

10. *Is he or she uncomfortable and fidgety when not using the Internet?*

Yes ☐ No ☐
If yes, how does this behavior affect you?

_____

_____

_____

GAMBLING ISSUES

1. *Has your loved one ever gambled until his or her last dollar was gone?*

Yes ☐ No ☐
If yes, how is this affecting him or her? How is it affecting you?

_____

_____

_____

2. *Has your loved one ever lost time from work or school due to gambling?*

Yes ☐ No ☐
If yes, how is this affecting him or her? How is it affecting you?

_____

_____

_____

3. *Has gambling ever caused trouble at home or with relationships?*

Yes ☐ No ☐
If yes, what are the problems? How have they affected you?

_____

_____

_____

4. *After winning, does your loved one ever have a strong urge to return and win more?*

Yes ☐ No ☐
If yes, how does this affect you?

_____

_____

_____

5. *After losing, does he or she want to return as soon as possible and win back the losses?*

Yes ☐ No ☐
If yes, how does this affect you?

_____

_____

_____

6. *Has your loved one ever sold anything to get gambling money?*

Yes ☐ No ☐

If yes, how is this affecting him or her? How is it affecting you?

_____

_____

_____

7. *Has your loved one ever gambled with borrowed money or a loan (including a credit card cash advance)?*

Yes ☐ No ☐

If yes, how does is this affecting you?

_____

_____

_____

8. *Has your loved one ever neglected his or her welfare, or the family's welfare, due to gambling?*

Yes ☐ No ☐

If yes, how is this affecting you?

_____

_____

_____

9. *Has your loved one ever committed (or considered committing) an illegal act like stealing, embezzlement, or forgery to get gambling money?*

Yes ☐ No ☐

If yes, how is this affecting him or her? How is it affecting you?

_____

_____

_____

10. *Has your loved one's gambling ever made him or her consider suicide or other self-destructive acts?*

Yes ☐ No ☐
If yes, how is this affecting him or her? How is it affecting you?

_____

_____

_____

DISORDERED EATING

1. *Does your loved one tend to experience dramatic weight loss or weight gain?*

Yes ☐ No ☐
If yes, how is this affecting him or her? How is it affecting you?

_____

_____

_____

2. *Does he or she wear baggy clothes or layer clothes, hoping to disguise weight loss or gain?*

Yes ☐ No ☐
If yes, how does this make you feel?

_____

_____

_____

3. *Is he or she obsessed with exercise (for example, always wanting to exercise after eating)?*

Yes ☐ No ☐
If yes, how is this affecting you?

_____

_____

_____

4. *Does he or she complain about being overweight, even though he or she is very thin?*

Yes ☐ No ☐
If yes, how is this affecting you?

_____

_____

_____

5. *Are large amounts of money being spent on sugary or high-fat foods?*

Yes ☐ No ☐
If yes, how is this affecting him or her? How is it affecting you?

_____

_____

_____

6. *Does he or she base self-worth on weight and body image?*

Yes ☐ No ☐
If yes, how is this affecting him or her? How is it affecting you?

_____

_____

_____

7. *Does he or she frequently make excuses to avoid eating or to skip meals?*

Yes ☐ No ☐
If yes, how is this affecting him or her? How is it affecting you?

_____

_____

_____

8. *Does he or she get weighed often and overreact to tiny fluctuations in weight?*

Yes ☐ No ☐
If yes, how is this affecting him or her? How is it affecting you?

_____
_____
_____

9. *Does he or she avoid social situations where food is available?*

Yes ☐ No ☐
If yes, how is this affecting him or her? How is it affecting you?

_____
_____
_____

10. *Have you observed or found evidence of behaviors such as bingeing, purging, or laxative abuse?*

Yes ☐ No ☐
If yes, how is this affecting him or her? How is it affecting you?

_____
_____
_____

ANGER/ABUSE ISSUES

1. *Are you ever fearful of your partner?*

Yes ☐ No ☐
If yes, how is this affecting you?

_____
_____
_____

2. *Do you avoid certain topics (or spend a lot of time figuring out how to talk about certain topics) so that you do not arouse your partner's criticism or anger?*

Yes ☐ No ☐
If yes, how is this affecting you?

_____

_____

_____

3. *Are you afraid that your partner may try to hurt or even kill you?*

Yes ☐ No ☐
If yes, how often do you have this fear? What is it doing to you?

_____

_____

_____

4. *Has your partner ever threatened to hurt you or kill you?*

Yes ☐ No ☐
If yes, how often? What is it doing to you?

_____

_____

_____

5. *Has your partner ever physically hurt you?*

Yes ☐ No ☐
If yes, what happened? How did it make you feel?

_____

_____

_____

6. *Has your partner ever threatened to commit suicide as a way of keeping you from leaving?*

Yes ☐ No ☐
If yes, how did you react? How did it make you feel?

_____

_____

_____

7. *Has your partner ever forced you to have sex when you didn't want to?*

Yes ☐ No ☐
If yes, how did this affect you?

_____

_____

_____

8. *Has your partner threatened you at work, either in person or on the phone?*

Yes ☐ No ☐
If yes, how did this affect you?

_____

_____

_____

9. *Does your partner try to keep you from seeing your friends or family?*

Yes ☐ No ☐
If yes, how is this affecting you?

_____

_____

_____

10. *Does your partner verbally abuse you?*

Yes ☐ No ☐
If yes, how? How is it affecting you?

_____

_____

_____

FINANCIAL ISSUES

1. *Do you distrust your loved one's ability to handle money?*

Yes ☐ No ☐
If yes, how does this distrust affect you and the relationship?

_____

_____

_____

2. *Are credit cards a problem for your loved one?*

Yes ☐ No ☐
If yes, how is this affecting him or her? How is it affecting you?

_____

_____

_____

3. *Does your loved one often purchase items impulsively, knowing he or she doesn't need or want them?*

Yes ☐ No ☐
If yes, how is this affecting you?

_____

_____

_____

4. *Does your loved one's shopping behavior cause you emotional distress?*

Yes ☐ No ☐
If yes, describe the distress.

_____

_____

_____

5. *Has your loved one often hid purchases, or lied about what he or she purchased or how much money was spent?*

Yes ☐ No ☐
If yes, how is this affecting you?

_____

_____

_____

6. *Does your loved one ignore the consequences of his or her shopping habits, such as mounting debt or tensions between you?*

Yes ☐ No ☐
If yes, how is this affecting him or her? How is it affecting you?

_____

_____

_____

7. *Have you gotten into arguments or had a damaged relationship with your loved one because of the time he or she spends shopping, the deception about shopping, or any poor money habits?*

Yes ☐ No ☐
If yes, how is this affecting him or her? How is it affecting you?

_____

_____

_____

8. *Is your loved one using credit cards to buy things he or she normally would buy with cash?*

Yes ☐ No ☐

If yes, how is this affecting him or her? How is it affecting you?

_____

_____

_____

9. *Has your loved one begun to receive repeated notices and calls from creditors regarding late payments, or have accounts gone delinquent or been turned over to debt collectors?*

Yes ☐ No ☐

If yes, how is this affecting him or her? How is it affecting you?

_____

_____

_____

10. *Has your loved one taken out loans to consolidate debts and/or drawn on savings to pay regular bills that used to be paid from his or her monthly paycheck?*

Yes ☐ No ☐

If yes, how is this affecting him or her? How is it affecting you?

_____

_____

_____

EMOTIONAL ISSUES (DEPRESSION, ANXIETY)

1. *Does your loved one often feel sad or irritable?*

Yes ☐ No ☐

If yes, how is this affecting him or her? How is it affecting you?

_____

_____
_____

2. *Has your loved one lost interest in activities he or she once enjoyed?*

Yes ☐ No ☐
If yes, how is this affecting you?

_____
_____
_____

3. *Has your loved one lost interest in sex?*

Yes ☐ No ☐
If yes, how is this affecting you?

_____
_____
_____

4. *Have you noticed changes in your loved one's weight or appetite?*

Yes ☐ No ☐
If yes, how is this affecting him or her? How is it affecting you?

_____
_____
_____

5. *Have your loved one's sleeping patterns changed—for example, is he or she having trouble falling or staying asleep, or sleeping too much?*

Yes ☐ No ☐
If yes, how is this affecting him or her? How is it affecting you?

_____
_____
_____

6. *Does your loved often have feelings of guilt, or cry easily?*

Yes ☐ No ☐

If yes, how is this affecting him or her? How is it affecting you?

_____

_____

_____

7. *Has your loved one let his or her appearance run down—caring less about cleanliness or neatness?*

Yes ☐ No ☐

If yes, how is this affecting you?

_____

_____

_____

8. *Does your loved one seem overly critical of things, or does his or her temper get out of control easily?*

Yes ☐ No ☐

If yes, how is this affecting you?

_____

_____

_____

9. *Does your loved one often feel hopeless and worthless?*

Yes ☐ No ☐

If yes, how is this affecting you?

_____

_____

_____

10. *Has your loved one had thoughts of ending his or her life?*

Yes ☐ No ☐
If yes, how is this affecting you?

_____

_____

_____

OTHER ISSUES

Your loved one may be having trouble with issues other than the ones covered by the above questionnaires. For example, workaholism, inhalants, cutting, sexual addiction, intimacy problems, to name just a few. If any of these, or others, are troubling you, simply write down the answers to the following

As the result of my _____'s behavior, I have lost out on:

1. _____
2. _____
3. _____
4. _____
5. _____

If you're being affected and your math proves it, now it's time to listen to your own inner voice, which is often silenced in the clamor. You can call this voice intuition, conscience, a divine spirit, higher consciousness—whatever fits your belief system. That small voice is your built-in guide. It must be listened to, respected, and followed. To find that voice, remove yourself from the chaos. Find quiet. Be still and listen. Then follow that inner voice. You'll discover in the stillness that it's better to deal with your loved one sooner rather than later. And that's being honest. Honesty is the absolute fundamental foundation of helping people you love to get out of the hole they've dug for themselves. By understanding the costs in personal terms, you can move forward with a clear sense of the deficit that's been created in this whole big ball of bad.

One more thing: If it's any consolation, in the thousands of people I've worked with, there has never been a person, an employer, or a family who said they intervened without cause. Never. Not one.

Now it's time to learn how.

PART II

My 4-Step Program for Creating Change Now

This isn't an ordinary book on change. It's not a book on how to coerce, manipulate, or force people to do what you want them to do, and it runs counter to the conventional wisdom that you're powerless to change another person. What you're about to learn is a unique four-step process, crafted with love and caring, that has a remarkable effect on people. It works whether you're trying to influence your spouse or kids at home, get a loved one to break a crippling addiction or devastating problem, deal with difficult people at work, or just persuade people to make better, more life-affirming choices. The four steps, in a nutshell, are:

STEP 1. *Craft a Circle of Change*
Use the natural influence of friends and family and claim your unmatched power to move a resistant loved one toward change.

STEP 2. *Deliver the Invitation to Change*
Ask someone you love to take the actions necessary for lasting change.

STEP 3. *Champion the Change*
Support your loved one through his or her transformation so that change sticks.

STEP 4. *Care for You*
You have to take care of yourself. Your life is valuable. You were not put on this earth to deal forever with someone's self-destructive behavior. This step shows you how to nurture yourself so that you stay physically and emotionally strong, mentally alert, and spiritually centered.

You are uniquely poised to step in and act with love, passion, and purpose. Give these steps a chance, and you will change someone you love.

FOUR

STEP 1
Craft a Circle of Change

You are about to see that by following my simple four-step change process, you can change someone you love for the better. This powerful process begins with Step 1: Craft a circle of change. Here is where you'll bring together a group of people who care about changing your loved one and are willing to help you do it.

Helen Keller once said, "Alone we can do so little; together we can do so much." Nowhere is this beautiful thought more apt than in Step 1. For change to begin, you can't—you mustn't—go it alone. Sure, your instinct will be to try to do this on your own, but you must resist this. Successful change depends on the help, love, and support of a hand-selected group of people. There is strength in numbers. I call this group the circle of change.

The circle of change is powerfully influential. When someone faces several people, it's not as easy for him to dismiss the whole affair as a personal disagreement, or ignore the heartfelt wishes of parents, children, their spouses, and friends. He'll better grasp the gravity of the situation. And more people can present evidence that a problem really exists. Be it an addiction, overeating, anger or abuse, depression, anxiety, or an obsession, the first step toward motivating change is circling around your loved one with words of encouragement, truth, sincere gestures of unselfish care and support, and most of all, the warm protective embrace of love.

THE FAMILY MEETING

The circle of change engages your loved one in a very special process traditionally called an intervention. You probably know it best as a technique used to help people who have addictions. Yes, an intervention works well for that, but its principles can be broadly and practically applied to any behavior that needs changing.

Mistakenly, an intervention is frequently thought of as an event preconceived as a forceful, confrontational, emotional, and ambushlike episode. What you'll learn to do here is quite different. In fact, I rarely call it an intervention; I call it a "family meeting." It's very strategic, and it's carried out in a caring, loving manner. The family meeting is a statement to your friend or loved one that you love him or her enough to want to see change. This is key. It makes no difference how deeply seeded the trouble, because there are few problems that love cannot conquer or heal. All those in the circle of change demonstrate their love, give indisputable reasons why change must begin, and clearly point the way toward help as the only option.

TEAMWORK

The circle of change is all about teamwork, not about you forcing, begging, bribing, or manipulating someone to change. In fact, the circle is not about you getting your way at all. It's about a group of genuinely concerned people working together to help reset someone's life.

The top priority of all members, for example, is reaching team goals, not personal ones. On an all-star sports team, the expertise of individual players means nothing if it doesn't help the team achieve its goals. If the team doesn't win, no one wins. Likewise, there are no individual heroes in the circle of change, but rather a collection of influence and strengths made available to the group. The success of the circle relies on teamwork to achieve a common goal. And that goal is to have your loved one accept help so that change can begin.

FORM THE CIRCLE

The first challenge, then, is to get the right people in the circle. When I advise families, the main criterion I use for selecting the circle is based on bringing together *the voices that matter most to your loved one*; in other words, who is he or she most likely to listen to? Who does he or she respect most? Love most? Depend on most? Admire most? Who carries weight with your loved one?

Honestly, everyone you consider for the circle will carry *some* weight. Some will carry more, however, and you might not discover this until everyone actually gathers together. A family I met with recently in Ohio is a perfect example. We were working to get Jack, a fifty-three-year-old diabetic father of five, to see a doctor and get back on insulin regularly. Jack's diabetes had become a matter of life or death. His family had grown weary of badgering Dad to do all the things a diabetic must do to control the disease and manage his health: test blood sugar, inject insulin, and take care of himself. At the same time, they wanted to save his life. Admittedly, the situation was frustrating. Jack had said no nine times to our plan. At one point in the meeting, Jack's wife, Alicia, turned to me in utter defeat and shouted, "Goddammit! Can't you hear him, he said NO! He doesn't want our help. I'm through!"

Then, from amid the circle spoke a quiet but forceful voice: Jack's seventy-six-year-old former piano teacher, the diminutive, gray-haired Mrs. Bittleton, who lived one town over. "If you lose your fingers, Jack, you won't be able to play like I know you love to do, and that I'd sure miss." Jack immediately promised to get the medical help he required. Mrs. Bittleton was the strongest voice in the circle. She reached Jack in a way the family could not.

For your circle to be truly effective and successful, select voices like Mrs. Bittleton's that matter. Look over the social landscape of your loved one's life. Ask yourself: In a perfect world—without considering schedules or geographical problems—if you could bring together people with influence and power (past, present, and future) in this person's life, who would they be? All close family or friends, and anyone else with an influential, meaningful relationship to your loved one, should be invited to attend—even children. Start picturing those people now and draw up a preliminary list for your circle. That list most often will include:

▶ *spouse and siblings*

▶ *parents*

▶ *grandparents*

▶ *children*

▶ *cousins, aunts, uncles, and other extended family*

▶ *pastor, rabbi, priest, or other clergy*

▶ *friends and neighbors*

▶ *teacher, past or present*

▶ *boss, past or present*

▶ *coworker, past or present*

▶ *ex-spouse, partner*

▶ *parole officer*

▶ *doctor, counselor, or mental health professional*

While the team is gathering to get your loved one help, there are times when adding someone to support you yourself may be critically important. In Boston recently a family of six sisters gathered with me to help their mom, Jackie. The youngest sister, Maggie, was leading the charge to change and really felt having her best friend, Kristi, present would support her own ability to navigate the personalities and dynamics in that family meeting. In fact, Kristi's support was key, even though she had no relationship with the identified loved one, Jackie.

I introduced Kristi in a simple way. "Kristi is Maggie's dear friend and is here with the blessing of the group to support her friend. We're glad you're here, Kristi."

Involving Users and Enablers

If you're dealing with a substance-abuse problem, it's often best *not* to choose people who are active substance abusers themselves. But there are exceptions, and I'll tell you about one I encountered last year. I was working with a family in Montana, the McKennas, whose eldest son, thirty-five-year-old Anthony, was a commodities trader. Anthony was a chronic pot smoker who no longer cared much about his personal appearance, his job, or even his life. Marijuana can do that to you. It has been associated with a number of mental conditions, including schizophrenia, depression, anxiety, and suicidal thoughts. All day every day, Anthony smoked pot.

Anthony's family protested when I suggested that we invite Anthony's buddy Kenny to the meeting, but I persisted. Kenny was a heavy pot smoker; he could speak from the trenches of experience. When Kenny talked during the family meeting, he said, "Anthony, I know I smoke a lot too, but you've lost more than I have. You are falling apart. Your situation has forced me to look at my own life." Kenny turned out to be the most powerful voice in the room—the voice and the example that tipped Anthony over the line to saying yes to help. Sometimes, the person you think might be the weakest link turns out to be the strongest.

People like Kenny who are users themselves might also be "enablers." Those are people who make it easy for someone else to gamble, drink, take drugs, and you name it: the woman who pays off her partner's debts or bounced checks; the mom who feeds her depressed, overweight kid comfort food; the husband who turns his back on his wife's addiction, pretending there isn't a problem; or the parent who covers for an addict when he misses work or school. The list goes on.

Part of enabling, just like active addiction, is denial. There is a desire to keep family secrets, not rock the boat, or sweep things under the rug. Enablers also make all sorts of rationalizations and try to minimize the problem, to ignore it and hope it goes away. While these intentions are mostly admirable (protecting and rescuing the loved one from perceived harm), the net result is a perpetuation of the disease or problem.

I believe it's vitally important to involve enablers in the change process. An enabler is often a voice that matters very much to the person in trouble. The enabler could be a parent, spouse, girlfriend, or boyfriend—someone the troubled person really loves. I remember clearly the situation with Marcus, a thirty-year-old guy in Georgia who was addicted to cocaine, booze, prescription drugs. You name the drug, and he was on it. Marcus's girlfriend was Karin, a twenty-two-year-old stripper, size two, with big, new breasts and long, thick, sexy blond hair—and she was the primary enabler, and as much into the drugs as he was.

Marcus's family did not approve of Karin, so she was not invited to the family meeting. I learned very quickly, because she called me about not being included, that Karin was probably the most important voice in Marcus's life. Even though their relationship was enmeshed in doing drugs, at its core, they really cared about each other. There was a sexual intimacy, a physical intimacy, and an emotional intimacy that no one else in the family had. We ended up including Karin in the meeting, and she ended up being the person who convinced Marcus to go into treatment. Not only that, Karin later admitted herself to a drug treatment program. Two lives changed for the better!

Leaving out enablers like Karin will not serve you well in helping your loved one. Enabling, at its core, is really a form of love. It is giving, helping, protecting, caring, nurturing—and yes, loving a person with a serious problem. My four-step change process is built on love—it is infused with love—so you need people in the circle who love the person in trouble. So do not be afraid of including the "stripper girlfriend" or other enablers. Yes, that enabler may have given your loved one drugs, bailed him out of jail, paid off her debts, and otherwise allowed negative behavior to continue. But because enablers truly love and care, we need to include them, listen to them, respect them, and draw upon their loyalties to encourage change.

Involving Employers and Coworkers

Here's where things can get sticky—involving people from work. Should you invite someone's boss? Coworkers? Someone from human resources? And if you invite someone from the workplace, will your loved one get fired once the employer finds out about the addiction, the alcoholism, or other problem? Will you be violating your loved one's trust and loyalty if you invite his boss? Or will you risk enraging and alienating your loved one?

These are important questions, and let me say up front that it may not be appropriate to involve the workplace. Consider whether the problem is affecting a person's job and causing sloppy work, missed deadlines, misbehavior at company functions, safety issues, or an increase in sick days, as is usually the case with a substance abuse problem.

As for the concern about someone getting fired, companies typically stand behind someone while they get help, particularly for a drug or alcohol problem. Employers have a vested interest in the health and productivity of their employees. Substance abuse, in particular, entails many costs for employers, including those stemming from absenteeism, workers compensation, decreased productivity, and increased medical insurance claims. For example, the U.S. government's Office of National Drug Control Policy estimates that substance abuse costs U.S. employers approximately $180.9 billion in lost productivity each year. Typically, some aspect of an employee's job performance will trigger concerns in a boss or supervisor anyway, and the company will want to help.

In fact, it's actually more cost effective for an employer to help a person get help than to fire him. The cost of firing and then replacing an employee can be several times the fired person's annual salary. These costs can ultimately include severance pay, a possible retaliatory lawsuit under the Americans with Disabilities Act, executive-search and training fees, and the loss of the fired person's valuable outside contacts and relationships. Some experts estimate that one dollar spent on intervention and rehabilitation results in a savings of four dollars for a company. And companies often conduct company-authorized interventions with my group and other interventionists, because they understand the value.

How then do you decide whether it's appropriate to involve the workplace? I help people answer this important question by applying a litmus test to the situation. Ask yourself the following questions:

▶ *Does the problem involve substance abuse or an Internet addiction?*

▶ *Has your loved one had documented job performance issues related to this problem?*

▶ *Has there been a history of absenteeism stemming from this problem?*

▶ *Is there a history of any on-the-job discipline in the previous two years?*

▶ *Is there a history of legal issues stemming from the problem?*

▶ *Will treatment or rehab involve time away from work?*

▶ *Will company insurance be used to pay for treatment or rehab?*

▶ *Does your loved one's job encourage or enable the problem (e.g., bartending when he or she has an alcohol problem)?*

▶ *Will Employee Assistance Program (EAP) resources be used to help get your loved one into treatment or rehab?*

If you answered yes to any of these questions, please consider involving someone from the workplace. Besides, if the problem is life threatening, don't fret over saving your loved one's job reputation over his or her life! Dead folks don't get fired or hired.

There are always exceptions. If someone's boss is unaware of a problem like substance abuse, it may or may not be a good idea to invite him. The people you choose to be in the circle have been affected at some level by your loved one's behavior, and are often aware of it and the damage it has caused. They're more informed and better equipped to participate in the change process. But you can still involve the workplace, if you need to, by contacting the company's Employee Assistance Program or H.R. department. EAPs have been in existence for decades. They help employees and their families untangle complex webs of problems ranging from substance abuse to parenting, relationship issues, stress, depression, and financial and legal troubles, to name just a few.

There is no charge to the employee and services are voluntary and confidential (except as required by state or federal law).

Keep in mind, too, that the workplace is the area in our lives where we have our greatest daily contact with others, where we expend creative energy, and where we form relationships. We generally enjoy other people we work with. The workplace is where the need for connection, common purpose, and a sense of friendship find a special place. So whenever you consider who will make up your circle of change, at lease consider coworkers or a colleague who cares.

Involving Professionals

You may also want to involve a doctor, therapist, or some other health-care professional in the circle of change. They are often powerful voices for change, and one reason is that they represent legitimate authority. We're naturally inclined to obey a figure who is seen as having some sort of authority due to professionalism, knowledge, and prestige. Marketers have known this for decades: People tend to buy products, services, or ideas from experts who carry the aura of power and knowledge. So if you need a voice with medical or mental health expertise in the circle, consider inviting an expert. He or she can join in person, or even on the phone or online via a service like webex.com.

Including proper authority figures helped trigger agreement in a client I had several years ago. Sharon, age forty-eight, was a high-powered industry exec, a type A personality who got things done and made things happen around her, except in her own life. For instance, Sharon had not been to a doctor (any doctor, for that matter) for more than thirty-three years! Turns out that many years before, Sharon's beloved mom was diagnosed with late-stage ovarian cancer. She died within days. Sharon internalized the trauma around her mom's death, associating doctors with bad news, and decided that she'd never, ever see one again. Sharon was pathologically afraid of doctors.

Her family was worried and disturbed by this behavior, and so they organized a family meeting. Their goal: to get Sharon to go to a doctor. Included in the circle of change were two doctors who just happened to be friends of Sharon's aunt and uncle and graciously agreed to help. The doctors counseled Sharon about the benefits of regular medical checkups. They allayed her fear of doctors. They were potent motivators. Sharon agreed to schedule a medical checkup and promised to see a doctor on a regular basis.

Another professional worth inviting might be a mental health therapist. If you've got an inkling that your loved one might be suffering from a serious mental disorder like an anxiety disorder, mood disorder, or a personality disorder, consider working with a therapist. A little background: There are many different types of anxiety disorders: panic disorder, obsessive compulsive disorder, posttraumatic stress syndrome, phobias, and generalized anxiety disorder (GAD), all of which are best diagnosed by a professional. When health care professionals are involved, documentation must be in compliance with Health Insurance Portability and Accountability Act (HIPAA), a health-care privacy rule. You'll find an example of a HIPAA document in Appendix II, at the back of the book.

As for mood disorders, these include major depressive disorder, chronic mild depression, and bipolar disorder (also called manic depression). There's a difference between these and feeling sad. People with mood disorders may characterize their moods as one of hopelessness or pessimism. They may also be drawn to thoughts of suicide as relief from their depression.

But remember this truth: Disordered behavior and crisis is a depressing, anxiety-inducing way to live. Often families will describe a loved one who is "depressed and drinks too much." Nine times out of ten it's the other way around. He or she drinks too much and from that comes depression.

A term you may increasingly hear is personality disorders, which are on the rise and estimated to affect 2 percent of adults. One of the better known is borderline personality disorder (BPD). Someone with BPD develops exceedingly stormy and volatile relationships. They whipsaw between great affection for family and friends and devaluing them with anger and hatefulness. The person may be intensely afraid of being abandoned and react savagely to the mildest of separations, such as a vacation, a business trip, or a sudden change in plans. Not surprisingly, friendships are difficult to maintain and may result in the abandonment that is so feared. Anyone with BPD can act impulsively in other areas, too, such as excessive spending, binge eating, and having risky sex. Whereas people with depression or anxiety disorders generally acknowledge their problem, people with personality disorders believe that their behavior is a normal and fair response to the way the world is treating them—all the more reason to involve a therapist.

COMPLETE THE CIRCLE

Remember to brainstorm and compile your list without editing. You can cross people off later; but for now, just put pen to paper, and write, write, write. Keep an open mind and be creative as you build this preliminary list. I once did an intervention in which we placed in an empty seat a picture of a child who had been killed as a result of the loved one's drunk driving. The absent child's voice was the most powerful in the room. Sometimes a deceased member can join through a video, story, photo collage, or again that empty chair.

Next, prioritize your list to include those you believe have the most influence on your friend or loved one. Get your list down to more than a few but less than a dozen. Larger than twelve, and the meeting can get unruly. Smaller than three, and it can lack power. I have had family meetings with higher numbers of people participating, but if you do this yourself, work to keep it manageable and below a dozen.

Set a date for the meeting. I advise folks to have the family meeting within ten days of the decision to intervene. Setting the date quickly activates the power you hold. The momentum is in place. Delay, on the other hand, breeds second-guessing, bickering, dissent, and procrastination. Your loved one is in crisis. Don't push pause; push the fast-forward button and get moving.

Then begin contacting the people you've picked for the circle. Simply begin the conversation with something along these lines:

I'm very concerned about Susan. I see that things are getting worse with her. I've learned about a way we can help her that we've never tried before. It's called a family meeting, and it's conducted with a lot of love, care, and concern. The goal is to have Susan agree to get help and begin to change. I know you're as concerned about Susan as I am. We're getting together to discuss this on [date], and it's important you are there. Can I count on you to join us?

If you're contacting someone from work:

Hi John, this is Richard Miller. I'm a friend of Tommy Drucker's. You're aware that Tommy has been struggling with some issues. I'm working with Tommy's family to get him some help. Is this a good time to talk with you? I trust we can keep this call confidential for the time being? We're having a family meeting, and we're inviting Tommy to participate. Tommy has a great deal of respect for you, and I wonder if you might be able to participate with us in the meeting. . . .

As you ask people to attend, be prepared for a variety of reactions. Sometimes people are too unsure or too frightened to participate. Some may flatly refuse. Others may just want to be there to show support but are not interested in expressing how the problem, behavior, or difficulty has affected them. Still others may be willing to do whatever it takes.

When someone is opposed to joining the circle, it often means they need more information. I suggest you educate them about the process. Ask them if they'd be willing to learn more about how the change process works. Offer to follow up with some information you'll e-mail, or suggest this book. Normally, after you explain the process to them, their concern and love for the person in trouble compels them to get involved.

Of course, sometimes people can't participate because of schedule commitments, geographical distance, or for other personal reasons. These situations can be accommodated also. People who can't be present may choose to make a contribution to the process through a letter, or they can join in on the meeting through technology such as conference calls or webex.com, which lets you make video calls over the Internet and even meet together using webcams.

PREPARE THE CHANGE PLAN

The circle's goal is to have your loved one accept help, which I call the change plan. That means you've got to have that plan lined up. And yes, it is up to you to line it up. This is because there's a very high rate of denial with most negative behaviors. People often don't want to accept that they have an alcohol problem, a gambling addiction, a spending problem, or any problem for that matter. People in denial just don't usually line up help on their own. So it's reasonable and makes perfect sense that you'll be the one to find the right program. You'll also be explaining to your loved one that you're not equipped to help her, and she needs someone, or some program, trained to deal with these kinds of things. The group is a powerful motivator for change, and for helping your loved one to say yes to a change plan.

Prior to the meeting, you and some of your team members must do some research. You'll want to identify a therapist, program, or support group that will help get your loved one back on the right track. Selecting the right one does take some legwork, and depends on the nature of the problem you're dealing with.

WHO NEEDS REHAB TO CHANGE,
AND WHO DOESN'T

If your loved one's behavior is destructive or dangerous (e.g., she's going home with strangers, doing dangerous amounts of drugs or alcohol, gambling or spending a lot, or logging untold hours on the Internet), the change plan should involve a strong program, possibly even at an inpatient residential facility for addiction. Signs that someone might need rehab include:

▶ *An increase or decrease in appetite*

▶ *Changes in eating habits and/or sleep patterns*

▶ *Unexplained weight loss or gain*

▶ *Extreme hyperactivity*

▶ *Excessive talkativeness*

▶ *Needle marks or bruises on lower arm, legs, or bottom of feet*

▶ *Obvious negative changes in overall attitude or personality with no other identifiable cause*

▶ *Changes in friends; for example, new friends are drug users*

▶ *Change in activities; loss of interest in things that used to be important*

▶ *Drop in school or work performance*

▶ *Skipping or lateness to school or work*

▶ *Difficulty in paying attention; forgetfulness*

▶ *Lack of motivation, energy, self-esteem, discipline; an "I don't care" attitude*

▶ *Defensiveness, temper tantrums, resentful behavior (everything's a hassle)*

▶ *Unexplained moodiness, irritability, or nervousness*

▶ *Violent temper or bizarre behavior*

▶ *Secretive or suspicious behavior*

▶ *Car accidents, fender benders, or more frequent household accidents*

▶ *Chronic dishonesty; trouble with law enforcement*

▶ *Unexplained need for money; inability to explain where money goes; stealing*

▶ *Unusual effort to cover arms, legs, and even feet*

▶ *Change in personal grooming habits*

▶ *Possession of drug paraphernalia*

On the other hand, not everyone needs rehab to change. The circumstances that precipitate selecting a change plan vary by the individual, and the problem at hand. You've got to zero in on what kind of help you need. Is your loved one a teenager with a food addiction problem? A guy with financial and legal issues because of a gambling problem? A spouse who needs marriage counseling? A relative with anger management issues? A child who is depressed? A mom who is stressed-out because of competing responsibilities at home, work, and school?

The change plan can include simpler sources of help: a credit counseling program at your local credit union; a weight-loss group in your community or at a local hospital; a smoking cessation class; participation in a 12-step program; a tutoring program at school; a marriage counseling program; a support group; sessions with a therapist; or stress-management classes. These are all important and effective ways to provide professional resources to change someone you love.

To make this part of Step 1 easy for you, I've listed many programs, treatment centers, counseling services, support groups, and other resources in Appendix I. You can also check the Internet or your local phone book for resources. Word of mouth is another effective way to find a therapist or a program. Ask your friends, relatives, or coworkers. You might be surprised at how open people are about having been in some sort of counseling. At this point, go down all avenues, make a list of all possibilities, research them, and learn more about their approaches.

If therapy is a part of the change plan, it will be up to you to research and check out therapists on your loved one's behalf. Check to make sure the therapist is licensed by the state, and find out just what academic and professional preparation the therapist has. Some have master's degrees in social work or counseling, some have Ph.D.s in psychology, and some are medical doctors. Ask them about their experience: How long have they been in practice, what kind of training do they have, do they have a specialty, are they affiliated with an academic institution, and so on. Find out whether the therapist has ever dealt with your particular problem before. If so, how often? If the therapist doesn't have the expertise you need, he should be willing to refer you to a therapist better able to handle the issues you're facing.

There has to be a certain fit between a therapist and a client. If you're not sure this is someone your loved one can work with, don't waste time trying to figure it out. Move on to someone else on your list. Sometimes you have to look around a little before you find the right fit.

Much of the same holds true for a rehabilitation facility: Choose the necessary expertise, experience, and licensing appropriate to your situation. Look into a few treatment facilities, read through their treatment programs carefully, and make sure you understand them. Treatment options vary along many lines—location, cost, mission, length, treatment philosophy, detox availability, and insurance compatibility to name a few. You have to find the program appropriate to your needs. Questions you may want to ask include:

▶ *Is the program run by personnel who are board certified in the field?*

▶ *Is the program licensed by the state?*

▶ *Is it accredited by the Joint Commission on the Accreditation of Healthcare Organizations (JCAHO) or Commission on Accreditation of Rehabilitation Facilities (CARF)? JCAHO and CARF set standards for health-care organizations and issue accreditation to those who meet those standards. If you are looking at acute care, almost without fail, insist on one of these two accreditations.*

▶ *Does the program provide an after-care program? This is necessary to maintain the treatment, prevent relapses, and provide recovery support after the main part of treatment is over. Ongoing case management is critical to helping people stay better. In my practice we call it Assist In Recovering (AIR) which is modeled on the Airline Pilot monitoring and accountability program that has shown to be the most successful way to encourage change through accountability. Treatment centers offer different degrees of this kind of program. Demand this. It counts.*

▶ *Can it be covered by your existing health plan? If not, is there a comparable choice?*

▶ *Can your loved one take time off from work through a combination of sick and vacation days? If your loved one has schedule conflicts or can't sacrifice time away from the job, an option is to get him or her to attend support group meetings like AA first.*

You may want to visit the facility first and see what's happening inside the walls. This will help to make your decision a little easier. The best way that you can help someone you love is to do your research, and eventually you will find a program or facility that will suit your needs.

If you're dealing with gambling, a spending addiction, or other financial problem, I urge you to include a financial counseling program as part of the change plan. A good financial counselor should be accredited or certified, and have years of experience working with all kinds of financial situations. An experienced financial counselor can help your loved one take an honest look at a particular situation to figure out the causes of financial problems. The counselor will then come up with a plan to work through them. Some financial problems are situational, such as a divorce, a death in the family, unexpected health-care expenses, job loss, or identity theft. Others are behavioral, like unwise use of credit or inappropriate spending habits. They're rooted in other problems and require a change in thinking and action to amend the problems. A qualified financial counselor should be able to help people sort through any financial situation and coach them to make better day-to-day choices.

Whatever change plan you decide upon, look into its price and whether it is covered by insurance. Some insurance companies pay for therapists and programs only under certain licensures, while others pay for only treatment options within their network. You'll also want to ask about co-payments required and number of sessions covered. If your loved one isn't covered by health insurance, ask for a listing of options for people without insurance.

Certain faith-based programs are often willing to serve people without insurance or financial resources. People who work in these programs often share a deep commitment to serve at little to no money. Understand that faith-based providers usually make their general religious tenets known from the beginning and use the language and teachings of religion to reach clients, instead of relying on clinical language alone. If this doesn't sit well with you—or, more important, with your loved one—then a secular program may be better. But for many people, if there's no insurance, no money, no family support, and no job, this is an alternative worth looking into.

Anonymous Support Groups

The forerunner of the self-help movement is Alcoholics Anonymous. Founded in the United States by two alcoholics struggling to remain sober, the organization today boasts chapters throughout the world. The AA approach is based on a 12-step program in which participants learn to admit their powerlessness over a certain problem, be it alcohol or something else. They come to believe that there is a Power greater than themselves that can help restore them to sanity and they make a decision to turn themselves over to that Power. Besides helping recovering alcoholics, AA has also become the model for numerous other self-help programs. You may want to locate support groups in your community that address the needs of your loved one. Among the many groups patterned after AA are:

Anorexics & Bulimics Anonymous

Batterers Anonymous

Celebrate Recovery (Christian Recovery)

Cocaine Anonymous

Debtors Anonymous

Depressives Anonymous

Friends in Recovery (Christian Recovery)

Gamblers Anonymous

Narcotics Anonymous

Nicotine Anonymous

Overeaters Anonymous (and its more structured offshoot, Greysheeters Anonymous)

Pill Addicts Anonymous

Rape Anonymous

Sex Addicts Anonymous

PREPARE THE CHANGE MESSAGE

Everyone in the circle agrees on your mission statement, which I call the change message. It recounts how the person's behavior has affected you and is expressed at the family meeting. It's about presenting reality to someone in a way they can receive it. The change message basically says, "We love you, and have seen you struggle with this for a long time. You are not alone in this process, and today we have begun change. We can picture you healed and better and whole. We are moving ahead in a new way because we need change! We would like you with us in this change." The change message does not say, "You're a crummy person . . . you're a jerk." That type of recrimination only raises everyone's emotional temperature and thwarts change. The change message expresses love, while initiating change.

Crafting the change message is a key part of the personal renovation that is about to take place. And like all renovations, it requires the use of delicate tools; bringing in the bulldozers may wreck the whole contraption. The tools you'll use to write your change message are the *eyewitness account*, the *flash-forward*, and the *resolution*. With these tools, you'll calmly paint a picture. In other words, you'll verbally offer a visual scene of how you want someone to change. You'll persuade someone to get help before he or she completely crumbles. Here's how these tools work:

The Eyewitness Account

Few things are better than an eyewitness account at the scene. It adds veracity to what has occurred. I know that from my days as a TV reporter. So ask, and answer, the question, "What have you seen?" (Give details!) Your answer forms your eyewitness account. Whatever you do, don't call your loved out for his stupid antics or blame him for being crazy and irresponsible—it'll just make him defensive. Put the onus on you and say something like "It freaked me out when you . . ." or, "I felt afraid for our family because . . ." "I haven't seen you for a long time, but your sister has been confiding in me that . . ." This will clue him in to the fact that his actions are affecting others. Often, the eyewitness account alone is enough to turn the tide. The proof of how powerfully this works is in the following story.

Michael Bartlett's thirty-nine-year-old sister, Marlene, was a sixth-grade school teacher and a divorced mother of two. Her kids were four and ten years old, beautiful little blue-eyed girls with freckles and wide grins. Following a wrenching separation and divorce, Marlene moved quickly from being a nightly drinker to a terrible, chronic late-stage alcoholic, who was going to die unless she went somewhere for intensive treatment. Marlene would pass out most nights drunk; just get into the bed and be out cold within minutes. Her children would go without food. Ironically, if you asked her what was most important to her, she'd say, without fail, her kids. In talking to Michael, I coached him in the process of using the eyewitness account.

At a family meeting with Marlene in Michael's living room, Michael looked at his sister and described what he had seen just two days earlier:

I walked in your house after your ex-husband called to say he couldn't reach anyone there and he was supposed to pick up the kids for the weekend. There you were, locked in the house, television blaring, with dirty dishes piled in the sink and mold growing in unwashed juice glasses. There was smelly laundry shin-deep on the floors and empty vodka bottles were strewn around your room. I've never seen so many bottles anywhere. A ceiling leak left a puddle on the floor. I was shocked and depressed when I found you drunk and naked in the shower, holding your four-year-old, who was sobbing inconsolably.

The Flash-Forward

The second part of your change message is the flash-forward. Ask yourself, What do you worry about that will happen if your loved one doesn't get help? Or, in other words, what are your fears? Be specific. That he'll die? Lose her job? Get physically sicker? That it's just a matter of time before she drives home drunk one night and runs someone down or ends up in jail? That he'll lose limbs due to poorly managed diabetes?

Using Michael's example again: *I love you, but I'm worried that you'll get so drunk again that something terrible will happen to you or to the children. Alcohol has become the priority in your life over your children.*

Using the flash-forward tool, you paint a picture, an honest though usually a grim one, of the future. Let your loved one know that she may not only be hurting herself but also the people she cares about. This tool is a spiritual time machine that shows everyone where the problem behavior is headed if left unchecked.

The Resolution

I've been playing the piano for some thirty-five years, and in many musical selections, there is the need to move from a dissonant, or unstable, tone or chord to a more final or stable-sounding one—a sequence referred to in music as "resolution." When we deal with a loved one who is troubled, we want to see that person move from instability to stability, don't we? We want to pave the way to a harmonious resolution. Using the tool of resolution, you describe to your loved one how you'd like to see this problematic behavior resolved. Basically, you spell out how you want the person to change—and where to get help to make it happen. In a perfect world, how exactly do you want the behavior to change? What is the "after" picture in your mind? What does your loved one look like, feel like, and act like after resolving his or her problem? What is your hope?

Here was Michael's resolution: *I cherish you so very much. I want to see you become the mother of these children that I know you can be—a loving mother they can look up to and feel protected and loved by. Your drinking is confusing and changing them. It will kill. There can be a new life ahead of you. Will you accept the help we're offering and start a treatment program today?*

So powerful was Michael's change message that Marlene saw just how addicted she had become, and within one hour, she was on her way to rehab. Michael's honest, from-the-heart eyewitness account opened up a whole new way of life for his sister—even though she had repeatedly resisted getting help. But after listening to Michael's eyewitness account, her no became yes.

"I" Messaging

The key to using these tools effectively also lies in your approach. We usually confront and communicate one of two ways. One of these is to use statements that are critical and put others on the defensive. These types of messages are called "you" messages. Examples are: "You're crazy." "You're just trying to get your way." "You are deliberately trying to hurt me." "You're screwed up."

A more successful way to communicate is to use statements that express your needs without attacking or criticizing the other person. These are called "I" messages. Examples: "I was terrified when you were two hours late for dinner Tuesday, because I knew you had been drinking." "At the party last Friday, I was humiliated because you passed out." "I feel overwhelmed by all the debts we have around us."

An "I" message has three basic parts:

▶ *An expression of how you feel: "I feel . . ." Follow "I feel . . ." with a feeling word: "I feel afraid . . ."*

▶ *A description of what the other person did or said that caused you to feel that way: "I feel afraid when you drive under the influence."*

▶ *A statement reflecting what you want to happen: "I feel afraid when you drive under the influence. I want you to stop this, and get help for your drinking. I feel it's out of control."*

"I" messages can include a fourth part telling why you feel as you do about what happened—a "because" section: "I feel afraid when you drive under the influence, because something tragic could happen."

"I" messages work because they relay how you feel without putting the other person on the defensive. Use "I" messages whenever you talk to your loved one about changing.

Your change message must be wrapped in love. Any action taken in love and with purpose and passion to address a crisis will deliver.

DECIDE WHO SHOULD LEAD THE MEETING

When you meet to rehearse, the circle should decide who will lead the family meeting. The leader should be someone who is least likely to get emotionally hot, and the most likely to persevere and encourage the group in dealing with a change-resistant loved one. This person should be someone who can remain calm, stay courageous, and has the ability and patience to move your loved one from saying no to change to saying yes. If the leader is someone your loved one highly respects, and wouldn't want to let down, all the better. We tend to comply with the wishes of people we like.

Most families I work with know instinctively who makes the best leader. But if they're struggling with this issue, I list some personality traits of good leaders for them. For example:

▶ *Ability to rise to the occasion in a crisis*

▶ *Willingness to stand up for what is important*

▶ *Action oriented*

▶ *Relationship oriented*

▶ *Ability to keep a group focused on the task at hand*

▶ *Ability to inspire respect and loyalty from others*

▶ *Ability to reconcile conflicting opinions and brings folks to agreement*

▶ *Cool under pressure even when the chips are down*

▶ *In possession of a clear-cut vision of the outcome*

Once people hear these traits, they'll come to know who should lead the family meetings.

SHOULD YOU USE A
PROFESSIONAL INTERVENTIONIST?

To change someone you love, you have the power, the support, and the love within your heart to do it all on your own. There are times, however, when you might want to consider a professional interventionist. Think about using a professional interventionist if your loved one:

▶ *Has a history of mental illness (anxiety disorder, mood disorder, or personality disorder)*

▶ *Has a history of violence*

▶ *Has previously engaged in suicidal behavior or has recently talked about suicide*

▶ *Is known to be taking several unknown mood-altering substances (this can produce erratic, unpredictable behavior)*

A professional interventionist is trained to handle these situations, while serving as a neutral, unbiased coach. He or she can even escort your loved one to the treatment facility. See Appendix I for more information on finding an interventionist or visit www.BradLamm.com for additional resources.

Your circle of change has powers you never imagined. It makes no difference how deeply seeded the trouble, how hopeless the outlook, how frustrated the feelings, or how tangled the web. A loving circle will move through this. So hold on, have faith, and know that change is beginning.

RECAP OF STEP 1

▶ *Decide who should be included in the circle of change and ask them to participate.*

▶ *Research programs and resources that will help your loved one change and identify the appropriate course of action for the change plan.*

▶ *Have all members of the circle prepare their eyewitness accounts. These messages describe how your loved one's behavior has affected you and offer a visual of the change you want to see.*

FIVE

STEP 2

Deliver the Invitation to Change

To change someone you love, the next step is to ask them to change. That's what you'll do in Step 2: Deliver the invitation to change. I know you're probably nervous about this, as most families I work with say this is the scariest part. But don't worry. This is a normal reaction, certainly understandable and to be expected. I've had people who've wanted to put the brakes on at the last minute, and not meet, because they were so apprehensive that their loved one would just get up and walk out. That happens rarely, and remember, "no" is a conversation starter in this work you are doing.

If you're the one requesting participation, write it down first—in the form of a script—then live with it. Get to know the words, because they're unlike anything you've said in the past, and you want to deliver them perfectly. I don't expect you to win an Oscar on the first reading, but recite and practice a few times until the words become cemented in your brain and you have the courage to speak them. Here are several examples:

Script #1

Bobby, we love you and we're having a family meeting this morning at eleven, with your mom and me and your brothers, along with Aunt Vicki and Uncle Bob and your boss, Thomas, because we are afraid for you. We're going to have the meeting with or without you, but it's important that you be here with us. We haven't known quite how to handle this, so we've come together and have begun working to change as a family. We're going to be talking about you, and it'll be better for all of us if you're here so we can talk with you, rather than just about you. Will you join us, please?

Script #2

Casey, your mom and I have been praying about what to do about your food disorder. It's been hard to even talk about it among ourselves—because we've been so afraid of how sick you are. I've been telling myself you'll get better if we just give you a little more time, but time's up. The time to do this on our own has passed. We love you! Your mom and I need help, so we've decided to have a family meeting. So tomorrow after school, Ms. Sallberg, your lit teacher, your mom and I, and your sister Kelly, who's driving up from Dayton, are going to meet. You're not the first one in our family to struggle with addiction of some kind, and we're going to break this cycle. In fact, we've already started. We're changing with or without you—so we sure pray you will join us, right here, with others who love you so much.

Script #3

We love you, and we have been struggling with how to help, and what to do. We have been afraid of what's going on with you. We have been afraid of doing the wrong thing. We asked Pastor Gregg for help—his son is in recovery too—to help sort things out. A former drug user, he has been clean and sober for many years. He suggested we have a family meeting, so that's what we are doing. Remember last year when you stopped for three months and we got our son back! Well, he's gone again, and we are all together on beginning change. We will meet this Friday at 11 A.M. at our apartment . . . to talk about changes we are embracing and how we can help you. We ARE family, and we love you. *We want to talk* with you *instead of just* about you.

Your Loved One's Response

After you ask your loved one to come to the family meeting, one of three things will happen: He or she will respond positively, negatively, or somewhere in between. Sometimes the person will be very agreeable, ask questions, and ask, "Wow, what took you so long?" Other times, the person will say "F——— you" and hang up the phone. He or she may even call you back, ask who will be there, and want more information.

If your loved one responds negatively or hangs up, that's okay. Send an e-mail or leave a voice mail that reiterates that you're having the meeting, but don't go into great detail. In other words, don't have the family meeting before the family meeting. Stick to these points: (1) We love you, (2) we need a change, (3) we're getting together to begin change, and (4) it is really important that you come.

Rehearsing

Between now and the meeting, it's a good idea to rehearse the meeting with everyone in the circle. You can get together and do this over coffee at someone's house, via webex.com, or over the phone. Have everyone share their eyewitness accounts, then make constructive suggestions if needed. The point is to just touch base, and get everyone comfortable with the process.

Let me reassure you that you're about to engage in one of the most loving experiences of your life. You're going to repair a relationship, help someone have the best life possible, or even save a life. As long as you've prepared yourself, and all members of the group know what they are going to do and not do, the meeting will go smoothly and your stress level will drop considerably. The power you have to begin change in the lives of those you love is enormous and already present. It's not something you have to discover, locate, or purchase. There is power inside your circle of change. I'm reminded of this in every family meeting I do, and I experienced it very recently in my very own family.

It broke my heart when I realized that my fifty-one-year-old brother, Gregg, was dying right in front of my eyes, while as a family, we stood by and prayed. Gregg is the kind of guy everyone loves. He's always smiling and trying to get others to be at ease. Gregg, who struggled for years with ups and downs in his weight, has diabetes. A chronic disease, diabetes occurs when the body doesn't produce or properly use insulin, and thus is unable to maintain normal blood sugar levels. It's often genetic, but neither my mother nor my father has it, nor did my grandparents. Uncontrolled diabetes can lead to very serious and often life-threatening complications, which include blindness, kidney disease, lower-limb amputations, heart disease, and stroke.

In our home, growing up, food was the center of family life. Our mom sure could cook. Roast beef with potatoes and gravy, beans cooked in lard, German chocolate cake—these were our favorites. Like many families, we ate to celebrate, commiserate, procrastinate, and do just about anything ending in an *ate*. The rich food seemed to affect Gregg more than the rest of us brothers, and when Gregg was a sophomore in college, the problem got worse. He packed on 100 pounds. He'd diet down, only to regain it back, plus interest, in fairly short order.

Eventually, he tipped the scales at 300 pounds. A Quaker minister and father of three boys, Gregg ate to celebrate the triumphs in his life and mourn the sorrows, often in secret. He ate to survive and to socialize and to escape. Food was no longer sustenance; it was a drug of sorts.

So when diabetes started taking a toll on his life, he fought it silently. He felt jealous that other people could just put a bite of food in their mouths and never have to think about it. He struggled to comply with the rigid prescription of managing the disease, and eventually decided to give up trying. Things got even worse.

Diabetes began to consume him in destructive ways. Gregg's blood sugar got so out of control that he had skin infections, and constant illnesses that surfaced and silenced him. The deep dark circles under his eyes, the way he shuffled his feet, his sickly pallor—my brothers and I could see that the illness was threatening to take his life. Gregg landed in the hospital in critical condition—the result of his diabetes, which stemmed from his disordered food habits. So we stepped in to save him.

Because we live all over the world—different countries and different coasts—my brothers, parents, and Gregg gathered together on a conference call, to have a family meeting. We did not start off by saying, "Get ahold of yourself. You're not taking care of yourself," or "You're a grown man, why don't you get your act together?" We did not nag Gregg endlessly to listen to his doctor. We did not beg him to go to the gym. We did not argue about what an extra slice of cake would do to his health. None of that.

Instead, we delivered a loving, upbeat invitation to change.

When you want someone to change, don't just say, "You've got to change." This is confusing and poison to the relationship. Instead, you'll use your picture-painting tools that I discussed in the previous chapter. You'll give your loved one a clear picture of what you've witnessed and the change you'd like to see.

In delivering our change message to Gregg, we presented the consequences of his compliance in a positive way. We shared our love, our hopes, and our eyewitness accounts of what his long, exhausting battle looked like to us. We brought to light how this struggle was affecting his entire family in enormous ways. We flashed forward and described what our "after" picture of him looked like in our minds. We reminded Gregg of his potential to be the great father, husband, and minister of which he was capable, and that we couldn't wait for him to look, feel, and be that way again. We made sure our concern didn't come across as criticism or as a sign that he had somehow failed in our eyes. Again and again, we told him how much we loved him and we wanted him to be happy and healthy.

Our change message motivated him to join Celebrate Recovery and Overeaters Anonymous, where he got a sponsor and began working hard to get better. He got it. Then he lost it. After twelve months of ups and downs we talked with him again and suggested in strong terms that he go to inpatient treatment for the problem. Within weeks he entered inpatient treatment at Shades of Hope, to save his life. His blood sugar is now fully under control with diet and exercise. He takes only one pill a day now—no insulin injections. He has a program of recovery that is working for him a day at a time.

WHAT HAPPENS AT THE FAMILY MEETING

You've drawn together a group of people close to your loved one—spouse, parents, grandparents, siblings, children, relatives, friends, and maybe coworkers—and now it's time for action. Own this—we know how to get together as friends and family, so while the stakes are different here, you are applying something you already know! Whatever the situation is, you're not going it alone. You've surrounded yourself with others. All of you are upholding, sustaining, and strengthening one another. Everything will move forward because your efforts are grounded in deep, genuine love.

The Setting

You'll want to hold the family meeting in familiar surroundings, usually someone's home, where folks will feel comfortable. As important is where each person sits. The seating arrangement makes a huge difference in the tone and atmosphere. The person who holds the most emotional punch and will speak last should be positioned next to your loved one. Position the person who will speak first, also an emotion getter, on the other side of your loved one. Sometimes when working with a family, I will sit lower than the rest of the folks, sometimes even on the floor when the identified loved one is a dominant presence. You might consider this for your leader, who will be ready to connect with love and hugs at any moment. This arrangement creates a sense of bonding and belonging.

Open the Meeting

If you're the leader, open the meeting with a welcome to everyone in the room. I always recommend that if your loved one is present, that you thank him or her for the courage to attend. Here are two examples of how to start:

Welcome, everyone. We're so glad you're here, Tommy. I know last night when we spoke with you, you were feeling a lot of different emotions. Your seat is the toughest in the room. So we applaud your courage in stepping out in faith and stepping up to join us as we walk through this time together.

Thank you all for coming. When we started comparing notes about [insert loved one's behavior or situation], our concern grew and we said, "Hey, let's get together to discuss in a really thoughtful, loving way how we can help and support Tommy. We're all going to speak directly from our hearts, lay out our eyewitness accounts of what we've seen, what's causing us fear and pain, and then we'll share with you what we hope will be the beginning of positive, lasting change. There will be a chance for you to talk in a bit. How does that sound?

Ground Rules for the Family Meeting

▶ *Participate in a climate of love, acceptance, caring, safety, and mutual respect.*

▶ *Have your BS meter set to HIGH. Denial can be strong!*

▶ *Do what you normally do when you get together as a family or group. Some families eat pizza together; some gather in the den; and others like to sit around the kitchen table. Gather where you graze. In other words, whatever your social dynamic is, do it. The exception is having alcohol or drugs present. If that's your routine, put it on the shelf for now.*

▶ *Turn off all cell phones, pagers, or beepers (unless there's a doctor on call in the meeting).*

▶ *No tissues allowed! Let the tears and emotions flow.*

▶ *Don't argue, yell, or otherwise raise your voice.*

▶ *Don't preach, belittle, or bad-mouth.*

▶ *Don't use the family meeting as a forum for hostile attacks or recrimination.*

▶ *Keep the tone honest but loving and dignified.*

▶ *Show patience and respect for all members in the circle of change.*

▶ *Conduct the meeting with calmness and love.*

▶ *Keep connected to your loved one. If he or she wants to go outside, have a smoke, or get some fresh air, someone should accompany him. (The only exception is a trip to the bathroom, and sometimes I suggest the door stay cracked.)*

▶ *Work to get a YES, and be determined.*

▶ *If your loved one says, "I'll think about it," respond by saying, "Fine. Let's get back together in two hours to decide." In other words, reschedule the meeting at a specific time, in order to give your loved one time to think it over. Stay with your agenda, which is to get this person to agree to the change plan.*

If Your Loved One Refuses to Attend

Your loved one may not attend the family meeting, at least not initially. This is okay and not an indicator that your efforts have failed. Please understand that the family meeting is not a one-shot deal, where you get together once, deliver a get-help ultimatum, and hope for the best. The family meeting, and its circle of members, function as an ongoing support group for everyone who has been struggling to cope with your loved one's problem. Participating in the circle helps heal you and others who have been scarred by someone's troubling behavior. The pain of an addiction, a troubling habit, or corrosive behavior ripples through a family, and indeed through a whole social network. There can be a lot of anger, resentment, and recrimination, directed at both the troubled person and at you and other relatives and friends. By speaking openly and candidly about pain, worry, and the negative emotions, a family can unite in concern and begin to heal any rifts created by the behavior. Whatever the outcome, the circle empowers you. You'll never again be so negatively affected by the behavior or actions of your loved one. With the support of one another, everyone in the circle gains strength, confidence, and courage that a brighter day has already dawned.

If Your Loved One Stands You Up

In some situations, your loved one may stand you up, even though he said he'd be there. What do you do now? Start the meeting on time; thank everyone for joining the circle. Then poll the group to see if anyone has any information. Where is he? Who talked to him last? Then begin the meeting without him or her. Seriously. You said you would have the meeting with or without him: DO IT. This is important.

The statistics in my practice are this: In about nine out of ten cases they say yes or no to coming then show up to the meeting. But just because he said yes doesn't guarantee he'll come, nor does his declining of the invitation mean he won't show up.

So, like I do, you have the meeting.

Begin the meeting the same way. Thank everyone for coming. Note that your loved one has not come to this meeting, then acknowledge the courage and love represented in the room. Ask for each person there to say out loud the positives of this moment:

▶ *We are together to help.*

▶ *We have strength in numbers.*

▶ *We can do together what we cannot do alone.*

▶ *In spite of our differences, we are agreed and together on beginning change right now.*

Take your group-strengths inventory, share your change message out loud with one another, and then share your eyewitness accounts with one another, going in turn. Don't just sit on your hands either: If anyone knows where your loved one is, I suggest that a couple of people in the group get up and go get him. Make a phone call to him or her.

To give you an example, I once worked with the family of a forty-five-year-old alcoholic, Jim, who said he'd be at the family meeting but didn't show up, even though he lived only a few blocks from where we were meeting. His brother and I went to get him. Jim opened the door, let us in, and we began the meeting right there. The more we talked, the more receptive Jim became, and he went with us to continue the meeting with the rest of the circle. You must be persistent, never give up, keep your focus on the goal—which is *change*—and ultimately you will get a different person than you had before.

Give Your Change Messages

Next, one by one, each person gives their change message. Don't read your message; this only breaks eye contact with your loved one and can ring of insincerity. A better method is to have a few bullet points on a piece of paper to prompt you if necessary. Speak from the heart.

For an emotional crescendo, it's good to have a talking order in place. This means that the person who speaks last has the most dramatic message. One of the most touching meetings I ever did involved an alcoholic grandmother with her adult children and grandchildren. The six-year-old granddaughter said to Grandma, "I'm not going to get in a car with you. I don't have fun with you anymore. I'm not going to come over to your house anymore." Tears started streaming down everyone's faces.

Everyone takes a turn speaking, saying, in effect, "I love you. I care about you, and I'm not going to lose you or let you self-destruct." Remember, the message is threefold:

The eyewitness account: You offer specific instances during which the person's behavior was destructive, damaging, or just plain out of control—and how the specific behavior has damaged your relationship. In short: What have you seen?

The flash-forward: You paint a clear picture of how you see your loved one's life ending up if the problem goes untended and how you would like to see the person change. Again: What are your fears?

The resolution: You ask your loved one to accept help and begin a plan of change, or: What is your hope?

All members share their thoughts and feelings openly but without judgment. Each message should end with a personal expression of love.

The Wrap-up: Present the Change Plan

After everyone has shared from their heart, then the question is called: We have a plan in place (explain treatment plan, show brochures, accentuate the positives) and have an appointment to get you there in a short time. Will you accept the help we're offering now? Seek acceptance now, not later:

We love you very much and we are all behind you. Are you willing to get help (go to treatment, enter this program, sign up for this workshop, make an appointment with this doctor, and so forth) and do it now?

WHEN YOUR LOVED ONE SAYS YES

Most of the time, your loved one will say yes. If you hear no, keep at it. Trust me on this. Please realize that the change process has been a time of bonding and expression of love among everyone in the circle, and together, you have set in motion an absolutely miraculous process. So it's no wonder that your loved one will say yes. When that happens, you follow up by getting your loved one into the preplanned program right away.

In a suburb of Seattle I had a group in which, after the identified loved one said, "Yes! I'll accept the help you're offering," her father chimed in with "I've got a few more things to say . . ." before sliding into a speech on this, that, and the other unimportant item for that moment. So, when he or she says yes: QUIT YAKKING AND GET PACKING! Whatever has been left unsaid can be written in a letter and then considered for a day or two before sharing it.

When you hear yes, congratulations are in order!

I am so proud of you for taking this step!

We are so happy you've trusted us enough to let us help you!

I love you so much, and am grateful you have said yes to our help, honey.

One or two people should offer to help her pack or get ready for her appointment. If your plan includes inpatient treatment, get a "What to Pack" form from the treatment center you have lined up. I have included a general one in Appendix II.

All that said, sometimes the yes will be a halfhearted one. I'm speaking from personal experience. When my friend Paul intervened with me and asked me to go into drug treatment, I was neither keen nor excited to go, but I packed my bags anyway because I had told him I would go. A person in crisis may not have the mental clarity to make definite commitments or good judgments, so you can't always expect your loved one to answer with a strong yes. The weakest yes is still a yes and will crack open the door to real change.

A REAL-LIFE FAMILY MEETING:
SHOP TILL YOU DROP TO DEBT

To show you how this all plays out, I'd like to introduce you to a couple I recently had the opportunity to work with, Tom and Rita.

I had just finished a Change Seminar for a community group when Tom, a tall, dark-haired man, pulled me aside. He was concerned about his wife, Rita. As he talked, it became clear to me that Rita was a junkie. But she didn't crave cocaine, alcohol, or any other drug. In fact, her addiction was to something completely legal and even socially acceptable—she was a shopping addict.

Her typical routine was to purchase something, hide it, then donate it. Suspicious when he found a receipt for a $5,500 donation to Goodwill, Tom was puzzled, so he asked Rita about it. She lied to him, claiming she had cleaned out the closet and donated clothes to the charity. In truth, Rita had a compulsive urge to buy. Like other compulsive behaviors, the purchase generated a mood of satisfaction, seeming to give life more meaning and allowing her to put aside, at least temporarily, her feelings of inadequacy, sorrow, or depression. Further, Rita rationalized her out-of-control behavior by telling herself that at least her donations to charities were doing some good.

It's estimated that 10 million Americans suffer from spending addictions like Rita's. For many, irresponsible spending habits can be brought into check by learning sound financial planning, but for others the never-ending cycle of "charge it and pay for it later" transcends being a bad habit to become a dangerous obsession, tearing apart relationships and driving people to financial ruin.

Tom's family was deeply in debt, and bill collectors were calling every day. Over the previous five years, Rita's parents had bailed them out to the tune of $180,000. But now the cycle of buy, hide, donate had worsened, with no end in sight. Tom and Rita were on the brink of losing their home. Her addiction was threatening to destroy their family.

Rita took out several credit cards in her mother's name and proceeded to rack up $40,000 in charges within a couple of months. Her mother discovered the ruse, but rather than turn her own daughter in to the authorities, she and Rita's father stepped in and bailed her out—again. They paid off her credit cards, closed her accounts, and sent her a cold e-mail criticizing her behavior.

Soon afterward, Rita was suspected of breaking into a neighbor's home and stealing the proceeds from a cancer fund-raiser in order to access more money to fuel her spending habit. The neighbors put the word out that she was a thief, and the family suffered the ensuing shame and embarrassment. Yet this did not stop her crimes. It was then discovered that Rita had embezzled money from her daughter's marching band fund-raiser. The police became involved. Tom was terrified that Rita would be put in jail, and she could have been.

Tom asked me what to do. I urged him to craft a circle of change. I told him to gather together at least two other people—family, friends, or both—who knew about the problem and were being affected by it. I explained to him that we do together what we cannot accomplish alone. Have each person prepare their eyewitness accounts, using the tools of flash-forward and resolution. Everyone's individual account brings to light how her addiction has affected the people present.

Invite Rita to attend the gathering. Whether she attends or not, build consensus around how her behavior is bankrupting the family—financially and spiritually—so that when she does join, everyone will be prepared to share the negative effects of her behavior. Support one another; this is one of the benefits of forming a circle and having family meetings. Agree that the family is in dire straits financially, that there's virtually no money saved in the bank. Then show on a graph or dry-erase board everything she's been spending and what she's been spending it on. If Rita is present, one by one, give your eyewitness accounts and urge her to accept help. Ask her to get into a financial counseling program, a debt workshop, even Debtors Anonymous, or all of the above.

Speak the truth with purpose, love, and authenticity, I told him. This is not gossip. Nor is it butting in. It's nothing short of restoring a family's future. It took all of five minutes to explain this process to Tom. Although he understood it, he was reluctant to follow through. He still feared that Rita would go to jail, and so he dragged his feet. Fortunately, two concerned friends of Rita's—Christine and Maya—came to the rescue and got involved in the process.

They helped Tom craft the circle of change and change message. They e-mailed the participants instructions on how to prepare their eyewitness accounts. Their eyewitness accounts described Rita's behavior in a factual, firm, and loving way—the compulsive buying and hiding of the merchandise, the fraud, the theft, and the impaired relationships—and how it had spiraled into emotional disaster for the family. Circle members described their fears—that the family would lose their home, that Rita would land in jail and end up with a criminal record, and that relationships would be torn apart forever. They asked Rita to change, to stop spending, stop stealing, and stop neglecting her responsibilities, and most important, to enter an intense program for help at a nearby university hospital.

Everything worked. Rita accepted help and accepted the change plan the group had set up for compulsive spenders. She also agreed to marriage counseling. It was hard, but the couple was determined to get beyond their problems and learn to trust each other again. After undergoing treatment and counseling, Rita refrains from using any credit cards, logs any purchases in a notebook (so she pays attention while shopping instead of numbing out), volunteers at charities (rather than making donations), and has begun making financial reparations to those she harmed.

THE CHANGE AGREEMENT

After your loved one says yes, as Rita did, I encourage you to use another powerful tool called the change agreement. It gets your loved one to agree in writing to certain commitments (to start therapy, take a workshop, attend a support group, enter treatment, and so forth). The agreement involves certain expectations along with consequences if the terms of the agreement are violated. It may also state that the person agrees to take part in the family meetings whenever they're scheduled. It is signed by everyone in the circle of change, and everyone gets a copy.

Something special, almost magical, happens when people put their commitments in writing. When human beings commit in writing to an idea or goal, they are more apt to honor that commitment. You know this yourself, if you've ever filled out a pledge form as part of a fund-raising drive. Donors to a fund-raising drive are much more likely to fulfill pledges that are public and put in ink. What's more, studies have shown that if an individual signs an agreement, stating, "I'm going to change my behavior," it cements motivation, especially if there are witnesses.

Written commitments produce inner change. Once someone has made a choice or taken a stand, and put it in writing, he or she will encounter personal and interpersonal pressures to behave consistently with that commitment. Agreements are therefore powerfully effective in changing a bad habit, behavior, or lifestyle. So I always encourage the use of a change agreement to solidify a commitment to this fix.

The change agreement is a living document. It can be revised if necessary. It creates accountability, keeps your loved one to his or her word, builds in added motivation, and is a concrete way to measure progress. It is a living, breathing road map representing your group's agreement to get well.

Should your loved one fail initially—say, for example, he starts maxing out his credit cards again, she resumes shoplifting, or he stops attending anger-management workshops—part of the agreement should state that he or she will agree to a higher level of care or treatment. Be sure to develop fail-safes for what will happen if the agreement is broken or someone doesn't follow through (not a punishment, just an action that everyone agrees is respectful to all). The change agreement is an important foundation of accountability and support that carries the changing or recovering person through the storms that are almost to certain to come. This agreement is a powerful tool for succeeding!

Here are six examples of a change agreement:

Example #1: Compulsive Spending

THE FIX

Change Agreement
February 2010

We agree that we are working together to help Mary become happier and healthier, and free from compulsive spending.

Joe, Audrey, Peter, and Lillian

I, Mary, agree to the following:

1. I promise to surrender my credit cards and checkbooks to the group immediately.

2. I promise to take all the steps in this agreement, in an honest effort to stop spending.

3. I agree to attend three Debtors Anonymous (DA) meetings each week.

4. I agree to obtain a DA sponsor by February 20, 2010.

5. I agree to work with Peter to help me monitor my spending and stick to a reasonable budget.

6. I agree to participate in our Family Calls every week.

7. I promise that if I am unable to this stop behavior, I will enter the intensive compulsive-spending treatment program at Wilson Heights Treatment Center without negotiation or delay.

Signature   *Date*

Example #2: Explosive Anger

THE FIX

Change Agreement
March 2010

*Our extended group of friends has shown resilience in
challenging times and made it through them together over the
years. Today, we choose to continue on in a new path of recovery—by
adding accountability and structure to the plan. We agree that
we will stay supportive, communicative, and loving as we work
together in this effort.*

Cindy, Paul, Michael, Daniel, Theresa, and Paula

I, Rory, agree to the following without negotiation or delay:

1. I agree to begin and participate in anger-management group therapy once a week (Wednesdays, 7 P.M. to 9 P.M.) at the Regional Counseling Center.

2. Between sessions, I promise to apply anger-reduction skills and record my efforts in a journal.

3. I agree to participate in a weekly conference call with the group.

4. If I do not comply with this program of recovery, I agree I will vacate my home and immediately undergo mental evaluation at the Waring Institute without further negotiation.

Signature   *Date*

Example #3: Smoking

THE FIX

Change Agreement
April 2010

We agree that smoking is not just a health hazard but also a threat to life, which is why we have come together to support George in quitting smoking and to demonstrate our love. We are his support system and we will help him with his progress and any tendency to deviate.

Marta, Debbie, Tommy, Katherine, and Bill

I, George, agree to do the following without negotiation or delay:

1. I will quit smoking on _____. (Date)

2. I will attend smoking cessation classes at Tri-State Hospital once a week (Tuesday nights, 7:30 P.M. to 9 P.M.).

3. I agree to follow the stop-smoking plan as outlined by this group, including altering my lifestyle in positive ways (exercise, proper nutrition, deep-breathing exercises, and other coping strategies).

4. If I relapse or abandon the above commitments, I agree to see Dr. Wayne Todd to begin a medical therapy program to stop smoking.

Signature   Date

Example #4: Drug Addiction

THE FIX

Change Agreement
May 2010

We have come together in love and support for Connie, and with this agreement, we clearly define concrete behaviors from which she has committed to abstain in order to define sobriety. We are here to support Connie.

Mark, Randall, Julie, Michelle, Warren, Christine, Carol, Henry, and Rachel

I, Connie, agree to do the following without negotiation or delay:

1. Begin, attend, and complete the Jefferson House outpatient program three times a week as scheduled.

2. See my individual psychotherapist once a week.

3. Submit to random drug screens.

4. Begin attending Narcotics Anonymous, doing 90 meetings in 90 days.

5. Check in twice a week with my circle of change and stay accountable.

6. If I do not comply with this program of recovery, I agree to enter Seabrook House for their 30-day program and understand that all the consequences we talked about previously will begin immediately.

Signature   *Date*

Example #5: Sober Living and Financial Support

THE FIX

Change Agreement
Date:_____

We, Sally Duncan and her family and friends, agree to the following:

1. Sally agrees to get a temporary NA Sponsor, and attend five 12-step meetings per week. She agrees to have a Meeting Card signed at meetings and returned to Dad's office each Friday, in a supplied postage-paid envelope.

2. Sally agrees to stay clean and sober while crafting a resume and working on job leads to pursue after finishing 90 days at the Sober Living House on _____ (date).

3. The family will provide a laptop computer for use and safekeeping by Sally.

4. Sally agrees to make every effort to obtain legitimate employment in the Boston area.

5. Sally agrees to register for college and take courses while maintaining a B average to continue receiving financial support from the family.

6. Sally agrees to see her therapist and sign a HIPAA release form so that the family can help her stay accountable with this. The family agrees they will not ask about personal details of therapy, but instead check on attendance and progress in general terms only.

7. Sally agrees to participate in the weekly Family & Friends Call with _____ moderating.

8. Sally will report to the family weekly by e-mail on her progress in meeting educational and financial independence objectives.

9. The family agrees to support Sally in the following financial ways while she is fully engaged in this path of change:

    a. Health insurance

    b. Cell-phone service

    c. $125 weekly spending money

    d. The cost of agreed-upon random drug testing

10. The family agrees that upon successful completion of 90 days at the Sober Living House, they will provide:

    a. Essential financial support for housing costs on a month-to-month basis while Sally secures part-time employment

    b. An earnings match of Sally's documented earnings so that she can move toward self-sufficiency; choice of housing will depend on Sally's ability to earn money to support her portion of housing expenses

    c. A vehicle for Sally's use after 90 days of continuous employment

    d. Therapy co-pay costs for weekly sessions

The fundamental design of this agreement is to provide Sally's financial and emotional support while she is attaining greater degrees of self-sufficiency in recovery.

We agree this path will not be easy, but have worked to make the process doable. We are committed to this process.

_____   _____

Sally   Date

_____   _____

Family   Date

Example #6: Therapy, Outpatient, or 12-Step Program

THE FIX

Change Agreement
Date:_____

We agree that we are working together to help Jackie become happier and healthier, and free from depression and the cycle of drinking dependency. Understanding that there is not just one way, we commit to support her in this process of discovery and wellness.

Bobby, Walter, Ozzie, and Ruth

I, Jackie, agree to the following:

1. I promise that I will not drive after I have been drinking.

2. I promise to take the steps below, in an honest effort to stop drinking alcohol.

3. I agree to go to three AA meetings each week.

4. I agree to participate in an assessment to get a clinical opinion on outpatient treatment options by _____ (date).

5. I agree to get an AA sponsor by _____ (date).

6. I agree to participate in our Family & Friends Calls moderated by _____.

7. I promise that if I am unable to stop drinking, I will go to inpatient treatment without negotiation or delay at Caron Treatment Center.

Jackie   Date

Ozzie and All   Date

PREPARE FOR CONTINGENCIES

What If Your Loved One Storms Out of the Meeting?

Yes, your loved one may stomp out of the room, erupt in anger, insist that he or she doesn't need help, be resentful, accuse you of betrayal, or maybe never even show up. Your loved one may flatly refuse to do anything. Hornets get mad, but they get tired and quiet down. People don't stay mad when invited into a family meeting in a loving supportive way. Some people run, but they too, get tired, and slow down. Then they're walking before you know it, and next scene, they're sitting with you talking and crying and working with you instead of against you.

These four steps to change I share with you are not easy, but they are *simple*. Simple to carry out in most cases if you follow them completely.

I remember the first time my heart was broken as a young man. I'd been broken up with and I hurt, my heart hurt, and it felt like it would stay broken forever. Hearts heal. The moments when you feel like "forever" is in front of you, remember that emotions level out, hornets get tired, and your loved one won't keep running forever, no matter how it feels at that moment. Emotionally prepare yourself for these situations, while remaining hopeful for positive change.

I remember clearly one of the mothers I worked with a few years ago, Tammy, who asked me again and again what we would do if her son Kip "headed for the hills." I encouraged her by explaining that, in the many hundreds of family meetings I had led, no one had yet run for the hills. Well, there's a first for everything. Sure enough, Kip headed for the hills.

His father, Monte, had invited Kip to the meeting; afterward, Kip wanted to talk to me by phone. "Why are you doing this to me? Isn't this a little premature? This is a private family thing. Butt out!"

A little background: Kip was twenty years old, a good kid and an only child who had been smart as a whip right out of the womb, according to the family. He'd skipped second grade, then fifth grade. Tammy and Monte had union jobs in a local factory in Davenport, Iowa, and their home was a happy one. Neither addiction nor chaos of any sort darkened their lives.

Kip had gone off to a university on a full-ride scholarship for excellent academic achievement. His first two years passed without incident. Prior to his junior year, Kip switched majors from math to biology, with aspirations of becoming a vet. He loved animals.

Suddenly, without warning, Kip started missing family dinners, which he'd attended like clockwork in the past. The family was notified that he was missing classes. They were baffled. Well, it turned out that Kip had started experimenting with drugs at school, and got hooked fast. He didn't run away from the drugs, but toward them. Within a month, he had gone from taking pills to crushing pills and snorting them.

Kip did join us for the family meeting, but stormed out after his mom began her eyewitness account. I helped his mom refocus the urge to run after him. While he didn't exactly head for the hills, he did head for I-129, but we continued our meeting anyway. We shared with one another our common emotions, we built further consensus on the change message, and we bonded as a group. Before long the phone rang. It was Kip. He couldn't come back to the meeting because he had been arrested. Pulled over for speeding, he had landed in jail when the police officer had spotted his "drug kit" on the floor of the car. We piled in several cars and headed straight to the jail where he was being held. We asked to speak with the arresting officer and explained that we were having a family meeting to discuss Kip's substance-abuse problems when he'd left in a huff. We told the officer that we had a ninety-day treatment bed on hold for him that very moment. Kip was released to my care, and the family meeting became a part of the record, and ultimately part of the solution. The judge offered Kip a suspended sentence if he completed treatment, and promised to wipe the record clean if he stayed out of trouble for two years.

While not every family will end up on the jailhouse steps, some will . . . or in a hospital. The point is that you don't walk away or disband the meeting when your loved one is resistant. Sticking together in a situation like this one sends a message to your loved one that you're serious and mean business. That message alone is a positive motivator for change. When your loved one leaves, they do so for many reasons; but the truth is this: You have not failed if they walk out. Doors swing both ways, and just as sure as a door closes, it will open again!

What If Your Loved One Says No?

When I work with families, "no" is just a conversation starter. We literally do not take no for an answer, and neither should you. No is nothing more than a word, and it holds little power. Behind that no is a yes dying to come out.

Strategies for Responding to No

When someone we love, whom we want to help, says no, it sounds like it is *forever* NO. It's not. It's a word at a moment in time, and it is not the end, but for many situations will be the bridge to YES. This is key: We keep moving forward in the face of a no. With or without agreement, we continue making the change we seek. I have a family I am working with right now whose son Brian we took into treatment four days ago for opiate addiction. Brian sold drugs, too, and at the family meeting Brian pulled out $42,000 in cash from his bag as an example of how drugs weren't the problem—they were his answer! He was making money and living large.

When his dad relieved the twenty-year-old of the cash, Brian agreed to treatment, but left it against clinical advice just three days later.

At most spots along this road to helping change someone you love for the better, we continue taking action in the face of no.

If your loved one says no to coming to the meeting, to treatment, counseling, or other prescribed course of actions, there are several strategies you can use. Prepare yourself and your group ahead of time to deploy them.

Strategy #1: Use a technique designed to get a lesser commitment. Suppose you've asked someone to enter a thirty-day inpatient addictions program, but he said, "I will do anything you ask, but not that" in the meeting. Keep working for full agreement, but if after a couple of meetings you remain stuck, consider compromise and a change agreement. After the refusal, make a smaller request but one that's equally as helpful in motivating change. For example, you'd propose: *Okay, I'd like to take you to a 12-step meeting. Why don't we start there? It's just five blocks away. Would you be agreeable to going?* Or: *Okay, instead of six months of treatment, how about we begin with ninety days?*

In many cases, he'll view your second request as a concession, and feel inclined to respond with a concession of his own—to agree to attend the 12-step meeting or smaller step. This spot of concession and negotiation is often the first really tough spot you'll come to during the family meeting. Do not concede too early, as accepting help will often take some time. After all you want to encourage the beginning of change in a tangible way with your loved one.

Agreements go both ways, so seek to break through the no and get to the yes of full agreement before negotiating. And by giving your love and care, you will most often get acceptance before you must negotiate. There's a very simple rule of human conduct at work here: the rule of reciprocity. It's a code that obligates individuals to repay in kind for what they have received. Reciprocity is a level of indebtedness we feel toward those who give us something, and it even applies to concessions.

Also, offering to attend the meeting with him carries weight. Knowing that you're there for him may make it easier. Typically, he'll recognize that you're doing what any person who cares would do and heed your advice.

Another form of no is if she says, "I can do this on my own." In response, tell her, "We don't think that will work, but let's try your way for thirty days and see how things go." Of course, after the thirty-day trial period is up, and she's failed to get help, you'd meet with her again and ask her to go into treatment.

Strategy #2: If you hear no, take a break for a bit. Set a time to reconvene. Give everyone a chance to cool their heels and chat. Get together again and calmly restate the case for change. Reiterate the behaviors that concern you and your desire that your loved one get help. Keep it simple. Stick with your major points and documented, observed behaviors of concern.

Strategy #3: Try again. Schedule further family meetings and invite your loved one. Deliver updated change messages. Bring additional people into the circle of change. There's no such thing as a failed family meeting. Each time you gather, you plant a seed. Your loved one may come back the next time and admit, "Everything you say is true. I'm ready to give it a go."

No Eventually Yields to Yes

Last summer, I was working with a family in Texas who were concerned about their daughter Lisa, who suffered from an eating disorder. They held family meetings to get her into treatment. Lisa said no forty-three times. I counted. Here is her story.

Lisa, a lovely blond girl with piercing green eyes, was overweight as a child. She found solace in food. It was how her mother showed her love. As five-foot-six-inch Lisa ballooned to 182 pounds, her mother would praise her for eating all "that good food." Yet the voice at home conflicted with the very loud voices at school—the ones who called her "pig" and "fatso" and "fatty catty."

For a while, Lisa found comfort in her fat suit; it insulated her from relationships. The food soothed her emotions. But at age thirteen, she decided that it no longer suited her, and she decided to lose weight. As people began to comment on how great she looked and how pretty her face was, and the boys paid more attention to her, Lisa kept dieting and exercising. Slowly, her attitude toward food began to grow unusual. She'd put food in her napkin while her mother wasn't watching. She'd keep some food in her cheeks until she could spit it into her napkin. She started purging after eating meals by making herself vomit.

Eventually, Lisa developed a gag reflex to food. The very sight of someone cooking would make Lisa's stomach turn. By age eighteen, her relationship with food had become dangerously disordered. For six years, her weight yo-yoed: 92 to 113, 120 to 86, 132 to 83. She married in her early twenties and became the mom of a little girl. Lisa weighed 91 pounds and was proud of the weight gain, but she was still scary skinny. Lisa had breast implants to make herself "perfect." She was top heavy, but the rest of her was sickly thin.

As you might imagine, her disordered eating took a toll not only on her body but also on her family. They repeatedly urged her get help—but she refused every time.

The family never gave up. They kept repeating their central message: *What will your daughter do if something happens to you? You need to be there for your daughter.*

Finally, after five family meetings, that change message broke through. Lisa waved the white flag of surrender and agreed to a compromise: seven days of intensive treatment at a disordered-eating clinic. The shorter treatment led to a full forty-two days of treatment, where she finally began to fight her illness—and eventually won. There was something miraculous in the loving persistence of her family.

When You Must Not Take No for an Answer

If the person is a danger to themselves or others, you should not take no for an answer. However, by law, you cannot drag adults off to a hospital or treatment center or admit them to a mental health facility without their consent. If you must get help for someone who may not want help but needs it immediately, a legal alternative is to call 911 and request that law enforcement do a welfare check to determine whether the person needs to go to a hospital for a seventy-two-hour hold. Laws differ from state to state, but in many of them, a person can be hospitalized for no longer than seventy-two hours against their will, if it is proven that they may do something harmful to themselves or to others. Usually, a person must show one of three conditions to be placed on a seventy-two-hour hold:

▶ *Being a danger to him or herself (for example, there is risk of suicide or self-harm; or serious, perhaps life-threatening health problems have cropped up because of the behavior)*

▶ *Being a danger to others (for example, making threats to harm others, driving under the influence, being involved in criminal activity, or neglecting or abusing children)*

▶ *Being gravely disabled (unable to provide for his or her basic personal needs for food, clothing, or shelter).*

When a person is held, the hospital must to do an evaluation of that person, taking into account his or her medical, psychological, educational, social, financial, and legal situation. By the end of the seventy-two hours, the person may be released, sign in as a voluntary patient, or be put on another type of hold for intensive treatment. (Again, this requirement varies by state.) The hospital does not have to hold the patient for the full seventy-two hours if the professional person in charge believes that the patient no longer requires evaluation or treatment. Frequently those held are released soon after admittance based on this hold being lifted by the medical professional. These legal remedies are used only as a last resort.

I recently did an intervention in which the loved one, who was an alcoholic, did not show up at the family meeting. We went to her house, only to discover that she was extremely intoxicated—to the point of requiring immediate hospitalization. She would not let us past the front door, however. Knowing that she was a danger to herself, we called local law enforcement to request a welfare check. The police and firefighters arrived and took the front door off its hinges to gain entry. They tested her blood alcohol level, which was .39. She was transported by ambulance to the hospital. Had we not stepped in, she could have died. While in the hospital, she told her family she wanted to be admitted to alcohol treatment. In this case, the welfare check served as a lifesaving bridge between resisting help and accepting help. The family began change that saved her life, no question!

The Leverage Strategy: Plan B

Don't give up if things don't go the way you want. Go to Plan B. I call this the leverage strategy. It sets up consequences of inaction. Yes, it's a little hard core, but it can be an effective motivator.

Money can be a great motivator when other things fail. Shelter. Food. Clothes. In other words, Plan B involves making use of consequences that help a person give change a chance. While I firmly believe we use only as much pressure as needed, at times, consequences are the way we help someone get unstuck from saying no. Saying that the "bank is closed: Today we begin throwing our financial and other resources and energies behind recovery and change instead of the crisis" is a powerful statement that can be made when there is consensus built to back it up and stand firm.

You apply Plan B by spelling out consequences firmly but kindly. Some examples:

We'll no longer be able to give you financial assistance unless you enroll in credit counseling. We'll support you but not your addiction.

Contact with the kids (or grandkids) will be cut off until you agree to go to treatment. We have a right to remove the children from destructive influences.

The police will be called when we fear for your safety.

You'll have to move out until you get your anger under control.

We'll have to close your accounts.

I will no longer cover up for you.

I'll have to take your driver's license.

You can no longer use the family car.

If you continue to resist change, you will lose your job.

Refusing to accept treatment means that we'll have to separate (or divorce).

Carefully prepared, structured consequences usually leave an individual with more motivation to comply. A caution: Don't ever bring up consequences unless you're willing to back them up. Usually, though, these situations are a last resort. Only 30 percent of the interventions I've done led to direct talk of consequences. When you use the change process as I've described, you usually won't need to use this sort of leverage. The idea of consequences hangs in the air. Only make them real if needed.

Change will happen. You have as many tries as you wish to take. As you work on developing alternative ways to interact with your loved one, take heart when things go well, but don't be overly discouraged when they go poorly. The next word, the next day, the next interaction is another chance for change to begin. And it will!

RECAP OF STEP 2

▶ *Invite the Identified Loved One to the family meeting.*

▶ *Gather together as a group in familiar surroundings and thank everyone for attending.*

▶ *One by one, have all participants give their eyewitness accounts, speaking from the heart.*

▶ *Present the change plan and ask your loved one to accept it without negotiation or delay.*

▶ *Have everyone sign a change agreement after your loved one agrees to the plan.*

▶ *Be prepared for contingencies.*

SIX

STEP 3

Champion the Change

You've put your loved one on the road to change. Congratulations! Now you've got to help that person to *stay changed*! This, too, is possible. The most effective tool for getting people to follow through on a promise, rid themselves of bad habits, or commit themselves to long-lasting change is *support*. Support is all about encouraging people and believing in them. I call this championing the change. It's Step 3, and its effects are lasting.

When people begin to change negative behaviors, we want their self-image to shift too. We want our former gambling spouse to see himself as a responsible, budget-minded provider; our once overweight sister to see herself as a trim, fit athlete; or our reformed-smoker girlfriend to see herself as a nonsmoker. As they come to view themselves more positively, they will begin to see other things differently, as if they've put on a new pair of glasses. And, rather than reverting to their old bad habits or behaviors, they'll be more likely to continue healthy, more positive behavior for as long as that self-image holds.

This is where you come in. You can help that self-image take hold—by supporting their positive change throughout, letting them know you believe in them, and that you will not give up on them. This is championing the change in a nutshell. By doing this, you invoke a powerful desire in someone to become a brand-new person with a brand-new way of being in the world. I know this not only from my work as an interventionist but from personal experience.

After I was well into recovery from drugs and alcohol, there was still one nefarious adversary I had yet to face: smoking. If I tried to ignore my intense physical cravings to smoke, I'd get fidgety and irritable. I was emotionally attached to my cigarettes. They were always just a reach away. They helped me get through the rough times. They calmed me down, they pushed my anxiety away, they suppressed my feelings. They were a good friend, always available, gathered together in a box courtesy of Phillip Morris.

If the subject weren't so serious, my repeated attempts to end my twenty-year, two-pack-a-day cigarette habit might make a good stand-up comedy routine. No matter what, I tried it. Nicotine gum? I didn't smoke for a few hours, but I chewed so hard, my jaw muscles locked up. Sugar-free hard candies? I developed such severe gas pains from eating so many, I had to stretch out in bed and munch on antacids. Welbutrin? I was so hopeful, I tossed my lighter and cigarettes in the Dumpster outside my office. After work, I fished them out of the Dumpster and lit up before I got back in my car. Defeated again! I depended on them so—and they were out to kill me.

For me, it took a dear friend—a person who had quit smoking years before—to help me finally, wholeheartedly commit to quitting. Janice, a real sassy redhead with a driving type A personality, took me into her bathroom, stood me in front of the mirror, and said, "Your God loves you so much. There will be a day when it will no longer be acceptable to love yourself any less, and that's the day you will quit smoking." I broke down and cried a little, knowing that each time I picked up a cigarette and lit it, I was giving in to an addiction craving and killing myself slowly.

A few months later, I was at the beach for the weekend. It was a blistering hot day on Long Island, and there I was, sitting on the roof deck of a clapboard shore-front house, having a cigarette. I hated the burning sensation of cigarette smoke curling up into my eyes on hot days like that. I went inside and looked at myself in the mirror. I wanted to live. I wanted to be a person who lives longer, feels better, and leads a great life. In my mind's eye, I saw all the casualties of smoking I had ever seen. I didn't want to be the guy on oxygen, strolling around the mall, hacking and gasping for breath. In that moment, I realized I was so in love with life that I couldn't smoke anymore. That was it. All the patches and pills and mints and gadgets for quitting would be history. It was just me and my Maker and the desire to live well and love myself. I quit that weekend.

Then panic struck, because I had to drive back to New York City. I used to smoke a lot when I drove, and I knew that driving was definitely one of my triggers. So I called Janice. She told me that if I didn't give in, if I just hung on for a bit, the desire would pass. Cravings rise and then pass away. It's okay to have a craving or a thought of relapse, but it's not okay to "romance" the thought. Cravings and thoughts simply arrive, and at some point they disappear. For months, Janice supported me through the quitting process by simply being there for me with strong but consoling words and a listening ear. "Don't even have one, no matter what," she'd warn.

Janice would also tell me, "I've always admired you for kicking your drug habit. That means you're the kind of person who can kick this smoking habit." Those words were so empowering! I began to see myself as being able to quit. Then I did quit. Smoking became inconsistent with my self-image. I identified myself as a nonsmoker, and I became grateful that I didn't smoke. In fact, if I see a smoker today, I either want to wrest the cigarette away from him and smoke it, or I am repulsed by it, thinking, "That terrible habit is killing him." I still crave that drug to this day from time to time.

From that experience, I realized the power of influence that someone's support plays in the lives of others. If you want to single out smoking and the importance of support, researchers at the Mayo Clinic found that one of the best stop-smoking programs is face-to-face encouragement from physicians, friends, and relatives. Beyond smoking, many studies show that peer influence plays a key role in people's decisions to change negative behavior, from overeating to drug and alcohol abuse. With few exceptions, humans are social animals. We want not only human companionship but also the companionship of those who are similar to us. And we tend to do what our peers are doing. Positive peer pressure can be a strong and positive reinforcer of healthy habits.

For too long, I think, Americans have attempted to be the one-person willpower machine, too independent to take on a support system or request a helping hand. The results are high stress, burnout, and relinquishing of goals that would otherwise have been attainable. Yet when people have a consistent, continuing helping hand—ongoing support—they're much less likely to give up and give in. They will stay the course and have a better shot at succeeding. Many research studies bear this out, which is why I've incorporated this vital third step into my system for changing someone you love.

Even after your loved one has agreed to change, has gotten outside help, or has just completed some type of program, your role continues with encouragement in weekly meetings, either by phone or as a group, to support the change that's under way, as well as to check in with one another to make sure all members of the family or group are taking care of themselves. Having people around who offer support and encouragement is one of the key elements to altering behavior patterns. There are so many beautiful ways to show support. Let's talk about them.

HOW TO SUPPORT YOUR LOVED ONE
THROUGHOUT THE CHANGE

Continue to Meet as a Circle

I advise the families and groups I work with to continue meeting as a circle once a week for at least six months. Definitely include your loved one in the circle. No secrets. The circle provides a safe and comfortable setting in which to demonstrate support, express love, share new ideas for coping, check in with one another, and provide comfort and help if there are tough times. Spending even twenty minutes a week surrounded by others who care can make you and your loved one feel more connected and cared for. Someone with free time during the day can help with shopping or doctors' or therapy appointments. The circle experience demonstrates love, support, and commitment to change, and it teaches an important lesson, that "We will get through this together."

I use a Cisco product called WebEx for this work (www.webex.com). It's a way for families and friends to gather, share pictures, exchange stories, and communicate in a dynamic way. There's even video capability. Everyone dials in on a conference line or online and clicks a link and voila!—you are connected. WebEx is a low-cost option for you to connect as a group in a more vibrant way than just a voice on the phone. Let this be a starting place for making your family-and-friends calls happen.

This process of connecting each week for a period is not rocket science, but sometimes it's very challenging for folks to commit. You may find, too, that the group that you had for the family meeting is less focused, and it's all right if not everyone can make it to the conference call meeting each week. The point here is that taking this step to make a commitment to connect and keep the energies of the group moving forward along the lines of change is important. It really, really matters.

Shine the spotlight on *change* as the topic, not just your loved one's recovery. Invite each person on this family and friends call to chime in with what they've been up to this week. Ask about their challenges and triumphs, what book they're reading, or what each person is doing to take care of him or herself this past week—and help identify ways they might make adjustments to make life better.

Encourage each other with these ground rules:

▶ *Speak one at a time and identify who you are—we're on the phone so we can't see you, unless video is part of the call.*

▶ *Stay calm and positive—let love and connectedness drive the conversation.*

▶ *No yelling, ever—if someone gets hot and disruptive, ask them to leave the call for this week.*

▶ *Think, dream, and do—focus on what you're doing to take care of yourself today, not just feeling.*

To the call leader I caution: Don't be bossy. The most important quality of the call's leader is being a good listener. So do it!

Give Time

It has often been said that when it comes to the people you love, love is spelled T-I-M-E. I believe that. When you give someone time, they feel your support in their heart, gut, and mind. Time can be as simple as the actual provision of services: driving people to meetings, doctors' appointments, or counseling sessions; or handling their money. Or you can join them in making lifestyle changes. Exercise with them or cook healthier meals together. Go to church together. Work on a hobby together. Do things with your loved ones that make life fulfilling. Accompany them to a 12-step meeting. This helps them get on with their lives.

Time also means being there emotionally. It's not uncommon for people in the throes of change to get depressed or go into denial. If your loved one becomes angry or withdrawn, or if you notice other major changes in his or her personality, talk it out together. Show your love and concern by a gentle touch, a hug, a caress, a smile. Provide a listening ear, empathy, and the sense that one is cared about and loved, not judged. And if you feel led, involve others in your circle. Even clergy members can help.

Provide Motivational Information

Another way to provide support involves giving helpful, motivational information, such as advice on whether to seek medical care, recovery information, or inspiration material. Most people love to play the role of teacher or preacher if given the opportunity. Feel free to put on either hat! But don't go overboard with information overload. You can inundate people with pamphlets, books, Web sites, and more. Too much can build resentment. The gift of one inspirational book or a copy of a single article is all it takes to provide this type of support.

Another word of strong advice here: If you decide to give helpful information, make sure it pertains to the problem or addiction at hand. Don't try to communicate some unrelated hidden agenda. Not long ago I worked with a family, the Montgomerys, whose alcoholic son Will had successfully completed treatment. Will was also gay. When he finished treatment, his mother started papering his apartment with biblical tracts on how he could "rehabilitate" himself and become heterosexual. This was not the kind of information or help he needed.

Support with Love

Adopt a loving, supportive attitude with your words and actions. This is a tough one. I know that you've probably got a lot of residual anxiety, pain, anger, hurt, and frustration right now, even though your loved one is in the process of changing. You're the one who has watched your loved one's downward spiral. You've possibly been ripped off emotionally and financially many times. It's easy to feel like you want to lash out with words like: "I knew you couldn't do it." "I don't know why I bothered." "I'm giving up on you."

Watch it! These are change-damaging words. Remember, once people commit to something, they try to make their behavior live up to that commitment and they act according to how they see themselves (their self-image). Words like those above do not reinforce a person's new, more positive self-image. They tear it down. Instead, express your belief in that person's ability to succeed and do well. As Janice did with me, say things like *You're the kind of person who can do this. I've seen you succeed before, and I know you can succeed here. I've always admired your ability to follow through. I know I can count on you.* These statements reinforce and strengthen your loved one's new, more positive self-image and helps them follow through on their commitment to change.

Practice Acceptance

The greatest need we have is to be accepted and treated as a person. Until change has begun (and it will), accept the person and the situation as it is today. Nothing reinforces defensive behavior more than judgment, comparison, or rejection. A feeling of acceptance and worth frees a person from the need to defend and helps release the natural growth tendency to change. When I say acceptance, I don't mean condoning a bad behavior. Rather, I mean affirming the intrinsic worth of other human beings. This preserves their dignity and self-respect, allowing them to respond and change without feeling threatened.

Support Versus Enabling: There's a Difference!

We often begin enabling as an attempt to be kind and helpful. For example, we may pay their bills out of our own pocket so that they won't get into financial trouble. By doing so, we help them avoid the consequences of bad money habits. We lend a troubled person money, often over and over again, and we are surprised when it's used to buy more drugs or alcohol, or gamble or shop compulsively. When we stop covering up for people, we let them experience the consequences of their out-of-control behavior. We no longer make excuses for them, lend them money, or bail them out of jail. We stop shielding them from the consequences of their behaviors. You can be helpful without enabling, by providing honest, productive support that leads to lasting change. Here's a look at the difference between enabling and support.

EXAMPLES OF ENABLING	EXAMPLES OF SUPPORT
Giving the person money (he or she might not yet be capable of handling it).	*Writing checks directly to a landlord or to pay bills.*
Lying for the person to employers, law enforcement officers, family members, etc.	*Refusing to lie to anyone or to cover up for the person.*
Making excuses for bad behavior, or creating alibis.	*Allowing the person to be fully responsible for his or her own problems and needs.*

Lax accountability of the change agreement.	*Following through on agreed-upon consequences of breaking the terms of the change agreement.*
Bailing the person out of jail.	*Letting him stay in jail and face the consequences.*
Joining in negative behavior with your loved one.	*Engaging in positive behavior with your loved one (not drinking or drugging; offering to exercise together; and in general, setting a high standard for healthy choices).*
Shielding him from negative consequences of his behavior.	*Detaching, but with love, and letting him face the music.*

HELP YOUR LOVED ONE PREVENT SETBACKS

Your loved one will make promises to stop drinking, quit smoking, stop spending, get help for depression, go to counseling, or take other positive actions. And most likely, he or she will make good on those promises. But what if the old ways return? What if there's a setback?

A setback happens when a person reverts to the negative behavior. Some people never experience setbacks. I had my last drink on February 4, 2003, and never looked back. Others have occasional setbacks, but eventually kick the habit. The process is like mountain climbing; they may need several attempts before they reach the top. Others still will have setbacks for the rest of their lives, choosing to view each one as confirmation that they're "just meant to be that way."

Setbacks aren't all bad. They can be learning opportunities. The individual can ask: What can I do differently? What can I learn from this setback that will help me strengthen and improve myself? How can I improve my results next time? People who ask, then answer, these questions see themselves as having made a mistake they needn't repeat. And recovering from a setback may give more confidence to resist a craving the next time around.

Helping someone prevent and overcome setbacks is one of the most important parts of Step 3. The key is to identify high-risk life situations, or triggers, that leave many folks exposed and vulnerable to setbacks. Triggers usually involve *old* habits, *old* friends, *old* attitudes, *old* fears, *old* stress, and the neglect of *newly* embraced change principles and programs. They move someone from new healthy living back into old negative living.

Two of the greatest triggers sending a person back to dangerous behavior are sex and money. Getting it. Keeping it. Worrying about it. Got it? And it's not always the easiest thing to talk about, these two topics. Be encouraged that opening up these topics in a safe and open way will help foster a relationship of openness with your loved one—so that when they feel pain about things they wouldn't normally talk about, they just might with you.

The great news is that triggers are often quite predictable—which means you can head them off at the pass. After all, forewarned is forearmed. It's mostly up to your loved one to learn how to deal with these triggers, often in concert with a therapist, but there's a lot you can do to help. Let me give you some examples.

Trigger: Money

Here's an interesting fact I've observed from my work as an interventionist: When someone is in recovery from alcohol, drugs, gambling, or spending addictions, his or her most likely day of relapse is payday. Why is that? Because money in their pockets and purses is a huge trigger for a setback. It's amazing how a person having no urges can suddenly have a setback once cash is available. The urge to use is now possible because of coins in the cup!

Strategies

▶ *Offer to handle your loved one's money and manage the bank account.*

▶ *Go with your loved one to the bank.*

▶ *Have your loved one delay getting or carrying an ATM or debit card.*

▶ *Help your loved one work out a written budget.*

▶ *Have paychecks deposited directly in the bank to avoid having cash instantly available.*

▶ *Have separate accounts so your monies are not commingled.*

Trigger: Social Situations

For many folks in the early stages of change, the thought of going out socially is downright frightening. ("How do I do that sober, refrain from smoking, or have fun without pigging out?") All of this, of course, needs to be challenged. Your loved one will learn how to have fun, socialize, date, and be in relationship with life without falling back into unhealthy habits. And you can help.

Strategies

▶ *Encourage your loved one to go to alcohol-free or nonfood events in the beginning.*

▶ *Don't accompany him or her to places with bars.*

▶ *Encourage her to talk to you or a therapist about fears.*

▶ *Encourage your loved one to associate with nonusers and replace unsafe relationships with safer ones. (Sounds harsh, but people are triggers, both positive and negative.)*

▶ *Rehearse tempting situations with your loved one. At holiday parties, where there will be people plying everyone with rich foods, or alcohol, or even drugs, have your loved one practice refusal. I ask clients to practice how they'll respond to the risky moments they face. By practicing, they learn how to deal with just about any high-risk situation.*

▶ *Be a positive example. Remember, people tend to follow what their peers do. So don't drink or smoke yourself, or otherwise engage in behavior that would set an unhealthy example.*

▶ *Avoid physical triggers. If you hang around a barbershop a lot, you are likely to end up with a haircut.*

Trigger: Forgetting

People with addictions, in particular, can be great forgetters. They can forget how bad their lives had become. They forget how their best intentions didn't improve their behavior. They forget that they have a progressive disease. They might tell themselves, "I'll drink, but I won't drive," or "I've matured. I don't need all those 12-step meetings." In short, they forget that they were sick, that life will get worse if they start the old behavior again. Here's how to help.

Strategies

▶ *Encourage your loved one to talk to a recovering friend or sponsor daily. With the help of a sponsor or other accountability partner, people can self-monitor for possible triggers, then ask for extra help.*

▶ *Make sure your loved one attends support group meetings and records attendance on an attendance card. (A sample is provided in Appendix II.) This is a great accountability tool.*

Trigger: Being Alone

Sometimes people will experience setbacks while they're alone or away on a trip. Suddenly, perhaps on the plane, the idea comes out of nowhere: "Who will know if I have a drink, smoke a cigarette, buy a lottery ticket, place a bet, or go on a binge?" My last drink was on a flight headed from New York City to rehab in California. Even back then, at the end of a six-month period where I had actively been working on stopping, going back and forth between days of sobriety and bingeing, there were setbacks and attempts at change. On that particular day, the day when I boarded a plane to take my first stab at inpatient treatment, I had made up my mind I was done! Determined I was, at least in my mind as I remember it. Then I was alone on the plane, anxious, afraid . . . I was an addicted fellow who was stuck in the storm before the calm, so I ordered a couple double Bloody Marys.

Here's what you can do.

Strategies

▶ *Encourage honest communication about fears, temptations, stressers, and triggers. Secrets and lies inhibit change.*

▶ *Increase telephone contact. Encourage your loved one to stay in contact with you or another support person such as a sponsor. Remind him, "I'm here for you," and that it's not okay to "romance" thoughts of old behavior.*

▶ *Help your loved one line up recovery meetings at his or her destination prior to traveling.*

▶ *Do an "Extreme Makeover" of your loved one's environment. Help remove all items directly associated with alcohol use or binge behavior (such as junk food or drug paraphernalia) from his or her home, office, and car.*

▶ *Offer to be there for your friend or loved one so he or she doesn't have to come home from work to an empty home or apartment.*

Trigger: Emotional Highs and Lows

Negative moods, such as anger, anxiety, depression, frustration, and boredom, are feasts at which people end up devouring themselves. So it's no wonder they're associated with huge setbacks! Foster positive emotional states like joy or celebration.

Positive moods often trigger setbacks too. The excitement of the good and the thrill of the great. The celebration of the extraordinary and the observance of special occasions.

Day in and day out, our loved one numbs out, at times to celebrate, and at other times to commiserate. Here are strategies for helping.

Strategies

▶ *Help your loved one develop alternate coping activities during emotional highs and lows. Examples include meditation, prayer, exercise, gardening, yoga, or a new recreational sport or hobby that adds fun to life. Participate with your loved one in these activities to show your support.*

▶ *If your loved one is a recovering addict, encourage regular contact with other recovering people. This often, but not always, takes the form of attending AA meetings or 12-step meetings, but can include church, therapy groups, or other kinds of supportive gatherings, including Celebrate Recovery and Friends in Recovery.*

▶ *Simply be present emotionally for your loved one. Support calms the brain circuits that produce stress hormones. By being supportive, you help someone you love stay relaxed and avoid the trigger of emotional stress.*

▶ *Encourage sound sleep, nutrition, and exercise habits. These habits mitigate stress.*

▶ *Catch your loved one doing well. Recognize situations in which they handled themselves appropriately. Tell them so. You'll help build confidence, strengthen motivation, and increase "self-efficacy" (the personal perception of mastery over risky situations).*

▶ *Talk about the importance of forgiveness and making amends. Both are emotional keys to a higher, better, changed self.*

Trigger: Neglecting Prayer or Spiritual Activity

We are hardwired for spiritual connection, spiritual conversation, and spiritual intimacy. Cut off from these things, we feel alone, in the absence of anyone or a higher power who loves us. There's no constant, guiding presence, and we are thus at great risk of slipping back into the behavior that is killing us.

Talk of spiritual things can be stressful in and of itself. So, easy does it, if this is the case. When newly sober, my connection to spirit was simple. In fact, it was so diffuse, it was basically: I am not alone. There is someone or something greater than myself, and maybe I can connect to whatever that is. Over time, this belief system deepened, changed. My connection to spirit evolved.

Today spirituality is a force that energizes me and gives meaning to my daily life. Each day presents new opportunities and challenges, but I'm never alone. I have a community and my faith to bolster me, and a God who loves me. Spirituality enriches my life and gives me hope and inspiration, even in the darkest moments—which is why I believe that surrendering to and connecting with a power greater than myself are critical steps to change. A higher power can refer to other things besides a deity: the universe, or a self-help group itself if necessary. Whether your loved one is dealing with addiction, something like depression, or a destructive habit, they need to have a sense of belief that they are not alone, and that they can reach out for help, in many different directions, including spirituality.

Keep it simple and encourage your loved one to give it a go. In the beginning of my recovery, I used the principle of "acting as if." I was *acting as if* I was a person of faith, *acting as if* I was a man with an abiding set of beliefs. I *acted as if* I could stay changed just for today. My developing faith did just that—it developed.

Strategies

▶ *Encourage regular attendance at a self-help group patterned after Alcoholics Anonymous.*

▶ *Invite your loved one to church, Bible study, or other faith-based gatherings.*

▶ *If you are so inclined, pray for your loved ones, and release any concerns about them into God's gentle care. Prayer can be an enormous source of comfort to you and your family.*

Practice HALT with Your Loved One

For nearly a hundred years, Alcoholics Anonymous has reminded people to keep the acronym HALT (and what it represents) at the front of their minds and daily choices.

The four letters that make up the word "HALT" stand for: Never get too <u>H</u>ungry, too <u>A</u>ngry, too <u>L</u>onely, or too <u>T</u>ired.

Great advice for preventing setbacks!

WHAT IF SOMEONE YOU LOVE HAS ALREADY HAD A SETBACK?

The best way to correct course after a setback is to reengage and participate fully in the change program. Call in your circle of change for help; you already know the drill. Try not to lose the momentum of the successes the person had before the setback. Help your loved one hold on to the identity of change. *He or she is a person who had a setback, not a person who failed to change.*

Help this person get back up as soon as you can. This basically involves, without negotiation or delay, placing back into action all the skills and tools you've learned thus far and helping get your loved one back on track. The last thing any of us, especially the person trying to change, needs to do is to allow the clutches of shame and guilt to snatch power away. We need all of the power we can muster to restart the change process. You, your loved one, and your circle of change need to stay in touch with your strengths. Don't get caught up in long, disempowering recollections about what happened. You've already seen the bruises, and you know where the scars are. Rally around with love to support the step back into change.

THE VITALITY OF "TRUST-BANKING"

Once a person begins change—by following a change plan, undergoing counseling, or finishing some other real course of action—it can be a very stressful time for you and your family. If he takes the patch off, will he smoke? Once she's lost seventy-five pounds, will she keep it off? Now that the ninety-day program is over, can I trust her with a credit card again?

Trust is at the core of strong, meaningful relationships. You and your loved one can't automatically create or rebuild trust; it must be earned, one behavior at a time. When I work with families, I use a tool called trust-banking. It means that you treat trust like a bank account, in which there are debits and credits. For example:

When I keep my word (like sticking to the change agreement), a trust deposit is made.

When I lie to you, a trust withdrawal is made.

When I use words to build us up, a trust deposit is made.

When I use words to wound or manipulate, a trust withdrawal is made.

When I honor confidences, a trust deposit is made.

When I take others for granted, a trust withdrawal is made.

Both you and your loved one have to understand how this "bank account" works and what the consequences are of a depleted or overdrawn account. When an account is empty, or even has a negative balance, trust has no foundation on which to build. Your loved one then realizes that he or she can't be trusted with money, credit cards, the car, food, shopping, the computer, relationships, social situations, or much of anything. A collapse in trust recalls all of the distrust and cynicism that had developed over time.

To rebuild trust, people have to stay accountable. They have to tell the truth or at least admit mistakes or apologize for making a withdrawal. They must treat others with dignity and respect. They must do as they've promised. All of this allows reserves in the account to grow. With greater reserves, your relationship will grow stronger, and change will have a better chance to solidify.

GATHERING UP THE PIECES OF LIFE

I often share with families the movie *The Wizard of Oz*. It is generally thought of as a children's tale, but is actually a wonderful metaphor for championing change. We all know the story. Dorothy, trying to find her way home, befriends three motley fellows who are all seeking something to make themselves whole: The Scarecrow is looking for a brain, the Tin Man a heart, and the Lion courage. The Kingdom of Oz is their destination. There, they believe, they can find what they need to be complete.

Dorothy and her newfound friends soon discover that they can only get what they desire by sticking together. They know they need one another. Solidarity and trust develop among them. They become genuinely interested in each other's well-being and fulfillment. Remember the part when the flying monkeys tear the Scarecrow apart? He literally comes apart at the seams, and there are bits and pieces of him scattered everywhere. And what do his friends do? They lovingly gather up the pieces and begin stuffing it back into him.

When the going gets tough, and dark forces threaten to strike, the group carry each other along with love, encouragement, and support. Either they all make it to Oz or none of them do.

We also need one another. None of us can walk alone if change and wholeness are desired. And like Dorothy, we will find our own way home to fulfillment and peace by gathering up the pieces of life and helping our loved ones on the road to change.

RECAP OF STEP 3

▶ *Support your loved one by giving time, providing helpful information, adopting a loving attitude, and practicing acceptance.*

▶ *Help your loved one prevent setbacks by strategizing together various ways of dealing with trigger situations.*

▶ *Manage setbacks by bringing your circle back together and putting back into action all the skills, tools, and techniques you've learned about changing someone you love.*

▶ *Work on building trust in your relationship.*

SEVEN

STEP 4
Care for You

This step might just be the hardest: taking care of you. Our natural inclination is to put ourselves on the back burner while we tend to the needs of others. We live in a time where it's virtuous to be a martyr, doing things out of duty or because we feel we have to. We often take on too many tasks because of a false assumption that we have more control over our lives if we do everything ourselves. We want to avoid saying no and looking like the bad guy. We don't want to be seen as selfish. Where does all this end? I will tell you where it ends—it ends with you worn out and jumping off the deep end at every little thing. I'm asking you to be selfish. No, I'm demanding that you be selfish, for some very good reasons.

Overextending yourself can damage your mental, emotional, and physical health. You'll get stressed out. You'll feel overwhelmed. You'll open the door to physical and emotional problems, like high blood pressure, bad moods, and insomnia. You might resort to self-destructive behaviors yourself, such as overeating, excessive drinking, and substance abuse. You're trying to cope with the stress you're under and you're using these things as escape valves.

In the area of substance abuse alone, it has been stated that for every person who is a drug or alcohol abuser, there are at least two or three non-using people directly affected by that use. They include children, siblings, friends, coworkers, spouses, and partners. Although resources to help an addicted person are predominant in the addiction field, the main caregiver in that person's life—that means you—also suffers and needs help. In fact, statistics show that if caregivers don't get help and support, they frequently suffer from depression, anxiety, physical illness, and low self-esteem. (The term "caregiver" usually refers to someone such as a spouse, partner, sibling, or adult child who takes care of an ailing person. I'll broadly apply the term here to mean *you*, the person who is living daily with someone's addiction, destructive habit, out-of-control behavior, or medical issue.)

Trying to do "people fixing"—being a caregiver—can leave you feeling angry, exhausted, and helpless. We can get pulled into other people's problems so deeply that we lose a sense of ourselves. This stuck cycle can become a nightmare that continues for months or years. For some, it is a generational cycle that they're up against.

I recently spoke to my dad, himself a caregiver for my mother, who had a stroke last year and now suffers from major impairment. While Mom has recovered to a certain extent, the Nancy of today is vastly different from anything we've known before: at times docile and loving, though often confused, anxious, critical, and demanding. Right after Mom's stroke, Dad announced he was going to retire from the country church he pastors. We encouraged him, as a family, to push pause, not quit his life's work so abruptly, and consider his own needs—financial, spiritual, and otherwise. "Stay with what you love, Dad! Stay with it for yourself—so that we can see and hear your joy," we told him.

And that is also my message to you. If you're a caregiver to someone with a serious problem, the most important thing you can do is take care of *you*. I am not saying put yourself first. That's unrealistic. Life demands that sometimes we put other people first—taking our kids to ballet or soccer practice, helping our elderly parents with errands, volunteering for something we believe in, or being there for a friend who is sick. Some days, you're at the top of the list and some days . . . well, you're fifth or sixth.

What I'm saying is that you must make a life for yourself, separate from your role as a caregiver, as my dad has done. Try not to use your loved one's problem or behavior as an excuse to isolate yourself or to join him in a joyless or ill existence. Find meaning in your life outside of this problem so that it doesn't become your whole world. Get out of the house and resume your life, or create a life if you didn't have one to begin with. Pursue activities that give you pleasure. Restore your sense of optimism and well-being. Enroll in a class. Meet new friends. Go on trips. Craft a life for yourself!

At first, this idea may seem shocking or, at the very least, self-indulgent. It's not. A commitment to others starts with a commitment to yourself. The challenge is to do your best thinking and move your life forward. When you take good care of your emotional, physical, and spiritual health, you can be there for others in a much healthier way.

So how can you draw the line? How can you back away to nurture yourself but still provide the love and support your loved one requires? What attitudes and strategies offer the best hope for restoring a normal balance in your life?

THE ANALOGY OF THE ROSEBUSH

I grew up in a house surrounded by rosebushes. A rosebush has beautiful flowers but thorny stems. If you're dealing with a tough situation as a caregiver, your relationship may prove to be a thornier rosebush than you thought it would be, but it is a rosebush nevertheless. Much of the beauty and strength of that rosebush comes from the care it has been given, the winds it has weathered, and the constant pruning it has received. Relationships are exactly like that, too. Their strength comes from love, the trials overcome together, and the nurturing of closeness.

Different people respond differently to thorns—the trials and the inescapable pain—in their relationships. The thorns make some people decide to give up on the relationship. The relationship gradually dies, and love is lost; the ignored rosebush turns into a bramble pile—prickly and no longer a joy to view. Some people madly yank out the bush, pulling up the relationship roots they have spent years growing. Others are gardeners who tend lovingly to the relationship. They know that the stem, though prickly, leads up to the rose, and they keep pruning the rosebush to encourage its growth and beautiful flowers.

Caregiving is a thorny task. How can we handle the thorns and enjoy the flowers of our relationships? How can we be better gardeners?

I believe the answer is *to find meaning* in being a caregiver.

A survey conducted a few years ago by the Family Caregiver Alliance brought to light this truth. Many respondents said that it was well worth the effort to be a caregiver. It helped them rediscover their relationship with their loved one. They were able to tap into the joy of that rediscovery and find rewards in caregiving.

I know this to be true from personal experience.

Years ago, my best friend Marvin died after a long, drawn-out battle with cancer. Marvin, a once robust lumberjack of a man, was a surrogate father to me in many ways, from nearly the moment I stepped off the plane onto the isle of Manhattan. His sons Freddy and Matthew were about my age, and they took me in, providing a sense of family, something I had once lost due to distance, drugs, and religious issues.

Marvin was a real rock in my life. But those tables turned when he was diagnosed with cancer. I had seen many friends slip quickly away in New York City in the eighties and nineties as a result of HIV, but I knew cancer was at least infinitely more treatable. And so, I was hopeful and joined Marvin in a spirit of "Let's fight this!" All of a sudden, I found myself a caregiver. I helped as I could, and gave as I was able, from a reserve I wasn't aware even existed.

Through his surgery and recovery, our friendship deepened and blossomed in ways both strong and soft. I was surprised by my ability to give him something I didn't know was there. Yet there it was, seemingly limitless, brimming with encouragement and hope. "You can fight this! You are doing great! What do we need to do to get over this hump? Let's make a list!"

But cancer can be formidable, and Marvin became sick again in 2004 after a brief remission. The cancer spread, and the future was suddenly quite short. I accompanied him to chemo appointments, and to the ER during the nights when the pain was just too great. I comforted and encouraged, prodded and fed hope, while keeping pills straight and schedules untangled. Then, when his life was running low on time, I helped select hospice care, and set up the home he loved for his final stretch. When the end was near, I called our friend Reverend Michael Ingersoll to come pray with us. Michael held his hand and encouraged him to "let go of this big beautiful life of yours." Within minutes, Marv's son Freddy and I were each holding one of his hands as he breathed for the last time, surrounded by love. Then he was gone.

I confess to being unsure that I was up for the task of caregiving. I had never gone through anything like that before. Yet the chance to love and care and give proved beautiful and without comparison in my life. I found true deep meaning in caregiving. And of course, my life was fuller because Marvin had lived. His is a memory that refuses to leave me.

Yes, caregiving can be a real litmus test of the health of a relationship. And yes, we hear a lot about its negative aspects. But I believe if you focus too much on those negatives, then that is all you will see, that is all you will get, and that is all you will experience. Like a magnifying glass, what we focus on gets larger and comes even more quickly into our life. If you look at your caregiving problems through a "mental magnifying glass," you'll grossly magnify the negatives. You'll blow things out of all proportion. You'll distort the way things really are. You'll set yourself up for feeling overwhelmed by every situation that crops up.

Studies indicate that we have about 60,000 thoughts a day. Unfortunately, about 90 percent of them are negative. Negativity is the last thing your loved one needs. It hurts that person and frays your bond. And if you're in the negative, you're making your caregiver journey much bumpier—on you! The longer negative thoughts occupy our hearts and minds, the more we believe them. When you think in negative terms, you believe in negative terms. It creates a vicious cycle that often leads to anxiety, stress, and depression. I believe you must replace any negative, self-defeating thoughts and behaviors with positive, motivating ones.

How do you do that? Here are my answers.

REFRAME YOUR VIEW OF CAREGIVING

Begin to look at caregiving in a different light. I don't know exactly what your relationship is to the person you want to change, but I do know this: You love and care for that person, or you wouldn't be holding this book in your hands. See caregiving as a demonstration of your love; reaffirm this daily. Love comes alive when it is sensitive to the needs of others.

Come to believe that by facing this experience together, you may actually be bringing the two of you closer together. Whether it is your spouse, another family member, or best friend who must change, it's important to understand that relationships can weather the challenge and grow stronger for it.

Try to find the positive side of everything you encounter. Remember, you want to do the very best that you can for your loved one. That should be a prime motivator for positive action. Look at your addicted child, for example, and tell yourself how lonely you'd be without him. Think of the joy your husband has brought into your life every day. Focus on the importance of your mom or dad in your life. Keep your thought train moving in this direction. Concentrate on the positive aspects of providing loving care for your loved one, and you'll work to erase negativity from your life. At first, you might literally have to dig out these positives, but after some time, they will automatically appear to you. Eventually, you'll see and experience only the good side of caregiving.

TAP INTO YOUR CIRCLE OF CHANGE

Keep yourself surrounded with positive, loving people, especially those in your circle of change. They'll help prevent negativity from creeping into your life. If you are around negative people, you can't help but be negative as well. There's no one to encourage you. Remove yourself from negative people and negative environments; surround yourself with positive people and positive environments. That is why I believe so strongly in support groups for caregivers, where there are people who have learned to deal with similar problems. One mother of a heroin addict explained to me how she coped: "Before I got myself into a support group, I'd cry, I'd pray, I'd call up everybody I know to vent my emotions. Now I call up somebody in my group and figure out specifically what I need to do." You think you're all alone in this, but if you can join a support group for caregivers, you'll realize there are many people in the same boat. Getting involved with other caregivers can really put your own challenges into perspective and ease your grief, no matter how tough your situation.

Be realistic. Don't fall prey to one of the great myths of today's society and believe that you should be able to "do it all." The truth is that you are only one person and you can't do it all. Determine which tasks are most important and set realistic goals for yourself. Enlist the help of other family members and close friends to help with care and errands. Chances are they are more than willing to help but just don't know what to do or how to ask.

So if caregiving overwhelms you (it can), ask for help, particularly from your circle of change. This is your health, your body, and your spirit. Pass some responsibilities on to family members or friends. Many people feel that they're letting others down when they say no, but saying yes to every-body is being cruel to yourself. When you start to feel guilty, remind yourself that it's okay to ask for help. In fact, think of this as giving somebody else the opportunity to say yes. Consult experts if you need help with financial or legal affairs.

When taking care of a loved one, family members often need to work cooperatively. The more people participating in care, the less alone you'll feel in your role. I think it's a good idea to divvy up responsibilities too. Start by figuring out, for example, what kind of support you need:

▶ *A break from caregiving?*

▶ *Help with meals, shopping, cleaning, laundry, etc.?*

▶ *Emotional support by telephone or e-mail?*

▶ *Help with chores—e.g., taking the care recipient to doctor's appoint-ments, therapy sessions, or support group meetings?*

▶ *Help with financial responsibilities?*

▶ *Help with enforcing boundaries in terms of money and living arrangements? If you suspect your child buys drugs while driving your car, for example, reconsider that privilege. Family members must build consensus and be consistent in the positions they take and limits they set.*

Once you've gotten commitments from those in your circle to help, I'd go so far as to write out a summary of what each person has agreed to do, then e-mail it to everyone. Being clear on needs and commitments is critical.

CULTIVATE LIFE-GIVING HABITS

Life is built in moments. The state of your life is the result of the choices you make and the actions you take, in each moment. Take care of your habits now, and they'll take care of you later. Ask yourself, "How can I best manage myself in this situation?"

What I'm talking about are the obvious and the not so obvious. You can get instant relief with some simple deep breathing, for example. Take ten deep breaths through your nose with your mouth closed. Deep breathing slows your heart rate, and focusing on your breathing brings awareness of how your body is feeling. Try other forms of relaxation such as meditation, yoga, tai chi, an aromatherapy bath, or relaxing music. The result is what it's like to feel relaxed.

I know that caregiving can certainly sap your energy—the life force that powers all aspects of our health—so you'll want to do everything you can to preserve it. While going through this potentially stressful time, it is even more critical for you to maintain proper eating habits. You don't need a nutritionist to tell you that your body looks and feels its best on a steady diet of fruits, veggies, whole grains, and lean protein. That's a no-brainer. But even though you know better, it's easy to grab junk food or fast food or even skip foods. Resist the urge to do this. The nutritional balance of your diet will give you the strength and energy you need during trying times.

Exercise is not only good for your physical health but it increases your endorphins, which help you feel better; and it's also important in terms of helping prevent depression. Plan exercise into your weekly schedule. Set aside time during three days a week to walk, jog, hike, visit the gym, or enjoy a spin on the bike. Keep these appointments to yourself. If you don't have a plan and a consistent weekly schedule, it can become difficult to balance the time you need for yourself with all your responsibilities.

Set aside time, even if it's just ten or fifteen minutes, for an activity you enjoy such as reading a book, writing in a journal, or having a massage. Believe in your value as a human being and your right to a few minutes of personal space at least several times a week. If you can take more than that, it's a bonus from which you will prosper. The trick is to start and to focus those few minutes on you, your interests, and your dreams.

And speaking of dreams, don't forget to sleep! Sleep allows your body to recover from everyday wear and tear. If you can relax and sleep well, your body can withstand great amounts of stress with little or no damage. Some of the most important hormones for body repair and healing as well as hormones for immune function are released during sleep cycles. When your mind is not at peace, it becomes difficult to enjoy a good night's sleep.

If you find sleep difficult these days, try this: Create a sleep-promoting environment that's quiet and completely dark. Engage in a relaxing activity in the hour leading up to bedtime such as reading, watching TV (nonviolent programs, of course), or listening to soothing music. Hop into bed only when you're tired. Turn off all lights. If you don't fall asleep in about ten or fifteen minutes, do some meditation exercises or create positive visualizations.

Sustain your spiritual health too. One's spiritual life can be defined very broadly and can range from religion to meditation to simply having a sense of hope that it is possible for change to continue and for good things to happen. The spiritual person in each of us is different, and we all need to find our own way of keeping in touch with it and developing that awareness of what fulfills us. When we find that, we can make it an identifiable piece of our lives that we can turn to for energy, solace, and validation.

IT CAME TO PASS; IT DIDN'T COME TO STAY

My dad reads scripture in his sermons, often quoting the biblical phrase *It came to pass*. Not until I was older, wiser, and sober did I realize that this innocuous phrase has a subtle, extremely meaningful inference. There are times in life, like right now, when you feel so hurt and frustrated that you're sure the pain will never pass. But it does, sometimes because of your efforts or sometimes because of the passage of time; but always, always, the pain goes away. It did not come into your life to stay; it came to pass.

Whatever your challenge, refuse to be stressed or immobilized. Life hasn't stopped, slowed down, or ended for you. It flows on in a healing and abundant river. In the face of any challenge, affirm: *I accept the reality of this situation, but not its permanence.*

When something comes into your life that is negative or not what you want, just say to yourself, "It came to pass." Maybe it came to teach you something or gift you with certain lessons. But it didn't come to stay. It came to pass. Don't let it weight you down. Instead, open your mind to the flow of wisdom and love that can help you deal masterfully with it. It has come to pass. Accept it, but accept it as an experience that is passing through and on its way out. Something better is on the way for you. Enjoy the use of this mantra: *It came to pass; it didn't come to stay!*

As a parting shot, I believe that if you find meaning in caregiving, you will save yourself a lot of tears. Renew your resolve to make sense out of this experience. Learn to take care of yourself, regardless of your loved one's behavior. Prepare your mind and heart. Gear your thinking toward the positive. Rekindle your special light by cultivating other parts of yourself. You have a right to be happy, which means the freedom and capacity to enjoy life again. You can live a happier life whether or not your loved one changes. Your ultimate joy does not depend on his or her recovery. The sun always comes out after it rains.

RECAP OF STEP 4

▶ *Find meaning in being a caregiver. There are emotional rewards in this role; look for the positives.*

▶ *Reframe your view of caregiving as a demonstration of your love.*

▶ *Tap into your circle of change. Remember, it is a support group. Join other support groups as well.*

▶ *Cultivate life-giving habits: good nutrition, exercise, adequate sleep, time for relaxation and meditation or prayer, and attention to spirituality. Remember that your life is valuable. Take care of it.*

▶ *Always remember that no matter what you're living through, it came to pass; it didn't come to stay.*

PART III

Overcoming Common Barriers to Change

EIGHT

What Are You Afraid Of?

Do you remember the first time you learned how to ride a bike? Did it take you out of your comfort zone? I'm sure it did. It was something new, exciting, but scary. You probably wondered, as I did, if you would ever be able to do it. I remember my dad running behind me, holding the back of my bike seat, saying, "You can do it!" Then he let go. After a few tries, and with my dad's encouragement, I finally got it, and it was cool. I did it!

As you get ready to motivate change in your loved one, it's going to feel like that first bike ride. You'll be scared, and you might not want to go through with it. But I'm here to tell you that you can do it! Don't let your fears prevent it.

Trust me; I understand how fear can put a choke hold on action. I remember the time my friend Trent came to visit me. I had not seen him in more than a decade, and I was startled by his appearance. It was early evening, and Trent, who was forty-five years old, was visiting me at my loft near Union Square in New York City.

His strawberry-blond hair was strangely parted. His khaki pants and white T-shirt were scruffy to the point of dishevelment. His unshaven face was pale and his fingernails chewed down to the quick. I had to collect myself for a moment because his looks were so unlike the kind of meticulous

detail Trent had always applied to his appearance. Trent, a history profes-
sor, used to count himself among the believers that clothes make the man.
He was always so clean and pressed and stylish. Now he looked as if he
didn't care.

Even more alarming to me was that he had a black eye and bruises on
his arms. I joked, "Who socked you?" He said he hit his eye while opening
a taxi cab door too fast, and the force knocked him on the ground. I
thought, "Either he is very accident-prone or something is going on at
home." I wondered if it was my right to say anything. Because I hadn't
seen him in ten years, I decided to stay silent.

We sat on overstuffed chairs in my living room, sipped on some spiced
green tea, and caught up with each other's lives. Head down, Trent mum-
bled that he was still with the same partner of a decade ago, a guy named
Andy, but that Andy had been drinking every day for the past three
years, from morning until night. Trent sat there, a cloud over him, broken, feeling hopeless while sharing parts of the drama he was living
through. I kept thinking, "What happened to the strong, active Trent I
used to know?"

It was getting late, and Trent said he had to leave. I told him, "Promise
me that if you need to talk, you'll call." He said, "Sure."

I confess I had been afraid to butt in. "It's none of my business," I rationalized. "What if I'm wrong and he gets upset?" I asked myself. "I haven't
seen him in a long time; surely someone has said something by now," I
reasoned. My mind was spinning, coming up with every possible excuse to
let things just be. My fears and what-ifs clouded everything, especially my
common sense.

The next morning I awoke with a fresh take. In this stay-out-of-it culture of ours, most of us are conditioned never to draw lines in the sand. We
hold back on what we really think, not wanting to "damage the friendship,"
or, I suspect, really not wanting to experience the discomfort of conflict.
But it's the silence itself that can damage the relationship or friendship—or
far worse, the friend or loved one. What are friends for? Why do we have
a family, if not to help keep one another from harm?

Believe me, I'm no advocate of general or unjustified butting in
("Shouldn't you work on that gut?" or "I'd never let my kids talk like that"),

but I knew I had to say something to Trent. I needed to trust my instincts. I didn't need permission to get involved in someone's life and speak up, especially if what was going on could be a crime.

I called Trent and invited him to lunch that day. We agreed to meet at a little Thai restaurant near my loft. We sat in a quiet corner of the restaurant.

"I'm worried about you. How are things really going in your relationship with Andy?" I began, after we had ordered a couple of appetizers.

At first Trent denied anything was wrong except the alcoholism, which he had mentioned the day before. He then sighed and the tears started coming. I reached over and squeezed his shoulder. He told me yes, that there was physical abuse, horrible, brutal beatings. His always drunk partner used wild, closed-fist punches to hit him. "For years, I worked so hard to keep the abuse a secret," he admitted. "I feel humiliated."

By now, I was vested in this situation, so I felt more comfortable speaking up. "I care what happens to you because you're my friend. And I'm grateful you trust me enough to let me discuss this with you. This isn't your fault, and you don't deserve it."

I didn't say anything like "Why are you putting up with this?" And I gave him time to process what I had said.

"I don't know what to do," Trent said. "I'm always terrified to go home, but more terrified not to go."

I reminded him of just how strong he was to be living his life in the shadow of abuse. "I know you're dealing with complicated stuff, but I'm beginning to feel like you might be in danger. You've got some hard choices to make." I didn't call Andy a jerk or resort to blame or name-calling.

I added that I wouldn't feel like a good friend if I didn't point him in the direction of people who could help him. I resisted saying "If I were you . . . ," because I couldn't truly understand the physical and emotional risk from his perspective. But I did hand him a note with phone numbers and Web sites where he could get help.

We ended our lunch in mostly reflective silence, and I knew he was mulling everything over. As we parted, I said, "Whatever decision you make, I'll be here for you."

A few days later, I heard from Trent. He had gone to one of the advocacy centers I had recommended. He had pressed charges, obtained an order of protection, and moved out. I felt relieved knowing I had helped, although I almost didn't, because I was afraid to.

Trent's story sheds light on another question I get from time to time: What do we do if there is violence at home? And my counsel is always the same: GET OUT, and then call for help.

Do not fall prey to attempting a family intervention on your own, with or without a circle of change, when the one who needs help has a history of violence. In cases such as this, involve a professional to work with you, as the emotions involved may distract you from doing what must be done. Namely, protecting the lives of those who surround the abuser.

In situations where violence is present, the spouse of the abuser will often have features of someone in a "suicide pact" with another. In these instances, the two can be so enmeshed in each other's chaos, violence, and pain that working to motivate the spouse to lead the charge in an intervention of any sort is nearly impossible.

There is an "I can't live with him, I can't live without him" belief system involved. In cases like this, the circle of care must work to intervene first with the battered spouse, to implore her to let the group act as the leader, or the board of directors, for her.

Fear will not always function as a motivation for change, and a battered spouse is frequently stuck in a cycle that has little to do with what is going on in real time, right now.

WHAT IS FEAR?

If you've been in a similar situation—reluctant to get involved—you may have been acting out of one of the most primal emotions known to humans: fear. Being scared of a specific thing or situation is actually a good thing; in fact, we humans are hardwired to be afraid, as a means of survival. Fear is an internal security system we're all born with. It helps us recognize potentially dangerous or threatening situations. It's part of the fight-or-flight response that prepares us to take action when we're in danger or to motivate us to address problems in our lives. Yet fear is an often pesky emotion marked by anxiety, pain, agitation, uneasiness, distraction, alarm, or dread.

While fear often protects us from danger, it may also cause us to act in ways that are counter to our best interests and the best interests of those we care about. My encounter with Trent, for example, opened my eyes and made me realize that it's what we don't do and don't say—and what we allow to go on—that could do the most harm.

Fear colors nearly every conversation I have with family members who want to initiate change in a friend or loved one. Everyone is afraid of something; and most families, no matter how strong, have some very big fears. One husband I worked with recently did not want to intervene with his depressed wife because he was afraid that she would leave him. I worked with a very powerful female executive who managed a hundred employees in a Fortune 500 company. She was afraid to talk to her live-in boyfriend about getting help for his gambling problem. She told me, "I'm scared he'll break up with me." I know of a fifty-seven-year-old manager of a large consumer goods store in Newark, New Jersey, who suspected one of his employees of coming to work high on occasion. On one hand, his compassion for the person and concern about the bottom line dictated immediate and decisive action. On the other, he was afraid of making legal, medical, and psychological mistakes.

Last year I worked with two parents, Mona and Frank Edwards, who were both prominent psychologists in Seattle. Their youngest daughter, Tina, had been diagnosed with depression as a teenager, and a psychiatrist friend prescribed antidepressants and antianxiety drugs to treat the disorder. Tina was now twenty, and the family suspected that she was smoking crack. She was emaciated and often looked strung out. She hung out with a crowd that ran fast and loose and had easy access to drugs. Her older brother and sister found crack pipes in her apartment and took pictures of them with a camera phone.

Despite the proof, Mona and Frank almost talked themselves out of having the intervention. Frank thought they were overreacting. "What if we're wrong and she gets mad?" Mona said, "Brad, are you certain those are crack pipes? They couldn't be something else?" I assured her that they were indeed crack pipes. Still, she argued, "What if they belonged to a friend?"

"Well, there were three crack pipes in her backpack, and another two in the kitchen cupboard. Given all those cash advances Tina took on her credit card along with her unexplained weight loss, the evidence is clear," I said. "Based on the facts, we are dealing with a very troubled twenty-year-old who needs help." (I was careful to frame everything in terms of facts, not emotion.) Yet the Edwards were afraid of confronting their daughter, afraid of losing their daughter's love, afraid of saying or doing the wrong thing, and so on and so on.

Let's talk about you. What are the fears that might stand in your way of helping someone? What are you most afraid of if you apply a little pressure? That he will leave you? That the daily tension around the house will be unbearable? That you will suffer financially? That you'll say something to her, and she'll tell you to butt out? That your child will hate you as only a child can? That you yourself will feel like a heartless interloper? Whatever your fear, it's an obstacle you've got to address to help change someone you love.

THE SIX FACES OF FEAR

There are countless fears we've all faced, such as fear of success, fear of losing one's job, fear of poverty, fear of flying, fear of criticism, fear of illness, fear of growing old, fear of being separated from loved ones, fear of death, fear of inadequacy, and so on. While fears come in many shapes, the ones I bump into most often in my work can be categorized into these six neat piles:

Fear of Rejection

Remember the anxiety you experienced when beginning a new love or applying for a new job? This is the fear of rejection. For many people preparing for a family meeting, nothing is more terrifying than the notion of being rejected, or hearing "no." None of us likes the idea of being turned down, turned away, or dismissed.

By nature, we all want to be liked, be accepted, and have lots of friends. Rather than risk rejection, most of us go to extremes to avoid confrontation. We don't like to argue. We don't like tense situations or even mild disagreements. We feel that confronting someone will get him or her angry with us, and we view confrontation as something negative. Usually, if we can't avoid it, we acquiesce. As a dad in Washington State told me several times while he anguished over the family meeting, "If I can't fix it, I put it away." He meant that in the face of his twenty-eight-year-old daughter's history of disordered eating and opiate addiction, he tried to love her by giving her things, and thus normalized the chaos resulting from her problems. Admittedly, this isn't the best way to be. To avoid confrontations, we sometimes tolerate behavior that we shouldn't (then later can't stop thinking of all the things we wish we had said or done).

When it comes to helping someone change, perhaps even saving a life, the desire to be liked can get in the way. There's no way to get around this; you just have to walk through it. If you have someone in your life who is self-destructing or causing chaos and conflict in all or most of his or her most important relationships, you've got to step up to the problem and be honest and constructive. Don't hold back. Move. Stir things up. Risk. Act. To stall is cheating your friend or loved one. You may have a long-standing relationship, but this person needs to know that your ultimate concern is for his or her welfare, quality of life, or simply a peaceful existence. Don't let fear keep you stuck.

Remember the Edwards family who were afraid to confront their twenty-year-old daughter about her crack cocaine use? The father was afraid she'd get upset. The mother tried to minimize the situation, brushing it under the rug, so she wouldn't have to go through with the meeting. I'm happy to tell you, though, that after some extremely difficult situations and emotionally trying times, the whole family is changed.

"I knew all my family was frustrated with me," daughter Tina told me later. "But no one hated me more than I hated myself. I knew I didn't want to live that way anymore." Through the family meeting we held, Tina realized that her addiction had to change and her life needed to begin. She got into a drug treatment program. Afterward, the entire family became involved in a support group for families of drug addicts.

If you want to help people be the best of who they are, this is one fear you've got to face. Your friend or loved one isn't rejecting the real you, so don't take rejection personally. He or she is rejecting the idea of being "talked into" something. Yes, you may hear "no." But this will occur less often as you continue to apply my four-step program to change someone you love. Once you've established that your fear of rejection is a roadblock, the best way to overcome it is to just go out and do whatever you know in your heart that you must.

Fear of Making Things Worse

I know a lot of people who struggle with this issue. It is a legitimate fear. You worry constantly that you'll make the situation worse if you tell the truth or let others know you're dissatisfied with their behavior. You cringe at any suggestion of conflict or confrontation, trying to avoid it at all costs. You avoid conversations for fear of making someone angry or hurting their feelings. You give in to what others want to do because you don't want to make them angry, but you're usually the one who ends up being angry.

I believe this fear springs from a lack of self-trust. If you feel fundamentally unworthy, if you don't feel it's acceptable to stand up for yourself, if you believe you can't survive the disapproval of others, then you will give yourself away over and over again. You'll end up feeling perpetually overwhelmed, resentful, and burned out. Overload and resentment are high prices to pay to keep peace.

The best way to overcome your fear of making things worse is to trust yourself more. When you learn to trust yourself, you know your limits and expectations and can express them to others. And you have the confidence to survive disapproval should it occur. You know deep in your bones that you can't possibly please all of the people all of the time, and so you come to understand that occasionally you will disappoint and upset others. The more you trust yourself and assert your autonomy, the more your love will come from a genuine place in your heart, rather than from some compulsion to please, avoid confrontation, or keep peace.

It is also important to develop a tougher skin, to get to a point at which you don't care so much about what others think. As the saying goes, You wouldn't care about what others think of you if you realized how seldom they actually do. Most people are so absorbed in themselves that they aren't thinking about you anyway. Even if you did confront them and they got mad, they'd probably forget about it in a short period of time. Remember, hornets get angry, but don't stay that way. They get tired. They simmer down.

Does this fear have any purpose? I think we should only feel the fear of making things worse if we are deliberately rude, mean, or offensive, or if we lie or cheat to intentionally harm someone else. The circle of change helps to dispel self-doubt, too, by building consensus, fact-checking, comparing eyewitness accounts, and verifying through its own inventory process that what you are doing is right, necessary, and good.

Changing someone you love is never achieved by tiptoeing around issues for fear of making things worse, or waiting for things to blow over. If something really important is at stake, be strong and take steps to change this situation. Don't let this fear stop you from taking action to save a relationship or a life.

Keep in mind, too, that it's difficult to predict how another person will behave. Your loved one could be very ready to change. Maybe he wants to break free from old patterns or is ready to stop self-destructing. So don't be afraid to rock the boat. It's better to rock a boat than to end up sinking in it.

Fear of Financial Insecurity

Your own fear may be the fear of financial meltdown. If someone in your family is an alcoholic, a shopaholic, or whatever, the loss of income is a very real threat. Yet some people tend to worry so much about money that they fear disclosing their loved one's condition or stepping up to it, for fear that the person might lose his or her job. This is counterproductive. Someone who doesn't get help is likely to ruin their health and not be able to work. Dead guys don't work.

A few years ago, I worked with a twenty-nine-year-old creative genius, Mark Sanchez, who worked at Fox TV. He smoked cocaine but remained a valued employee. His wife, Anne Marie, almost backed out the morning of the family meeting, even as the entire family was gathered. Mark's boss would be at the meeting, and Anne Marie feared that his attendance would result in Mark losing his job.

I had to allay her fears with some facts: If a person works for a company with more than fifty employees and has been employed for twelve months, they're covered under federal law while seeking treatment. And this fact is important: I've never had a person I've worked with lose his or her job because they got treatment.

Laws aside, in this case, the "aha!" moment for the boss was when I told him Mark was a cocaine addict and was losing his battle to the drug. The boss said that he knew something was going on, but couldn't put his finger on it. As is usually the case, many companies want to offer employees help, guidance, support, or treatment so that they'll maintain productive employment. With Fox's help and his family's intervention, Mark was able to get the proper treatment and get off crack.

In a different type of scenario, many spouses are afraid of losing a certain lifestyle. Their fear drags them back under the sheets of abusive relationships, without their ever trying to help the abuser change. Why risk being poor or not having a nice car to drive? The potential losses are too scary to think about. Anything is better than financial upheaval. If you're thinking like this, you're not only a prisoner to the fear of losing material things, you're also in serious harm's way. Why? Because abuse tends to escalate unless the abuser gets help. You could be placing yourself and others in danger. Do something before your own life runs aground.

Practically speaking, a financial squeeze is avoidable with adequate planning. A good financial planner can help you determine life, health, and disability insurance needs and how much protection is necessary in the event of a major financial impact resulting from job loss, job interruption, divorce, or a significant change.

In many situations, the fear of financial insecurity is a strong motivator for organizing a family meeting right away and getting someone help pronto. If you've got a spouse, for example, who is gambling away your family's life savings, I'm sure you'd want to stop the financial bleeding immediately. To see your way out of this situation, there is a next step forward, and it is the family meeting. Intervening is the best tourniquet.

Whatever the case, use this fear in a positive way to spring into action. Motivate yourself by what you don't want, financial ruin, to get what you do want: financial stability. Looking at your fear in this light will release you from its grip. Nothing feels better than getting your financial future on track.

Fear of Losing Your Sex Life

This is a fear I run into a lot. Whether you've been with someone for a long time or have just started a relationship, the fear of losing a sex life with that person can be very powerful. Why is that? The aftermath of sex is similar to the state induced by taking opiates—drugs with a sedative or narcotic effect. A mild but intoxicating mix of chemical changes occurs, including increases in the levels of serotonin, oxytocin, and endogenous opioids. The release of these feel-good chemicals serves many functions: to relax the body, induce pleasure and satiety, and to trigger warmer feelings of bonding. Sex, particularly in the context of a meaningful relationship, is a critical part of our well-being. It's a part of our bodies and our nature. And yes, it's scary to lose something that has been so important to your relationship. Sexual manipulation can keep you stuck. Break through it.

Martin and Samantha of Houston had been married for fifteen years, with a fairly healthy sex life. Both were attractive people in their early forties. Martin was the manager of a bank branch office, and Samantha was a working mom with a job as a buyer for a department store. She also took care of the couple's two children, Tommy, eight, and Laura, eleven, both of whom were active in after-school sports. Her work did require some travel, and so there was little flexibility in her schedule. Samantha was always asking herself the same questions over and over again: How will I get everything done? How can I do a good job at work and still be there for my family? How can I get Martin to help? And perhaps most important: How can I create a less stressed, more balanced life?

Samantha's life was also significantly challenged by the fact that Tommy was diagnosed with attention deficit hyperactivity disorder (ADHD) at age seven. He was given Adderall, a drug frequently prescribed for ADD and ADHD in both children and adults. It's a stimulant that heightens alertness.

Often frazzled, Samantha had trouble managing her daily life. She turned to food, mainly sweets, to medicate her anxiety. This resulted in weight gain, troubling because she prided herself on keeping a good figure. Samantha discovered that she could control her appetite and her weight by taking her son's Adderall, which some describe as a "legal" version of speed. The first time she popped one of the pills in her mouth, it immediately made her feel energetic, confident, attentive, and not hungry. She convinced her doctor that she suffered from adult ADHD and was able to wrangle her own prescription for Adderall.

But within about a month, Samantha built up a tolerance to the medication. Within two months of popping her first Adderall, Samantha was taking three times the prescribed amount daily. Soon she was polishing off an entire month's worth in one week and dipping into her son's prescription for extra pills. She would struggle through extreme physical and mental exhaustion until she could obtain more Adderall.

Eventually, Samantha's addiction forced her to leave her job. Family income was cut nearly in half. She began raiding the family's savings account to pay bills, until the account was down to nothing. Martin discovered the drained bank account. Although he suspected his wife was hooked on the prescription drug, he was reluctant to step up to the problem. His greatest fear wasn't the fact that her active addiction was robbing their children of a healthy home life; it was the fear of losing what little sex remained that stopped him going through with an intervention. Although the situation infuriated and exhausted him, Martin was afraid of losing the physical connection he had with her.

Despite Martin's fear, we did have the family meeting. Samantha admitted her addiction to her family and her doctor and quit Adderall. She is now working on putting her life back together. "I tried to fool myself into thinking that I had this problem under control, but it just had me under its dangerous spell," she told me later.

Fear of losing your sex life goes back to the fear of rejection by someone you find desirable, fear of letting go of a sure thing, and fear of being alone. But if you're sincere about wanting someone to change, put your concerns about your sex life aside, at least for now. Your partner values and needs you. Reassure him or her that you're in this together. Your patience and love will ultimately bring the two of you closer than ever before.

Fear of Abandonment

One of the fears I encounter most often in my clients is the fear of abandonment. It's something we all struggle with to a greater or lesser degree. It triggers the possibility of a painful separation and loneliness. The longing we all feel to be connected to another human being is a deep, primal drive, rooted in childhood. The most significant connection we can have as children is with our parents, and in adulthood, with our partners. Very few people, young or old, want to live in isolation. So when it comes to having a family meeting, the fears that crop up are primarily "He will leave," or "She will never talk to me again."

This agonizing fear was exemplified by two members of the Warren family of Long Island. It was a blustery winter day when I pulled up in the driveway of their one-story home, constructed mostly of stone. To my shock, the focus of the family meeting, Lindsay, age thirty-eight, was naked, screaming and flailing in a snowbank.

Present at the family meeting were her mother, Amanda; her dad, Richard; her grandmother Dorothy; and her sister, Susan. "Come on inside, hon, we're having a family meeting," I said. We all went back outside, invited Lindsay in, and got her dressed in some jeans and an oversized T-shirt.

Each family member knew Lindsay was disturbed, and each one had his or her own theory as to why. Susan, who was a born-again Christian, was convinced that Lindsay suffered from a spiritual malady. Her grandmother Dorothy believed that Lindsay had inherited her grandfather's love of drink. (Dorothy's late husband died of cirrhosis of the liver.) Amanda was convinced that Lindsay was a drug addict, and Richard felt his daughter was clinically depressed and suffering from bipolar disorder. Despite their differing diagnoses, the family members had a collective solution: put Lindsay's condition out to the Universe and trust that she would get well—a solution based on the doctrine of a well-known bestseller, copies of which several family members were clutching when I walked into the house.

It's important to add here that while I was on my way to the family meeting, Richard called me and said, "You have to call it off. We can't go through with this. It's too much for our family."

"Too much for our family" emanated from the fear of abandonment in Amanda and Dorothy. "Too much for our family" came, too, from embarrassment that their daughter was naked. The more I had talked to this family, the more they opened up and shared their concerns, feelings, and fears, as well as their frustrations, based on their not knowing what to do. Earlier in her life, Dorothy had confronted her husband about his alcoholism, and he left her temporarily. Dorothy's fear was studded with real-life experience. Based on her history, she was afraid Lindsay would leave, too, even though her granddaughter had nowhere to go. Lindsay had lost her apartment over an inability to keep up the monthly rent.

Some of your own fears may be exaggerated because of old emotional bogeymen from your past. For instance, if your father left your mother over some issue, you may fear that your mate might do the same. It's understandable that you don't want to bring that pain with you. You may attach more significance to that possibility than the actual situation warrants. But don't let yesterday drain value from today and tomorrow.

As for Amanda, she was Lindsay's primary caregiver. Her maternal, nurturing instincts had kicked in. In a mission of motherly love, Amanda put her life on hold to take care of her firstborn daughter. She was very afraid that her daughter would leave for good if confronted.

The entire meeting was tumultuous and explosive. Out of control, Lindsay tried to attack everyone in the room with her fists. Rather than try to subdue her ourselves, I suggested that we bring in law enforcement. Now I had their attention!

"Why would we call the police?" Richard ranted. "That will really get the neighborhood tongues wagging about us!"

Nonetheless, the police were called, and Lindsay hit a police officer. She was handcuffed and taken away in an ambulance that night. As a result of her arrest, Lindsay was admitted to a psych ward, where she accepted the plan for treatment. Doctors did a toxicology screen. It produced evidence that she was high on alcohol and opiates.

Are you afraid of abandonment? Then don't dwell on the limitless possible outcomes of the family meeting. The longer you entertain what-ifs in your mind, the longer you delay taking action. One lesson from the bike example: I know this is hard, but as my dad told me, "You can do it!" Learn to trust by practicing trust: Decide to trust a person or a situation. Let go of the outcome. You can deal with it when it happens. Stay with me here. Understand that this fear response was appropriate when you were a baby—when your fear that you would die if you were abandoned was justified—but realize that you're an adult now, and should the unlikely happen (abandonment), you will survive.

Fear of Failure

Here's a huge, scary fear that coexists with all the other fears: the fear of failure. A lot of people avoid doing a lot of things because they're afraid of not doing them well. The same goes for holding a family meeting. One of the main reasons people avoid doing them is that they fear the whole effort will fall flat on its face. If it's any consolation at all, I've never seen a family meeting fail to create change, and I have done hundreds and hundreds of interventions.

The philosophical conundrum that asks, If a tree falls in a forest and no one hears it, does it make a sound? can be applied to interventions. If an intervention is held but the troubled person doesn't show up, is it still an intervention? The answer is YES, in banner-sized capital letters. An intervention is a process, not a single moment in time, so regardless of what the person does, the intervention is under way.

If you find yourself immobilized by the fear of failure as you prepare to use my change formula, try any or all of these suggested antidotes:

▶ *Work as best you can on erasing your fear and failure statements. Examine your language carefully. How often are you using sentences like these: "She'll never go through with this." "He'll never recover." "She can't stick to anything." "Nothing ever turns out the way*

I planned it." Ouch—those hurt, don't they? They suppress optimistic attitudes too.

I believe optimism is vital. On a personal and practical level, I find assuming a can-do attitude about my work or personal aspirations always opens up possibilities. My mind begins to work in new, more creative ways—and I'm sure that, physiologically, the neurotransmitters in my brain are finding new pathways and enhancing my thought process. Optimism helps me concentrate better; and that automatically helps me solve problems, tackle new projects and ideas, and achieve my goals. You must have a high level of optimism to change someone you love. At interventions I lead, I am forever saying "She's going!" to the disbelief of those present who have seen their loved one's resistance.

▶ *Don't be too hard on yourself. Remember, one of the biggest worries people have is that they will get it wrong. We're all frightened of making a mistake. Our fear makes us tense, worried about upsetting the status quo, incurring the wrath of a friend or loved one, and we're pressured into playing it safe. It's okay to be afraid or nervous. As long as your intent is sincere and loving, the right words and actions will come.*

▶ *Put aside your what-ifs and if-onlys and think about what's going on around you. Sure, getting your loved one much-needed help may not be easy. What if he refuses? What if she promises to get help but doesn't follow through? Many what-if scenarios can be anticipated in planning and choreographing the invitation to change intervention. Use objective decision-making tools, for example. Map out the pros and cons, possible outcomes, desired outcomes, and likelihood of the outcomes on a piece of paper or white board. Stay focused on the results you want, not on the emotions surrounding them.*

▶ *Commit to acting versus reacting. How will you ever know what's yours to accomplish if you never take that first step to find out what's within your reach? Taking action is proactive and requires strength and confidence. When you're taking action, you have less time to be consumed by fear. Worrying doesn't solve problems. Action does.*

▶ *Keep trying. There is great wisdom in the familiar saying,* Winners never quit and quitters never win. *If you study the biographies of any successful person, you'll probably find a string of failures, rejections, and disappointments that infiltrated their lives before there was a celebration of triumph. Walt Disney went broke several times and had a nervous breakdown before he became successful. Albert Einstein failed math courses. Enrico Caruso had so much trouble hitting the high notes that his voice instructor advised him to give up singing. Instead he persevered to become one of the world's greatest tenors. The issue is not failure but your response to it. If you have a desire to succeed, don't let the fear of failure prevent it.*

FEARS: REAL OR IMAGINARY?

There's a distinction between rational fear and irrational fear. Here's a rational fear: You've just had a mammogram, and your doctor informs you that a small mass was detected on the test. You fear you may have cancer. That would be an example of a rational fear. On the other hand, if your doctor tells you that you're okay, and you still have a fear of cancer, that would be an irrational fear.

Most fears are imagined. In fact, 95 percent of the things we imagine through fear never happen. Much of the remaining 5 percent we often make happen ourselves. Like the person who has a fear of failure: he may get himself so anxious about failing that he will actually, somehow, make himself fail.

I heard once that fear is an acronym for "false evidence appearing real." Nowhere is this more true than with family meetings. The assumptions we make about our friend, spouse, loved one, relative, coworker, or employee may or may not be accurate, but we unnecessarily let those assumptions make us nervous and hesitant. It's merely your imagination telling you the worst is going to happen. But guess what? Even your worst fears may never come true.

Are your own fears real or imaginary? To find out, take a careful and honest intellectual inventory of your fears. Our imaginations can run wild, and need to be reined in with a reality check. My Fear Inventory below will help you assess whether your fears are fact or fiction.

FEAR INVENTORY

Everyone has fears. It's just that some people are more fearful than others. How is fear holding you back? Take this fear inventory to find out. Part A will help you assess your fear level and make you aware of how fearful you really are. Part B will give you insights into how to identify and control unfounded fears.

Part A: How Fearful Are You?

What follows is a list of twenty-five statements. If a statement is true for you, check the space next to the statement. If a statement is not true for you, leave it blank. Be honest in your answers. Don't think over any statement very long either. Mark your answer quickly and go on to the next statement.

☐ 1. When scheduled for a routine checkup, I'm sure my doctor will find something wrong with me.

☐ 2. If I see a police car cruising behind me, I wonder if an officer is going to stop me.

☐ 3. I rarely wear my best jewelry. I keep it stashed in a safe place.

☐ 4. If my company went out of business, I'd feel petrified over my bleak prospects for employment.

☐ 5. The approval of others is very important to me.

☐ 6. I don't like to fail at anything.

☐ 7. I usually put off important decisions.

☐ 8. I believe in the saying *A leopard can't change its spots.*

☐ 9. I avoid trying new things unless I think I can do them well.

☐ 10. I tend to worry over future events.

☐ 11. I feel that it is impossible to overcome the influences of the past.

☐ 12. I prefer to vacation at the same spot or resort each year.

☐ 13. From time to time, I've described myself as having a nervous stomach and uneasiness.

☐ 14. When my birthday rolls around, I feel depressed because I'm one year older.

☐ 15. I avoid confrontation.

☐ 16. When my boss makes changes at work, I feel apprehensive.

☐ 17. I hate to take chances.

☐ 18. I find it hard to express my opinion.

☐ 19. The last time I made a major change to my routine was over three years ago.

☐ 20. I dislike making mistakes.

☐ 21. I often get annoyed over little things.

☐ 22. I am uncomfortable around people I perceive to be richer or smarter than I am.

☐ 23. My parents were fearful of people, places, and things.

☐ 24. If I think the time might be right for a love affair, I often get cold feet and avoid the situation.

☐ 25. When someone tells me no, I usually feel upset and hurt.

Fear Inventory Scoring

5 checks or fewer: You're rational in your thinking and possess the ability to control your fears. Quite probably, you are also adept at planning what to do in situations that might feel threatening, rather than worrying about them.

6 to 10 checks: You have fears every now and then. Determine if these fears are imaginary. If so, admit it and refuse to continue to dwell on those fearful thoughts. What the mind dwells on, it magnifies and encourages. It will eventually begin to actually believe that your fearful imaginations are real and act upon them. If your fear is real, accept it and take whatever steps you can to change the circumstances that cause your fear.

More than 10 checks: You may be overly cautious in many situations. Work with your fears, whatever they are, not against them. Trying to limit or squelch fear only aggravates and perpetuates it. Instead, accept that you are experiencing feelings of worry and anxiety, but know that the outcome you fear is unlikely to happen. Recognize, too, that most fears exist only in your mind. You are worrying about something that has not yet happened and may never happen.

Part B: Reality Check of Fears

Let's get a little more specific. Look over the chart below. In the first column, catalog the fears you have about doing an invitation to change intervention: fear of rejection, fear of financial insecurity, fear of losing your sex life, fear of abandonment, and fear of failure. (I've provided an example.)

To the side of each fear category, in the second column, describe the fear in complete detail and with complete honesty, including how you react to this fear. An example of a detailed description is: "I can't go through this family meeting because I fear that I'll use the wrong words and that my wife will become angry with me, and threaten to leave and take my kids."

Next, look at your list of fears, and assess their rationality. Certainly consider the answers to these questions: What evidence do you have that things may go wrong? What is the probability? Are there ways to head off a bad outcome? Have you survived similar events before? Remember times when things worked out well for you and find similarities. Examine the assumptions behind your thought patterns, and see if they square up with reality. You might consider taking an external perspective. Pretend someone else wrote them, and they've consulted you, as a wise friend, for feedback.

Use this information to rate your fear. In the third column, give each fear a score from 1 to 5—where 1 means this fear is imaginary, irrational, and unlikely to happen; and 5 means it is still within the realm of reality. Analyzing the rationality of your fears will cut them down to size and inspire you to overcome them. In many cases, you'll find yourself amused by how unrealistic your fears are. Keep in mind, too, that fear goes away when you do the thing you're afraid of.

FEAR CATEGORY	FEAR REACTION	FEAR SCORE
Fear of financial insecurity	*He is the breadwinner; we will lose our home if he has to go to treatment.*	*1*

STAY EVER HOPEFUL

Over the eons, many inspiring words have been penned on the subject of hope. One of my personal favorites is this anonymous quote: When you get to the end of your rope, tie a knot and hang on. This simple axiom characterizes what's best about the human condition: More often than not, when paralyzed by fear or faced with seemingly insurmountable challenges, we're surprised to discover—or rediscover—our capacity for hope. Hope fills up the space fear vacates. Rather than give up or give in, do everything you can to fear less and hope more.

During family preparation for interventions, I say again and again these two things:

1. Lean into the Hope

2. She's going!/He's going!

NINE

Claim Your Number One Source of Power

Once you've worked through your fears and come to understand that change is possible for your loved one, it's time to devote some time and sweat to bringing about the specific changes you desire. Frankly, where will you get the necessary energy, especially when you're racing around and perhaps still living from crisis to crisis? It's not easy, because investing so much of yourself in helping another distressed person may make you feel guilty that you're taking time away from other important obligations, or because it doesn't seem fair that you are healthy and that your loved one is not. But let me tell you, this energy I'm talking about—the energy to begin effecting change—is not something you eventually "get"; it is something you already have. And it's right in your own family.

A Family Miracle

Gerald and Ann Martin lived in Westchester, Connecticut, and for a while, their life was big and blessed. The Martins' large home, with its Lexus out front and swimming pool in back, was the picture of clean-cut, upper-class life, and Gerald and Ann, both fifty-seven, easily blended in. She was a real estate agent, with blue eyes and light brown hair that feathered back to her shoulders. He was a dot.com millionaire, self-confident and trim, with wild brown hair and a square jaw. They had a strong marriage, a community they loved, and two grown kids—twins, a boy, David, and a girl, Devon.

If you met David at a party, the first thing you'd notice would be his eyes. They look above you, never directly at you, then dart away, scanning his surroundings as if looking for a place to hide. When David was growing up, he saw little of his father, who was often away on business. David remembered that his father never praised him for any of his achievements, nor came to see him play basketball in school—except once. He was the high scorer that day, and his father's sole comment was "Your teammates really played poorly, didn't they?"

Devon, on the other hand, was the jewel in Gerald's crown, favored and fawned over. She reminded me of a young Audrey Hepburn, a lithe, graceful beauty of a brunette. Sadly, in April 2000, Devon was diagnosed with an autoimmune disease that over time left her with cognitive problems and nerve damage so severe that she lost some of her fingers. In 2007, Devon was told she had acute kidney failure and would need a kidney transplant. The best match: her twin brother, David.

The problem was that David, now living in Seattle, and by his own will alienated from the family, was a cocaine addict, making kidney donation risky. Yet unless Devon received the kidney, she would die.

My team and I got involved with the Martin family because they wanted me to help them get David off cocaine. I had numerous discussions with the family, individually and in family conference calls. Many insights emerged from these discussions. The childhood David never had—that is to say, all the love and understanding and encouragement he needed but didn't get—had been haunting him. It undermined his capacity to deal with emotional hardships, and he was having trouble accepting that his parents cared enough about him to want him to get treatment. I said to him, "You think that's all behind you, but until you learn to forgive and let go, chances are you'll continue to be controlled by those same family patterns." My observation hit the mark. David's cool exterior began to thaw, and he was receptive to returning home to meet with his family.

I knew from experience in working with families that if parents have a rocky relationship with one child, or if there's an illness or a death in the family, siblings often wind up turning to each other for comfort. Whenever there's a failure at the parent level, or a crisis, siblings may become a source of love and support for each other. I asked David and Devon if this was true for them. They agreed it was.

When we were all together as a group, face to face, I asked, "What can this family do to help one another out?" They all looked at one another; everyone was in tears. Finally, a breakthrough came, and it was amazing for everyone involved. The Martins fully embraced the reality that if David got clean, he could save his sister's life.

It was a powerful, life-changing revelation. David moved home to Connecticut for good, got into treatment and off drugs, and donated his right kidney to his sister. The entire family, once fractured, came together to provide support for sister and brother. David, for his part, repaired his relationship with his parents and reinvested in the family. "It's hard to explain," David told me. "My love for my family has never been as deep as it is now."

With the love between parents and children rekindled—and two lives saved—a miracle truly occurred.

People can change. People do change. And the family—however you want to define it—is uniquely poised to help them change. The Martins are living proof.

FAMILY STRENGTHS

When I work with families, I always emphasize that their number one source of power is the naturally occurring influence of the family—its relationships, the bonds, the history, and the shared future. Family is the strongest and most enduring influence in any person's life, no matter how far down the ladder he or she has fallen. Sure, some days you feel like barely making it through, but you're sticking together as a family. Even if there's a fracture in the family, at least some members are still in communication with each other. In fact, research shows that if a family member has an addiction, he is much more likely to be in daily conversation with at least one parent than a nonaddicted child. We know, too, from decades of family research, that the family can offer protective factors that steer kids away from substance abuse and make children more educationally successful. People who navigate change the best say that those close to them, including a spouse or partner, were most important in guiding their change, according to a major study on change published in 2009 by the Southeastern Institute of Research (SIR). Think about the common sense behind the proof: No one knows your loved one like your family does. No one cares more about his success than your family. You've been there, through the good times and the bad. You're part of the most influential group of people in someone's life. And for whatever reason, your loved one always seems to gravitate back to the family—for comfort, shelter, resources, security, predictability, and more.

When I refer to family, I mean not only your family of origin (biological or primary guardian) but also your family "of the heart," those who are an important support for your loved one. This can include people such as family friends, spiritual mentors, neighbors, teachers, coworkers—those considered to be a significant influence. All of these people constitute a natural support system that has enormous influence and power.

THE SIX PILLARS OF FAMILY STRENGTH

Your energy to change someone you love comes from your family. And you plug into this incredible power by drawing on your "family strengths." Family strengths are a set of relationship qualities that:

▶ *Enhance the emotional health of the family.*

▶ *Contribute to a family's sense of well-being.*

▶ *Support and protect families and family members, especially during times of adversity.*

▶ *Influence and inspire positive, lasting change in family members.*

What makes families strong? In a nutshell, families who define themselves as strong say they love each other despite differences and disagreements. They find life together satisfying. They know how to solve problems productively, and live in harmony with one another.

I admit that, at first glance, that may sound a little storybook-ish, and maybe not at all like *your* family. For the record, I'm not describing the rarely obtainable *Leave It to Beaver* household here. In fact, today's family is just about any family that isn't headed by patient Ward Cleaver and his pearl-clad wife, June! Real families have stresses and challenges like never before. They have secrets, old family rivalries, guilt, resentments, unequal burdens, broken trusts, a "not-my-problem" mentality, and differing values and interests, to name just a few issues.

However, every family—including yours—has strengths, and they come in many forms. In my own work with families over the years, I've codified these strengths into six areas that I call the Six Pillars of Family Strength.

Pillar #1: Communication

Strong families talk to each other. They share themselves. They know that listening to what others say and feel is one of the most powerful ways of showing love. They don't just give lip service to each other; there is consistency between what is said and what is done. Family members are open and honest with each other. They discuss personal fears, stresses, complaints, and other feelings with each other, without criticizing or judging. They have a voice in family decision making and problem solving. Their opinions are respected.

Pillar #2: Caring

Do you let your spouse, children, parents, and siblings know they're appreciated? Do you give them positive attention? Can they tell by the way you treat them that you think they are pretty special? Strong families focus on one another's strengths, not faults. And when it comes to love, strong families excel at it. They show affection, love, warmth, and appreciation for one another. They're not afraid to say "I love you" or hug one another.

They're proud of one another and they express it. When someone is in trouble or in need, family members step in to help, unselfishly and with love. Even when a family member makes mistakes, members of caring families find ways to encourage and support that person. Strong families celebrate positive aspects of one another. For example, they pay attention to the talents, skills, achievements, special qualities, and characteristics that make the other person unique. Caring families make each member feel they are of value.

Pillar #3: Health

Families who value health recognize that there are benefits and pleasures to be gained from pursuing a healthy lifestyle. They eat nutritiously, stay active, keep up with doctors' appointments, and have healthy outlets for stress. The family's commitment to healthy living empowers them to establish priorities and make decisions that everyone can live with and by. These families know that habits impact others, so they try to live in such a way that everyone in the family is better off for it.

Pillar #4: Commitment

Families with this strength are committed to the togetherness of the family, and they are loyal to one another. They value the things that make their family special, such as family history and traditions. They spend quality time together as a family and enjoy being together. They work together, play together, and enjoy leisure time together. They may be very busy, but they don't let jobs, school, or personal hobbies steal family time.

Pillar #5: Resiliency

Resilient families are seldom surprised by trouble. They aren't problem free; they just admit to problems and do what they need to do to solve them. They are problem solvers, not problem makers. They anticipate problems and think in terms of multiple solutions. These families also think optimistically about their lives. Whereas pessimists say, "What a mess I'm in," and get paralyzed by it, optimists say, "I don't know how but I'm going to solve this problem." They have a strong sense of purpose, and view bad circumstances as opportunities to grow and learn.

One aspect of family resiliency is humor. Having a sense of humor helps families cope with life's stressors and crises and is very beneficial in strengthening families. It defuses the tension and has an immediate calming effect. Families who learn to find humor even in some of the grim realities and emotion-packed challenges of daily life have an edge on peace of mind.

Pillar #6: Spirituality

Spirituality is an important family strength, particularly during times of change, and it has diverse meanings. It can be a belief in a higher power. It can be an attitude—the state of being happy enough with what one has or is, not desiring something more or different. Or it might be a sense of gratitude and hope that recognizes even the little things of life as special events. At its essence, spirituality is a sense of purpose in life, a connection between the individual and something higher than oneself. People who believe in a higher power are more likely to respond successfully to change, and will connect more with that higher power during times of change. Another aspect of spirituality in some families is a belief in serving others, particularly those less fortunate. Whatever form it takes, spirituality provides a way to deal with successes and also failures in family relationships, build emotional support, and inspire connectedness, both at present and eternally.

As you read over the six pillars, maybe you're feeling a little discouraged because your family life isn't everything you want it to be. If so, I have good news for you: Every family has family strengths. You just may not recognize yours yet. I see this all the time. Not long ago, I worked with a family whose adult son, Raymond, was a $500,000-a-year cocaine addict and alcoholic, with a history of physical abuse. After he attacked his own father, the dad slapped a restraining order on him. That occurred in January, and the family didn't ask for help until May. It wasn't as if the behavior was new. The family just thought they were weak and powerless, and so they dragged their feet, not tapping into the strengths they had as a family.

And they did have strengths. At their core, they were loyal to one another and resilient when the chips were down. It was this resilient family solidarity that ultimately got Raymond into treatment. Talk about a miracle: Today he lives a productive life and works in the family business! If you feel like you have no strengths on which to draw, I'm here to tell you that you do.

IDENTIFY YOUR FAMILY STRENGTHS

What I'd like to do now is have you take a brief questionnaire. It will help you identify your family strengths, as well as see areas where you can help build or improve certain strengths in your family. Grab a pencil and, after each statement, circle the response that best describes your family.

Strongly Disagree (SD)	Disagree (D)	Agree (A)	Agree Strongly (AS)

PART A: COMMUNICATION

SD D A AS 1. I can openly share my feelings, opinions, hopes, dreams, fears, joys, sorrows, experiences, growth, and needs with my family.

SD D A AS 2. In my family, we listen to one another: When someone is talking, we give them our full attention with an open mind and heart.

SD D A AS 3. We respond positively; we use words and actions to show we are listening.

SD D A AS 4. If I have a problem, my family makes suggestions that are kind and helpful, without criticizing or judging.

SD   D   A   AS   5. My family makes me feel important, and that what I have to say counts.

PART B: CARING

SD   D   A   AS   1. My family exhibits genuine affection toward one another.

SD   D   A   AS   2. Members of my family notice the talents, skills, achievements, special qualities, and characteristics that make each person in the family unique.

SD   D   A   AS   3. My family is comfortable saying "I love you" to one another.

SD   D   A   AS   4. In my family, we ask one another for help and speak up when we need somebody to listen or just to know someone cares.

SD   D   A   AS   5. My family is proud of me, and I am proud of my family.

PART C: HEALTH

SD   D   A   AS   1. We get annual checkups and follow our doctors' advice.

SD   D   A   AS   2. We exercise, either formally at a gym, or informally, such as by walking, playing catch, hiking, or bike riding.

SD   D   A   AS   3. We eat nutritious meals together.

SD   D   A   AS   4. My family openly talks about, and steps up to, issues related to health, such as diet, exercise, smoking, or alcohol or drug abuse.

SD   D   A   AS   5. My family is supportive and helpful when a family member is depressed, anxious, or dealing with stress.

PART D: COMMITMENT

SD   D   A   AS   1. My family strives to spend quality time together.

SD   D   A   AS   2. We practice traditions such as an annual vacation, prayers before bedtime, movie nights, holiday get-togethers, and/or birthday celebrations.

SD   D   A   AS   3. I feel supported and encouraged by my family.

SD   D   A   AS   4. In my family, we are loyal to one another.

SD   D   A   AS   5. We go to one another's games, music performances, school events, and so forth.

PART E: RESILIENCY

SD   D   A   AS   1. Members of my family have a sense of humor that helps us cope with life's stressors and crises.

SD   D   A   AS   2. My family solves problems with cooperation, creative brainstorming, and openness to others.

SD   D   A   AS   3. My family encourages and fosters high self-esteem.

SD   D   A   AS   4. We're able to settle arguments, not let bad feelings fester, and we forgive one another.

SD   D   A   AS   5. Optimism, or positive thinking, helps my family feel hopeful during trying times. We tell ourselves we can rather than we cannot.

PART F: SPIRITUALITY

SD   D   A   AS   1. My family has faith in a higher power.

SD   D   A   AS   2. My family expresses gratitude for what they have, not complaining about what they do not have.

SD   D   A   AS   3. In my family, we talk about spirituality and what it means to us in everyday life.

SD   D   A   AS   4. My family attends religious services together.

SD   D   A   AS   5. My family believes in helping people in need—in our own extended families, in our neighborhoods, and in our communities.

Analyzing Your Results

In each of the six parts of this questionnaire, review the statements with which you agree and agree strongly. If you have two or more Agrees or Agree Stronglys in any one section, this indicates that your family is strong in this pillar. Even one Agree or Agree Strongly is a positive sign! These are strengths you can *build on*. Next, look at the statements with which you disagree or strongly disagree. These are areas you can *build up*.

BUILDING YOUR FAMILY STRENGTHS

Like all families, yours has room for improvement, even at the points where you're strong. My own family has always been strong in the areas of caring and spirituality, but less adept in communication. This was evident in a long-buried family secret. I was approaching forty years of age when the skeletons in my family's closet began to slip out. I grew up with the understanding that my maternal grandmother, Enid Trautman, had died when my mom was only two years old. It turns out that in 1937, my grandpa Elmer Trautman, Enid's husband, committed her to the Oregon State Mental Hospital (the same place where *One Flew Over the Cuckoo's Nest* took place). Enid was depressed, anxious, and possibly an alcoholic. In those days, you just locked alcoholics up in insane asylums. After my grandfather Elmer committed her, he went on to marry three more times, while Enid languished in the hospital without a single visitor. My brothers and I found out she had been released in 1976 to a halfway house close to our home. She died there, alone, in the fall of 1978. Although my parents had known about Enid, they decided to keep the "old truth" alive because my mother couldn't emotionally handle the real truth, and we learned of Enid after her death. Family secrets like mine always have a way of bubbling up to the surface. There is destructive power in a secret, along with the sadness for those who concealed the truth in shame, deceit, or denial. The word "secret" comes from the Latin verb meaning "to separate or sift apart"; and, in fact, secrets do break apart families and impede open communication and trust.

If you know you've got to build on or build up strengths, as my family did, it helps to write some action plans on how to do that, and this is an exercise you can do as a family. Families must work together for the family to work. Under each of the six pillars, I give you some ideas for simple actions you can do to strengthen your family. Read through these ideas and add some of your own.

Communication:

▶ *Talk more about feelings and experiences while driving in the car, while sharing household chores, or before bedtime.*

▶ *Encourage family members to share by saying, "Tell me more," or "What was the best part of your day?"*

▶ *Be better listeners. Set aside lectures and really try to understand from the other person's point of view.*

▶ *Make plans to eat meals together at home as a regular feature of your lives.*

▶ *Our action plan for strengthening family communication:*

_____

_____

_____

_____

Caring:

▶ *Compliment one another every day: "I really like the way you . . ." "You're special to me because . . ." "One of the things I like best about you is . . ."*

▶ *Write positive notes about these things and put the note under the person's pillow, or in a backpack, briefcase, or purse, or send caring text messages or e-mails.*

▶ *Establish a recognition night to celebrate family members' achievements. Serve favorite foods or go out to a favorite restaurant.*

▶ *Our action plan for strengthening the caring in our family:*

_____

_____

_____

_____

Health:

▶ *Exercise together. This doesn't have to be any more complicated than going for a walk, or playing basketball, badminton, or even tag.*

▶ *Set health standards: Eat well, sleep right, and manage your life so that you have time to enjoy and savor all that comes your way.*

▶ *Keep an eye on one another's moods. If someone seems down longer than usual, even kids, talk to a professional.*

▶ *Our action plan for strengthening the health in our family:*

_____

_____

_____

_____

Commitment:

▶ *Pick an evening and make that a standing family night. Consider it sacred time, and don't schedule conflicts with it.*

▶ *Go to one another's games, music performances, school events, and so forth.*

▶ *Establish and practice family traditions. A family tradition is any activity or event that occurs regularly and holds special meaning for that family. The tradition may be as simple as stories and prayers before bedtime, or Saturday-morning pancakes, or as elaborate as an annual vacation.*

▶ *Our action plan for strengthening our sense of family commitment:*

_____

_____

_____

_____

Resiliency:

▶ *Designate a time and place each week to resolve conflicts peacefully—a "safe zone." I use bedtime as a time to resolve standing conflicts to honor a goal of going to bed "at peace."*

▶ *Consider family therapy or team-building exercises to develop better problem-solving and coping techniques.*

▶ *Accept and believe in one another.*

▶ *Our action plan for strengthening our family's resiliency:*

_____

_____

_____

_____

Spirituality:

▶ *Worship together, and/or visit one another's houses of worship or ceremonies. This can be a bonding experience.*

▶ *As a family, participate in some community service like volunteering at a nursing home or soup kitchen, or collecting food for a local food pantry.*

▶ *Talk about spirituality and what it means to all of you in everyday life.*

▶ *Our action plan for strengthening our spirituality as a family:*

_____

_____

_____

_____

I hope you feel more empowered now by working through these exercises. Building on family strengths is an ongoing process. The important part is that you know you have them, and that they are always available to you. They give you the power to move through the decisions and actions that lie ahead.

Affirm Your Strengths

My father, the Quaker pastor, built up a tradition of repeating "affirmations" in our home and at church. Affirmations are short, positive statements that you repeat each day about what you want to accomplish. They trigger a new set of feelings and these new feelings set you on a positive course of action. They help erase self-doubt. They have tremendous power over our minds and actions. The affirmations below are my favorites, and the ones I like to share with families as they begin the change process. I suggest that you stand in front of the mirror and repeat your chosen affirmations. Deliver them with purpose and volume. Don't whisper. Speak so you can really hear yourself.

Change begins with me now.

Our family is equipped to create lasting change.

The miracle I seek is me.

As I demonstrate love, the love is magnified.

I exhale fear and breathe in hope and action.

I deserve wellness in and around me.

My history demonstrates resiliency and change.

Our stories spoken in love change lives.

We are resilient and loving.

I am patient. Change is a process.

Our family deserves healing and change.

I am a powerful agent of change.

BREAKING NEGATIVE PATTERNS: THE FAMILY MAP

I think it's essential to look not only at your family strengths but also at your family patterns. Family patterns are partly responsible for why people act as they do, drink as they do, take drugs as they do, and so on. The good news is, family patterns can be broken.

One of the best tools for breaking negative patterns is the "family map," also called a genogram (pronounced *jen-uh-gram*), and I use it often in family meetings. It's a psychological family tree, with the buds, bark, and creepy bugs still intact. It shows all family members, including pets, and their relationships and reveals significant family behavior patterns—divorces, addictions, suicides, violence, and other problems—that may have affected a person's life. Many behaviors tend to repeat themselves in families from generation to generation, and you can see this on a family map.

Family mapping is critical in helping us picture "just the facts" as we work to separate feelings, fears, or points of view from the work we do. Like they said on the 1950s TV show *Dragnet*, our family map illustrates for us: "Just the facts, ma'am."

The process of mapping out the past will help solidify for family and friends your own truth, past and present. Your family map shows the good and the bad, the trauma and the joy. How one feels about the past dictates how it is handled and viewed. As a result, editing of all sorts occurs. Exclusions. Additions. Minimizations. Amplifications. We seek neither more, nor less drama than the facts. Through family mapping you will become better equipped to act with purpose and truth. You will solidify your eyewitness account, which is so critical to the work we do.

Permit me to use my own family as an example again. My brothers and I were all addicted to something, from drugs to food to gambling. Many relatives struggled. For years, I wondered why there was so much addiction in my own family. So I sat down and drew my family map, tracing my ancestors back a few generations. I was amazed when I looked at my map. I could clearly see that there was a perpetuating pattern of addiction in my family. (See below for a copy of the map I drew.)

When properly drawn, the family map presents your family's history in a single image, making it easy to visualize how your relatives have affected you. Patterns of illness and addiction, or particular temperaments, will leap out at you. This puts your loved one's own depression or addiction into better context when he sees that his grandmother, uncle, and some cousins dealt with the same problems, for instance.

Brad Lamm Family Map

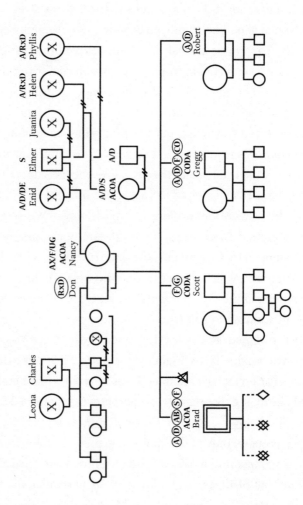

Family Mapping Legend

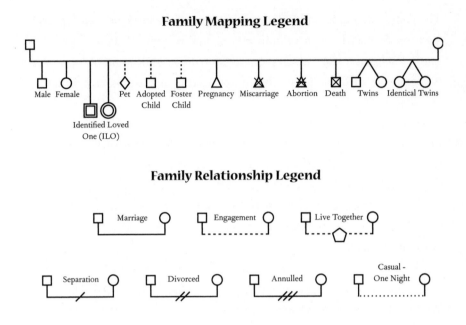

Male   Female   Pet   Adopted Child   Foster Child   Pregnancy   Miscarriage   Abortion   Death   Twins   Identical Twins

Identified Loved One (ILO)

Family Relationship Legend

Marriage   Engagement   Live Together

Separation   Divorced   Annulled   Casual - One Night

FAMILY ISSUES* LEGEND

A: Alcohol
AB: Anorexic or Bulimic
ACOA: Adult Child of Alcoholic
AX: Anxiety
CO: Compulsive Overeater
CODA: Codependent
D: Drugs
DE: Depression
F: Food
G: Gambling
RxD: Prescription Drug Addiction
S: Smoking
UG: Unresolved Grief/Loss

*Note: For a more comprehensive list of issues see pages 205–207.

Circled letters denote "in recovery," for example, a circled A means an alcohol dependent history, currently in recovery.

The Family Mapping and Relationship Legends illustrate how each person, alive or deceased, born or unborn (including pets), occupies historical space. Each has a story and a piece to contribute. Male symbol (upper left) is connected with female symbol (upper right) in the majority of family-building maps.

People believe that they choose a lifestyle of addiction, or they're weak. But just as you may have inherited your father's blue eyes or your mother's red hair, so, too, can you inherit addictive behavior. This helps you see why there should be no guilt on anyone's part for these disorders. They were no one's fault. They didn't start with your loved one. For many, they were passed down like silverware. Everyone is connected, all influencing each other all the time.

In a world where the victimization of self is commonplace, the family map is not intended to provide an excuse for addiction or hurtful behavior. We look for causes of disease as a way to prevent future disease as well as to help reduce relapse once remission is achieved. In my own process of family mapping, I was initially overjoyed by what I found. "It's their fault!" I howled. Then my mom and dad showed up to rehab, where they participated in the family program, and from that I understood they were doing the best they could with what they had.

I was not a victim of my past. I was a victim of my own behavior, behavior that had some very real causes related both to nature and nurture, or genetics and environment. Once I realized these patterns and connected the dots of my life, behavior, history, and problems, these truths enabled me to do something with this inventory.

If someone denies they have an addiction, then pull out the map. There, in black and white, are the patterns. It's hard to deny the possibility of addiction when you see it replicating itself through generations of a family. Apples don't fall far from the tree.

Anton Chekov once said: "Man will become better when you show what he is like." How true. The process of looking back is healing. When a person makes a conscious, more meaningful connection to his life path, it helps break negative patterns and motivates change. Life starts to get better, much better. The family map is a powerful tool in our effort.

HOW TO DRAW YOUR FAMILY MAP

How do you draw your own family map? One way is to do it online. You can go to my Web site at www.BradLamm.com and build your own genogram by dragging and dropping various symbols, entering names and identifiers. Another way is to simply take out pen and paper and start drawing. It's not complicated. Here are some guidelines for drawing a very simple family map:

1. Decide how many generations you wish to depict on your family map. You will probably want to keep it to three to four generations.

2. Gather as much information as necessary to draw your family map. Talk to your relatives about your ancestors.

3. Get paper, a pen, and a ruler.

4. Decide which issues you want to identify. The list below will help you decide what to look for. You can simply assign a letter code to each issue, as I did when I drew my family map.

Here is a comprehensive list of possible issues to include in your family map. They range from chemical dependencies to physical and mental illnesses, from behavioral problems to relationship and/or personality traits.

Issues

Abuse, physical, sexual, or verbal

Alcoholism

Alzheimer's

Anger (bad temper, hostility)

Anxiety

Autism

Codependency

Compulsive behavior/OCD

Conflicted feelings

Control/manipulation issues

Criminal behavior

Depression

Drug abuse

Eating disorders (anorexia, bulimia, binge eater, use of laxatives)

Enmeshment

Estrangment

Exercise obsession

Gambling

Grieving

Illnesses, chronic (diabetes, heart disease, cancer)

Job problems (e.g., maintaining employment)

Memory loss

Mental illness

Money-management issues

Obesity

Prescription-drug dependency

Sexual compulsivity/sexual issues

Smoking

Sobriety

STDs

Suicide (including talk or attempts)

Twelve-step program involvement

Unhealthy relationships

Violence

5. Represent males by squares and females by circles in your family map. A family is shown by a line connecting the generations. Label each shape with the person's name. Your Identified Love One (ILO)—that is, the person needing help—is identified with a circle within a circle (for females) or a square within a square (for males).

6. Draw a square or circle on the bottom half of the page to represent you and label it with your name. Add your siblings on the same part of the page, connecting all siblings with a line.

7. Draw a circle and a square to represent your parents and label the shapes with their names. If you have one parent, draw a straight line upward and one shape to represent him or her.

8. Above your parents, add your grandparents, and beneath and parallel to your parents, draw their other children (your aunts and uncles), all connected with lines. If there are any divorces, indicate so with two slashes on the line connecting the couple.

10. For those who are deceased, put an X through that circle or square.

11. Continue drawing each generation in this manner, connecting lines and shapes for siblings, children, and other relatives. Keep all members of the same generation on the same row.

Making a family map is an eye-opening experience. Use it at your family meeting. It reveals an enormous amount of data on family patterns. It cracks through denial. It helps change begin.

Understanding our family strengths and patterns brings clarity and focus to our relationships. If you are going to change someone you love, you must tap into your family's unique strengths. If you are to help one another, you need to know what drives them, and part of what drives them is your family background. All of this advances the journey toward change, and helps people open the doors of their heart. My hope is that you now understand your power and feel emboldened to act decisively. Remember: Change someone you love, and you profoundly change your life too.

TEN

Bring Down Blockades to Renewal

As you navigate the road to changing a loved one, you're going to find yourself stuck in the slow lane at times. This is simply the nature of the journey. Although deep down they want to change, people with hurts, habits, and hang-ups tend to put up blockades, consciously or unconsciously. You'll face their resistance at every turn, snarling your ability to motivate change.

The blockades I'm speaking of are self-deceptions or lies. Sure, more than a few of us tell lies about ourselves to ourselves. Sometimes, these are "little white lies," exaggerations or deprecations about our qualities, accomplishments, or values. But other times these are big whoppers that one is not an alcoholic (despite all evidence to the contrary), that one is not to blame (a form of the victim mentality), that one is helpless (even though experience suggests otherwise), and so on. Humans frequently resist change by rationalizing their behavior, by spinning the meaning of events to suit their needs, or even fabricating falsehoods to avoid change—even though they fundamentally want a better life. An existence constructed on self-deception saps one's heart and soul. As one client told me, "Lying to yourself is exhausting." At their core, self-lies are emotional caves where people take refuge from problems and pain.

You can help someone face the truth about themselves. Do this and you set the stage for real change, the kind that reshapes attitudes, behaviors, even lifestyles. Let's talk about blockades you'll be up against, and the strategies you can use to bring them down, so that change can begin.

THE BLOCKADE OF DENIAL

I DON'T HAVE A PROBLEM, OR

THERE IS NO PROBLEM

This type of thinking is constructed to rationalize, protect, or hide the negative behavior. Denial is very serious business because, as a delusionary belief system, it can control a person's life. And if it weren't so serious, sometimes denial can be downright funny. I'm thinking of a cartoon I once saw, showing a man buried in beer cans stating, "What do you mean you think I have a drinking problem?"

When in denial, people refuse to accept that something exists or happened. It's a form of psychological blindness that prevents one from seeing his own problem. Denial can also involve changing the meaning of an event to lessen its impact. If something goes wrong as a result of the behavior—say, someone loses his job—the person might say, "I hated that job anyway." Denial is basically a defense mechanism that people resort to all the time, a guard dog standing watch at the front door of troublesome behavior. And quite frankly, the impulse to avoid painful awareness is natural. No one is eager to know hurtful things. But the impulse toward denial offers only short-term comfort, or a kind of brittle, artificial ease that eventually falls apart.

I recall a client, Gerry, who spent months hoodwinking herself that she didn't have a drinking problem anymore. She had quit drinking three years earlier and remained sober and active in her church. However, about one year ago, when her husband became terminally ill with liver cancer, she began drinking again.

Sadly, her husband passed away, and Gerry increased her drinking even more. She had alcohol first thing in the morning, often heading to her job as a legal secretary with alcohol on her breath, according to a concerned coworker. She was bloated, her eyes were yellowish, she had no spirit. She looked deadened. Certainly, it was likely that the stress of her husband's terminal illness caused her to fall back into heavy drinking, and she was using alcohol to numb her grief. I believed, too, that Gerry felt humiliated and ashamed that her excessive drinking was apparent to others, and she just wanted to avoid and deny the issue entirely.

Family and friends asked me, "What can we say to her that will make her face the truth and take this seriously?" My strategy for smashing this blockade was twofold. First, I suggested there was a more pressing issue to address.

Gerry was in grief. I advised the family to meet her where she was and be empathetic. Focus on her grief and how she was coping with the loss of her husband. Empathy is a strong motivator. Why not suggest that she undergo grief counseling first? If she accepted that type of counseling (which she did), drinking as an inappropriate coping mechanism could be gently introduced and explored over time. Once Gerry came clean with everyone about the reality of her drinking, she experienced a liberation that swept through her life like a fresh breeze blasting into a stuffy room. Honesty helped her get sober again.

Addicted people like Gerry don't have a monopoly on denial. It's used by many people who have nasty or annoying habits, or by those with chronic illnesses such as diabetes or heart disease. Every situation involving denial is different, but here are some strategies to consider.

Bring Down the Denial Blockade

▶ Let him know what you've seen. *Use the eyewitness account in your day-to-day communications; you don't have to reserve this tool for a family meeting. Describe the situation as you see it. As you do so, don't let the conversation get argumentative or accusatory. Stay away from abusive language. All this does is drive the two of you apart. Your eyewitness account helps him step outside of his distorted world momentarily so he can see things for what they are. If others use the eyewitness account, too, all the better. He'll hear more than a single person's opinion that a behavior is bad news. When presented with a whole bunch of opinions all saying that same thing, he's more apt to face the truth.*

▶ Use your flash-forward tool. *Let her know what's ahead. Here's an example of how this works when dealing with denial. Suppose four of us hop in a van, and we're supposed to be heading south to enjoy a vacation on a sunny beach. There's no compass, but everybody except the driver of the car can plainly see that we're heading north. So we tell the driver that she's got to switch directions, but she won't, because she's in denial. Now what do you do? Try doing a flash-forward with the driver. And that would mean saying, "Okay, we all believe you're heading north, but you don't believe us. But if you keep going in this direction, we predict that it's going to start getting colder, and pretty soon we're going to start seeing snow, ski slopes, and a big sign saying 'Welcome to Vermont.' So if that turns out to be right, will you agree to turn around?"*

People tend to respond more favorably if they feel like they made the decision on their own, or the solution came from them. You have to predict for them that sometime in the future, they're going to lose something, *they're going to lose* someone, *or they're going to get in some sort of trouble. Somehow, in a measurable way, their life is not going to get better; it's going to get worse. And if you predicted this, they'll remember that, and their lightbulb will go on. They'll be motivated to break out of denial, to change, and to get help.*

▶ Bring out the family map. *It depicts in concrete terms the hereditary patterns of negative behavior. There's no denying the problem when it's portrayed clearly. Family maps break through denial, and help people change their dysfunctional behavior.*

▶ Let him experience the consequences of his negative behavior. *The wisdom of this advice is grounded in a basic psychological truth: When the consequences of doing something are good, a person will likely repeat that behavior. If the consequences are bad, he often won't. This is the old "hot stove" analogy. If you touch a hot stove and burn your fingers, this experience gets so seeded in your memory that you'll probably not make the same mistake twice. Most of the time we do learn from our mistakes.*

Here's a practical application: If someone has had too much to drink the night before and can't get up for work, he should be left alone. Don't call the office and say he's sick. The person will begin to recognize that there are consequences for his or her actions—job loss, demotions, financial issues, and others—and eventually stop denying the problem. Some people will not change until the pain of staying where they are is greater than the temporary pain they experience when making a change. They need to feel the pain of the consequences to get off dead center.

▶ Avoid escalating confrontations. *No one likes them, and they don't work. They just build up defenses even more. Instead, get your loved one to talk, and talk—while you listen. Don't fall for the idea that if you listen, you enable or encourage the negative behavior. You're being empathetic. Empathy is not enabling. Empathy is feeling what the other person feels, seeing the problem from his point of view, and walking in someone else's shoes. As in Gerry's example, genuine empathy understands, but it doesn't condone. Your goal is not to harshly confront denial, but to understand what drives it—which could be shame, fear of rejection, low self-esteem, or more. Most people open their hearts if they feel understood. And when that happens, you'll have a much better chance at breaking through denial and getting someone closer to change.*

THE BLOCKADE OF MINIMIZING
IT ISN'T WORTH WORRYING ABOUT, OR
IT'S NOT THAT BAD

Minimizing is viewing something as less important than it really is. It's twisted-up thinking, a kind of psychological junk food. It involves certain behaviors that continually flow from it, like lying and covering up. When someone minimizes the problem, they're diluting the seriousness of it, usually in an effort to protect their self-esteem or habit. They might also say things like:

You caught me on a bad day.

I should know better.

I didn't mean it.

I can keep eating this way and be okay.

I bummed the cigarette. I didn't buy it.

I can put more debt on my credit cards—everyone does it.

It's just another little bet. There's no harm.

I don't buy pot ever. I just smoke it!

I see minimizing all the time. You'd never think that your good-natured grandmother could be a drug addict, would you? When brother and sister Gene and Leslie Lawton came to me about their grandmother, they were concerned that she was addicted. She could barely function at home but put on quite a good appearance at a doctor's office when requesting prescriptions. When we met with Grandma, she told us, "I can't be addicted. My doctor prescribes the pills I take." That's a clear example of minimizing. The good news is that the blockade of minimizing is not as strong as you might think. There are ways to break through.

Bring Down the Minimization Blockade

▶ Ask him gently to prove that he's not addicted, not a spend-thrift, not depressed, or whatever the situation is that he's minimizing. *Suggest that he go on a one-month trial of abstinence, not use credit cards, or demonstrate a stable state of mind. Couch your request tactfully. Say, for example, "I'd feel so much better if I could see that you're not abusing . . . not spending . . . not being so unhappy. Could we see how things go for the next month?" A successful trial period may help him feel so much better that the problem eases up. An unsuccessful trial period proves that he needs help. You then may need to approach the situation more formally with a family meeting.*

▶ Make counterstatements that disprove her minimization. *Suppose she says, "Oh, I just had a bad day. It's not that serious." Evaluate the situation more realistically with her. Ask, "How can you say that passing out at the party, getting a DUI, or missing work is not that seri-*

ous?" Follow up with, "Can you see any problems with your reasoning?" You might again use your eyewitness account to help analyze the situation more rationally. This dialogue looks at, and neutralizes, the faulty logic behind minimization. You make it easier to come at the problem from a more objective, reasonable direction. Pretty soon, such people will be able to counteract these thinking errors on their own, and that blockade will be smashed.

▶ Jog someone's memory. *Many of the most serious problems (like substance abuse) are, at their heart, diseases of dishonesty. Anyone who has lived with an active addict, for example, knows how dishonest they can be. They live lives of denial and delusion, their perspectives warped by fear and self-centeredness. Recovery is really a process of coming back to reality—becoming honest with themselves and others. You can help bring them back. If someone is minimizing, give a reality check. Remind them of the pain that their addiction or behavior has inflicted. Review the negative things that have happened as a result of the behavior: bounced checks, alienation from family members, arguments, neglect of kids, depression, illness, sick days, loss of wages—basically the bad effects on someone's physical, mental, social, or spiritual health. This is not being negative; this is being rational. You can also revisit the benefits of recovery if this person has had a setback and is trying to minimize it. Ask him to talk about the benefits so far from being in recovery. Point out the benefits of positive change against the pain of the negative behavior. These approaches actively counter minimization.*

▶ Learn about the facts regarding the behavior in question. *Many families I work with feel paralyzed because they don't have the knowledge they need. Once they educate themselves about the problem, they feel so much more empowered. So where this blockade exists, make sure everyone is informed about the addiction (including symptoms) or behavior, including your loved one. Families must educate themselves, partner with the medical professionals, consult with specialists, and learn to properly intervene to address the problem. Knowledge is power, and in most cases, it breaks down the blockade.*

THE BLOCKADE OF ARROGANCE
I CAN HANDLE IT, OR I'LL QUIT TOMORROW

Arrogance is avoidance, and another form of delusion. Permit me to use another driving analogy. Arrogance is like driving down the highway and noticing that your gas gauge says you're running on empty. You keep driving anyway, while ignoring the gauge and pretending that your tank is full. Eventually, you will run out of gas. A lot of people go through life like this, sabotaging themselves, all because they refuse to pull over and fill up.

People with addictions are among the most arrogant on the planet. Many users, with all the best intentions, really believe that they can quit tomorrow; that they are strong enough or have the willpower to "just stop." The problem is that in most cases, tomorrow never comes or tomorrow becomes months and then years. Some may think they don't have problems because they only drink on the weekends. Others may go for long periods of time without touching a drop of alcohol, but once they get started, they may go on a binge that could last for several days or weeks or months. Addicts also rationalize their behavior in pathological ways that allow them to continue in their addiction. I once knew a guy who was promiscuous, a three-pack-a-day smoker, and a junk-food addict who considered himself health-conscious because he religiously took five types of dietary supplements every morning.

If you've ever been close to someone with a pattern of destructive behavior, you probably know all about this. Alcoholics and addicts want things to be their way. To get that, they can be charming, or intimidating.

It may surprise you to learn that some form of severe insecurity is almost always behind these attempts to control others. People addicted to alcohol, drugs, or compulsive behavior experience levels of daily insecurity practically unimaginable to those who don't have an addiction. Arrogance covers up the fact that they're actually some of the most insecure people around.

Bring Down the Arrogance Blockade

▶ Swing into action. *The major step in changing this person's negative behavior is to let him know the behavior has become a problem. These things don't get better on their own. Don't delay. Craft the circle of change, have a family meeting, and use the tools to get her into treatment. Treatment should focus not only on the behavior but also on restoring self-esteem.*

▶ Be an encourager. *As much as possible, remind him that with time and effort, he can change his habits, make improvements to troublesome aspects of his life, and reverse the course of his life. Encouragement engenders hope, builds internal security, and restores a sense of control.*

THE BLOCKADE OF "I CAN'T"

You hear people say either "I can" or "I can't." It's a choice made regarding being positive or negative about what they think they can do. If people believe it, they'll achieve it. I love the classic children's story *The Little Engine That Could.* As the engine choo-choos along, it sounds out, "I think I can, I think I can, I think I can." This attitude gives people the power to do whatever they set out to do. People who believe in themselves will change for the better.

The polar opposite are people who say they can't. They have a tough time changing because they don't believe enough in themselves, or they lack self-confidence. It's not enough to simply give this person a pep talk and say, "You can do it." You have to show them that they can and help them build their self-confidence. You can do this through a technique called modeling.

When we copy what successful people do, we are modeling. We find someone who is getting the results we want, and we do what they do until we get the same results. This is one of the easiest ways to achieve a goal and can be used to change someone you love. There are different ways to model. All of them work.

Bring Down the "I Can't" Blockade

▶ Set an example. *As the saying goes, Be the change you want to see in others. One way people change behavior is by watching others exhibit the desired behavior. Your kids probably resent it when you tell them what to do, but they might respond better to something more subtle. For example, putting your own dirty dishes in the dishwasher after a meal may work better in getting your children to do so than reminding them each time. Setting an example for what you expect is very powerful, especially in cases where people resist instructions from others to change their behaviors. If they see you managing your debt, they are more likely to start managing their debt. If they see you eating a healthy diet, they are more likely to start eating a healthy diet. If they see you successfully quit smoking, they are more likely to follow suit. Following your example also makes them feel more in control, because there hasn't been nagging or coercing on your part. People are more open to change if they feel they can do it on their own.*

▶ Tell a story. *If people think they* have *to, they won't. No one likes to feel as though they're being bossed around. This is a natural tendency. A great way to get around this is to tell a story to change someone's behavior. Telling a story works better than telling someone what to do because it provides suggestions rather than directives, and suggestions put people in charge of their own behaviors. For instance, suppose your friend or loved one confides in you that she's having trouble kicking a bad habit. Rather than directly advise her on how to overcome it, choose to tell a story. If you've been in therapy, treatment, or some other program yourself, relate how the experience helped you, or give an example of someone who has benefited.*

▶ Try video modeling. *Have you ever sat in a dentist's office and watched a video of a dental procedure? How about a video clip on breast self-examination? Or an inspirational film in which someone got off drugs? If so, you've been exposed to video modeling. It's used to help people get over fears of dental and medical procedures, overcome public-speaking anxiety, and conquer phobias, among other uses. With video*

modeling, someone is shown footage of people performing desired be-
haviors. The goal is to persuade a person that he, too, is perfectly ca-
pable of doing the same thing, and that he will be successful at it. It's
the idea of If he can do that, so can I.

As I wrote this chapter, I came across a fascinating experiment pub-
lished in the journal Women's Health. *It involved sixty pregnant*
women who were smokers. The goal of the experiment was to see whether
video modeling could help these mothers-to-be quit smoking or at least
cut down. The women were randomly assigned to one of two groups.
One group received some brief smoking cessation advice, plus a sheet of
tips on how to quit. The other group received the same tip sheet, but also
watched a videotape showing how other women had quit smoking, dealt
with stress in positive ways, and built support for quitting from family
and friends. Twenty percent of the women who watched the video were
able to quit smoking altogether. That might not seem like a huge im-
provement, until you consider the fact that nobody in the nonvideo
group quit. *The researchers concluded that video modeling was helpful*
and that doctors should use this technique in their offices and in public
maternity clinics. Clearly, video modeling worked.

Video modeling is a great form of help to employ in counseling sessions
or treatment programs. But you don't have to be a therapist to use it. Less
formally, there are actually many "video models" all around us, in the
form of great inspirational movies and TV shows that show people over-
coming the odds. Some good examples include the DVD My Name Is
Bill W, *the true story of Bill Wilson, who founded Alcoholics Anony-*
mous; the movies The Color Purple *or* The Hiding Place, *or the reality*
TV weight-loss show The Biggest Loser. *These productions and others*
like them inspire hope, positive thinking, and the motivation to change.

THE BLOCKADE OF BLAME

IT'S ALL YOUR FAULT I'M LIKE THIS, OR IF ONLY
YOU'D . . . , THEN I WOULDN'T HAVE TO . . .

During the spring of 2007, I worked with Wendell, who, at six feet and 525
pounds, was struggling with severe obesity. Twenty years ago, he was a fit,

strapping man of around 185 pounds. Now he's housebound, in chronic pain, depressed, and receiving food deliveries all day, while his wife, two-year-old twins, and three-year-old son are living upstairs—and getting on with life.

Wendell can't muster even the strength to put down the doughnuts that are killing him a dozen at a time. All the while, he blames others for his sad predicament: his wife for not loving him the right way; his parents for dying and stranding him with the failing family business; his brother, who got out of the family business, went to college, and made something of himself; his mother-in-law, because she sides with his wife; his genes—they're bad, because he looks at a doughnut and gains weight; and his car—the seat is not big enough (never mind that he outgrew the thing ten years ago!). But really, his problem is about the food and how he's eating to self-medicate the pain. Wendell is mired in pounds of blame. Unless he stops blaming, he will never be able to move forward under his own steam.

Blame funnels the problem away, to inadequate parents, uncaring spouses, insensitive bosses, a liberal government, a conservative government, and the like. We live in a society of blamers and victims. Have you noticed? They're always being "done to" by someone else. If someone is overweight, the cause is not self-control, but the food industry and advertising for pushing junk food. It's the gun's fault that the bad guy shot someone. It's the restaurant's fault that Johnny got drunk. It's Big Tobacco's fault that she's hooked on nicotine. Personal responsibility is sorely lacking in today's world; there's an excuse for every bad behavior you can think of. Blame has become part of our official culture. Ultimately no one is responsible for anything. Blame someone else, hire a lawyer, and live comfortably off the settlement.

Unfortunately, there are people in this world who have the victim role down to a science. They blame, they complain, they gripe and moan. In some ways, it is wickedly brilliant behavior. By blaming, they never have to be accountable for anything! On top of that, they seem to have no intention of making the changes they know are necessary to solve their problems. But if they're not going to do anything about their predicaments, they're not really victims; they are volunteers. Once they stop volunteering, their lives will change.

I think the worst part of blaming is that blamers like to make issues your fault. They never, ever take personal responsibility for their behavior. It's always someone else's fault—usually yours. You are the reason they yelled at you, treated you badly, or embarrassed you publicly. You're the one making them drive ninety miles an hour, gamble, or drink too much.

This behavior is really a form of verbal abuse—a way of shoving you around with words. It's designed to put you in your place, to control you, or to make you doubt yourself. Verbal abuse is the most prevalent type of battering that goes on in this country, and you have to treat it as such. It's never justified either, so you should never feel that it is your fault. Yes, it's hard to believe that people who say they love you would treat you this way, but they will. This blockade is somewhat different from the rest because it attacks you, and you have to protect yourself.

Bring Down the Blame Blockade

▶ Practice control. Stay cool. *When someone unfairly blames you, it says nothing about you but everything about that person's need to divert responsibility and shirk accountability. Do not give the person who has unfairly blamed you the satisfaction of knowing he has scored. If you react to such a person, you're rewarding him and letting him know he has power over your emotions. Don't allow him to have control over how you feel. Take back your power. When he learns he can't push your buttons, the blaming behavior will ease off.*

▶ Give the problem back to its rightful owner. *You can help others, but you can't own their problems. Emphasize to your loved one, "I encourage you to own your problem." Tell her, "I love you, and I'll be behind you." This offers the appropriate help and support. In essence, you're detaching from the problem but not from your loved one who has the problem. Realize that backing off will be tough—like taking your hands off the wheel while driving at a hundred miles per hour. It will be tempting to grab the wheel again.*

▶ Make the point that today is not about excuses, and it's not about asking, Why me? *If someone spends all their time (like Wendell) blaming their problems on things outside themselves, and asking, Why me? rather than looking at how he can change to solve his problems, he will continue to fail in life. So get him to ask how-can-I-change questions: How can I make this better? How can I stop smoking? How can I stop bingeing? These questions prompt people to reclaim their self-responsibility and go after what they truly want out of life.*

▶ Say no to blame. *Let him know how hurtful his words are. Discuss with him the fact that it is unacceptable to you. Set boundaries on what you will and will not accept from him. I think you have to be direct and hope that your message sinks in. Point out that you think he is a blamer, attributing his behavior to childhood, society, family members, feeling that he's never been given a chance, or some other external circumstance. Tell him that he is in charge of his life, accountable for results as well as for lack of results, and he has the power to make changes that will improve his lot in life. Soften your directness with love. A caution: Once you've made your position clear, he will try to get you to back down. Stay the course to break the cycle of blame and motivate him to improve his behavior.*

▶ Don't brood on blame. *Dispose of it quickly by judging it as unjustified. Do not let blame poison your day.*

▶ Never get in a fight with the blamer. *If he gets angry, stay calm, walk away. Don't give him what he wants: a reaction from you. If this type of verbal abuse (or any type of abuse for that matter) continues, particularly in an intimate relationship, seek professional help now.*

Your friend, spouse, relative, employee, or loved one will *not* forever put up these blockades. Don't let any of them dissuade you from taking the initiative and being the force for change. You can—and I hope you'll come to feel you must and will—help them face reality by implementing the four-step plan outlined in part 2 of the book. When you are finally ready to take that first important step of crafting the circle of change, it will be a time of liberation, when the hard work of denying, avoiding, pretending, and blaming is over, and the equally demanding but far more fulfilling work of being authentic is at hand. This is when you and your loved one will learn that truth really does set us free. Fundamentally, people do want to change. Once you bring down the blockades to change, you can and will help your friends and loved ones get their lives back.

PART IV

*Practical Applications:
Cope with the
People in Your Life
and Restore Your
Relationships*

ELEVEN

Stop People from Self-Destructing

Are you fed up with your husband's smoking? Scared that your sister is getting too fat? Afraid of going broke because of a gambler in the family? Convinced that your son is an Internet gaming addict? Frazzled by your wife's mood? Ashamed that your family is harboring a sex addict?

If someone's life is spinning out of control, you can change their destructive behavior, and you don't have to turn into a tyrant to do it. The big question is, how do you deal with it? Here I'll show you, with some practical approaches for applying my four-step program to serious, specific situations that are very common in our world today.

GET ANYBODY TO STOP SMOKING

The harmful effects of tobacco smoke—on both the smoker and those around him—are well known. Yet quitting smoking is hard because, for many people, nicotine is as addictive as heroin or cocaine. Nevertheless, you've got to urge your loved one to clean up his act, because his bad habits are more than an annoyance: they're hurting the health of everyone around him. Asking him to get help can be one of the most important requests you'll ever make.

Step 1 - Craft the Circle of Change

Gather together those people most affected by the smoking—you and your kids or grandkids, for example. Maybe you'd want to include your family doctor too. Physicians really do have the tools and the treatments to help people quit smoking. Have everyone prepare a heartfelt message on why your loved one should quit. Research some effective ways and programs to reduce and/or stop smoking, and decide on the best course of action for your loved one. There have been recent developments with some new stop-smoking medications. Have this information handy, and schedule your family meeting.

Step 2 - Deliver the Invitation to Change

Make the invitation to your family meeting, where each person will tell your loved one why he should stop smoking. Don't attack, nag, or otherwise slap him around verbally. Voice your concerns in a loving way. Here is an example:

Eyewitness account: *Kelly, your mom and dad both smoked, and most of your friends smoked too, all day, every day. Smoking has been part of your life without fail. I get worried about you because I see that you're smoking more than ever.*

Flash-forward: *I love you, but I am afraid you are cutting your future short.*

Resolution: *I see you as a grandfather, godfather, and dear friend to all of us here. I want you to stop smoking because all of us would like you around for a long time. We will support you through what will be a terribly challenging process: losing your "best friend" and choosing life.*

It's worth mentioning, too, that there's no more compelling and inspiring motivation than a child's request, when it's voiced something like this: *Daddy, please quit smoking. We don't want you to die.*

After everyone delivers the eyewitness accounts, ask him to enter a stop-smoking program. Help him set a quit date. Don't put it off. If something is put off, it will be put off again and again and again. Provide handouts (available from groups such as the American Lung Association and the American Cancer Society). Mention hospital- or community-based support groups in your area, along with meeting times and locations.

He may tune you out or get angry or sarcastic when you approach him on the subject. Or he'll do the opposite of what you're asking. This is particularly true of men. We have radar that goes up whenever we sense we're being controlled. Instead of doing what his wife wants, a guy will dig his heels in deeper. As with any family meeting, if the answer is no, take a break and reconvene in an hour. Repeat your request. Just try to motivate him again, but don't nag. With many people, the gravity of what people are saying takes a while to sink in. They have to think it over. Be patient.

Step 3 - Champion the Change

To quit, someone must overcome a physical addiction to nicotine, as well as a psychological dependence on smoking. Therapies such as the nicotine patches or medications help with the physical and chemical component. Beating the psychological addiction is the hardest part. For many, smoking is relaxing and part of daily activities. Change your family routine. Help your loved one avoid situations that set him up for failure. For example, if his morning ritual is drinking a cup of coffee and smoking a cigarette, then encourage him to have coffee later or not at all during those first few weeks. He may need to avoid certain situations, such as the local bar or the weekly poker game, until the cravings have subsided. Help him find alternative ways to reduce stress, such as exercise, fishing, yoga or meditation. Do these things with him whenever he feels frustrated and has the urge to smoke.

Provide psychological encouragement. Many people aren't motivated to change because they believe that they can't. Provide positive input: "Honey, you are doing great. I'm so proud of you." Try to focus on his good traits. Talk about how quitting has helped him: better health; money saved; more social activities; improved appearance of skin, teeth, and fingers; fresher-smelling clothes; more self-confidence; improved intimacy; and more influence with others. Congratulate successes and encourage continued abstinence. Reward progress with something special: a dinner, an outing, a gift certificate, or a present.

You might also get results by saying less and being a good model, so he can see what he's missing out on: runs and hikes, feeling fit, having more stamina, and so forth. Chances are, your loved one's interest in a healthier lifestyle will be piqued and hopefully, he'll catch on. Both men and women are more likely to develop healthier lifestyle habits when their partner participates in an active way with them.

The average successful nicotine quitter has failed an average of six previous attempts. So if there's a setback, don't get upset by it. Remind him only that it's a learning experience, and that relapse is consistent with the chronic nature of tobacco dependence. You don't want him to think of it as a failure. Encourage him to step right back on the smoke-free train. The slip was nothing more than stepping off the train at the wrong station. He'll need to get right back on and try again. Almost anybody, no matter how addicted, can quit smoking. You just have to hang in there with them. Without fail, the craving will pass and with time the space between cravings will increase.

Step 4 - Care for You

Clearly, your loved one must modify his smoking behavior before it's too late. Prohibit smoking in and outside your home, and anywhere in your presence. He may not like it, but reducing the opportunity to smoke helps people to quit. Ultimately, you may have to let him work this out with his doctor. Have his physician tell him repeatedly that the most important thing he can do to improve his health and yours is to stop smoking.

GET ANYONE TO LOSE WEIGHT

Your husband, your wife, your kids, your parents, or someone else you love is overweight, and the situation is getting worse. By now, we know all the alarming statistics about obesity and health, but most of us don't know what to say or how to say it or what might work. This is why people ask me all the time, "How can I help a loved one lose weight?"

I have to ask them, "Are you ready for a lifestyle change yourself?"

It often takes a group or family lifestyle change to help someone you love lose weight. The change must be made by those who are close and involved. Don't expect your loved one to develop healthful eating and exercise habits if you don't practice them yourself. You can't expect one person to eat apples while you and the rest of the group are munching on nachos. That's pretty much the bottom line.

One caveat here: If someone you love is hundreds of pounds overweight or in the throes of an eating disorder, you must intervene with a formal family meeting that possibly includes a doctor or a therapist, and definitely a prearranged plan for admittance to a treatment program or structured change plan. Morbid obesity and eating disorders are life-threatening and need immediate intervention. For less urgent cases, such as a loved one who needs to lose maybe twenty to forty pounds, and needs a lifestyle adjustment to reverse the trend, here's what I advise.

Step 1 - Craft the Circle of Change

Helping a loved one lose weight is challenging under the best of circumstances. It's tough to prod a family member or friend into taking steps toward a healthier weight, without stressing your relationship. Most overweight people know they should shed some pounds, and it bothers them. That's why broaching the subject dredges up negative feelings about themselves, and about you for mentioning it.

To get around these challenges, I strongly believe that you must make losing weight a family affair, and make the family your circle of change. If it's just you and your spouse or partner, that's fine. A recent study, drawing lessons from social networks, suggests that a spouse's successful weight loss can rub off on the other. This study, from the University of Connecticut, says that couples not only tend to gain weight together, they can also lose it as a pair, even if only one of them is enrolled in a formal diet program. The spouses of the patients who attended regular weight-loss programs lost about five pounds over the course of a year.

Whatever your situation, invite your loved one and other family members to come together as a group (or as a couple) to make some lifestyle changes—healthier cooking, more activity, less TV, and so forth. It doesn't matter if some family members don't need to lose weight. What matters is the support of those you live and eat with. Support can mean the difference between success and failure. Everyone can benefit from a healthier life-style, anyway, so everyone must get hip to this if you want your loved one to lose weight and succeed.

Step 2 - Deliver the Invitation to Change

Gather everyone together, including inviting your loved one. Keep in mind that most people are extremely sensitive about their weight. Let's be honest. Thinness is equated with attractiveness in our society. People who don't fit society's physical ideal may question their self-worth, especially if confidence is shaky to begin with. It may be better to approach loved ones about their weight in terms of how it affects their health rather than their appearance. This could motivate some to spring into action, particularly if being heavy threatens their health in the short term or if a defining event, like a heart attack, or an alarming cholesterol test result even, has served as a wake-up call.

Here is a suggestion on how to broach the subject with honesty, direct-ness, and without ridicule—and to do so as a family:

Eyewitness account: *We decided to meet as a family because we want each other's help in leading a healthier lifestyle. Some of us have been gaining weight over the years, and we've been frustrated about how to lose it. Others just don't get enough exercise. A few of us do pretty well, and I think we can learn from one another.*

Flash-forward: *From what some of us have read, being overweight and out of shape can cut our lives short. But even if our more immediate desire is to fit in a smaller size, wouldn't it feel great to meet that goal? Just think how much more fun it would be to shop for clothes. I can think of a hundred reasons to get thinner, but most of all, I'd love for us to be fit as a family. I see us doing a lot more things together—like biking, swimming, and living longer and healthier lives—if we made healthier choices.*

Resolution: *When we talked a few days ago, it looked like everyone was on board for making some lifestyle changes. It's been tough to do this before on our own. Now we're coming together as a family team. We're going to help one another eat better and exercise more, and we're going to support and encourage one another. This is our family's project, and we'd like everyone to be a part of it. We're starting right now.*

This is a productive way to broach the subject because it's honest, direct, and devoid of ridicule. I'd then have everyone in the room talk about how they feel—pros and cons—about this new beginning, and how they feel empowered by not having to go it alone. If you want to be a little more formal about it, you can say, "We've signed up for Weight Watchers, the program at church, Overeaters Anonymous, or the local weight-loss clinic, etc." Or: "We've taken out a family membership at the fitness center that everyone can use."

I'd also recommend that everyone sign a change agreement, saying that they'll commit to supporting one another and holding one another accountable for making lifestyle improvements.

If anyone resists, back down temporarily but continue with the family plan. The person will eventually come to his or her own conclusion of how to proceed. And as in the study I mentioned above, she may automatically lose weight because the family lifestyle has changed. In the meantime, look for signs she may be open to restart. When she's more receptive, seize the opportunity. Delve deeper by asking, "How can I help you?" Continue to encourage exercising, healthier eating, and other ways to lose weight.

Step 3 - Champion the Change

Provide support to each other in the following ways:

Change the scenery. It would be great to think that people make their own choices and follow through on them, without being too influenced by things around them. But this isn't what happens in real life. Behavior is situation specific. For example, if you go to an all-you-can-eat restaurant, you'll eat more. If you serve yourself on a big plate, you'll eat more. If you move that bowl of chocolates on your desk closer to you, you'll eat more. So don't let your loved one fight to change her eating habits in the midst of the wrong environment; just change the environment for her. Remove the fattening foods from the house and stock the cupboards with healthy foods. She'll lose weight because the environment supports better choices. In other words, help her control her environment. Don't let it control her. You want to make it easier to do something you want done and *harder not to*.

Reinforce desired behavior. Praise is more effective than criticism. Find ways to compliment her for any success—working out, making healthy food choices, joining you in a hike or bike ride. Compliment her when pounds are shed: "You look great!" or "I see you've got more energy" or "Those clothes fit really well." Accentuating the positive encourages good self-esteem (which may, in turn, encourage weight loss).

Help her build her self-image. Everyone has a self-image based on a combination of upbringing, day-to-day reality, and social influences. Self-image tends to mesh with negative thinking. People with weight problems often tell themselves: "I'm fat . . . I'll never lose weight . . . I'm a slob." You can help her stop this thought train by encouraging her to form an image of the thinner, more fit person she'd like to be. Have her write down some of her "fit goals." Ask her, "What type of clothes will you wear?" "How will your life be different?" "How will you feel mentally and emotionally when you are thinner?" Using the answers to these questions, she should create an autobiography of her life as a thin person and keep this new life in the forefront of her thinking. This exercise will help her form a stronger, more positive self-image.

Never reprimand. Saying things like "Don't eat all that stuff. You'll get even fatter," points up something they already know, and so they increase guilt and lower self-esteem (and possibly enable him to stuff in another bag of potato chips.) Likewise, don't tell your spouse, "When you were in shape you really turned me on." This hurts feelings and sends a message of rejection, destroying confidence (another perfect setup for a binge). Keep in mind that your spouse is the same person you cared enough about to marry. Letting her know you still care is the best way to encourage her to make positive choices.

Never, ever enable. Using a bowl of ice cream or a piece of cake to soothe your loved one's frustrations or disappointments or to show love teaches her to use food for comfort. Also avoid using treats as a bribe to get kids to put away toys or as a reward for eating carrots and broccoli. These actions will only push them deeper into emotional eating. Nurturing your loved one means supplying not only tasty food but also food that's nutritious and healthy. Remember that a hug and kiss and a few soothing words usually make the pain and stress go away without the calories.

Make fitness fun for the whole family. Everyone should get between thirty minutes and an hour of activity at least five days a week, according to fitness professionals. So do things you enjoy—swimming, playing basketball, taking a dance class, weekend hiking.

Don't overpolice food. As any dieter knows, the surest way to become obsessed with a food is to make it off-limits. However, some restrictions are important, such as one cookie instead of three at lunch, or ice cream after dinner every few days instead of every day. I avoid sugar and white flour. A food plan helps.

Show love and maintain respect. Through all of this, share everything in a way that demonstrates your unconditional love and your continued respect for him or her regardless of what he or she chooses to do. This advice applies to any behavior you want to change.

Step 4 - Care for You

Continue your own healthy lifestyle. That way, you'll motivate by setting an example. If nothing has happened so far, expect things to change when your loved one starts seeing your progress and how it has affected you. She'll get on board, and you'll be amazed by how well she does. Before long, you'll be motivating each other.

ELIMINATE SOMEONE'S GAMBLING HABIT

From playing bingo, video games, casino games, or the lottery to placing bets on horses and even sports games, a problem gambler is a person who gambles more than he or she can afford, and cannot stop. He or she may lie about gambling or may gamble longer than planned. Pathological or compulsive gambling is a chronic and progressive disease. It destroys families and financial futures. If someone in your life has a gambling problem, you can help turn it around.

Step 1 - Craft the Circle of Change

Gather together everyone affected by your loved one's gambling. Locate treatment or counseling options, such as Gamblers Anonymous. Its only requirement for membership is a desire to stop gambling. Identify a mental health counselor who has experience in treating a gambling addiction. Check hospitals and therapists in your area for a treatment program that will treat your loved one. Come up with a clear change plan. Schedule your family meeting.

Step 2 - Deliver the Invitation to Change

Gamblers have great difficulty accepting the fact that when it comes to gambling, they are losers; they have made bad choices, and hurt others and themselves. You have to be very clear when presenting the facts, so use your eyewitness account, flash-forward, and resolution tools.

Here is an example of how to approach the subject in your family meeting:

Eyewitness account: *Brandon, it's clear to us that you have a serious problem. Just last week, in an episode of binge gambling, we found that you lost more than $10,000.*

Flash-forward: *Once it was your secret, Brandon. Twice, it became a family affair because some of us joined in to help you pay rent. We can't bear to watch you lose everything, and we feel that's where you're headed.*

Resolution: *Brandon, we want to see you free of this addiction, so that you can live life more productively and fully, and contribute in a meaningful way to your family. Now we've banded together in a different way to help, support, and feed recovery rather than the addiction you're struggling with. Today, together, we are pooling our resources to support your recovery, instead of your problem. We stand together in support of change and healing.*

Ask the gambler to agree to the change plan you have put together and say that you'll take him today. Be sure to introduce a change agreement at the family meeting, for accountability. It formalizes the change plan, and spells out your loved one's follow-through responsibilities and the consequences of not sticking to the plan.

Step 3 - Champion the Change

To support the gambler through recovery, focus on helping him avoid risky situations and limiting access to money. Unlike many other problems, dealing with a gambling problem requires financial contingencies, so talk to a financial adviser or an attorney before you intervene. Ask what the best ways are to deal with the money side of the problem based on your own financial situation and then make it part of the addict's recovery plan. Although everyone's situation is different, here are some suggestions to consider:

Control access to cash. With the help of a financial or tax adviser, put the gambler on an allowance for essentials, with all other financial temptations put out of reach. Close any joint bank accounts and reopen them in your name only to prevent access, as long as addiction remains an issue. These decisions should cover everything from checking accounts to investment accounts and business assets. If it can be sold or liquidated easily, it's a target. Inform other family members of the problem in case your loved one tries to borrow money from them. While these may all sound like childish restrictions, it's important to remember that money is to a gambler what booze is to an alcoholic.

Applaud positive change as it comes, one day at a time. While the monetary changes may seem punitive, making real and fast decisions on how money is accessed has a direct and immediate impact on the destructive behaviors. So while one might read these championing behaviors as negative, they are enabling health and healing.

Money in a gambler's pocket will quickly go to his hands, then slip away in a variety of ways when on a run. I have a client in an inpatient treatment center right now for gambling, and her addiction caused crises as bad as any crack, heroin, or meth addict has caused. Addiction drives chaos, while moving into recovery creates the foundation for health and healing. I view "closing the bank" to be a rich, positive step in reclaiming the future.

Develop a tough-love repayment strategy. So often, families with means quickly pay off gambling-related debt to eliminate embarrassment that the gambler has caused. Such speedy bailouts are usually a mistake. Actions have consequences, and the addict must be made to reverse the damage he or she has caused. People who make bad decisions don't learn from them if the problem is quickly cleaned up by others.

Sign up for a credit-check program. Credit reporting services can send e-mail alerts whenever someone checks your credit report to approve a new loan or credit card. If your spouse opens a new line of credit to access fresh sources of gambling cash, these services are a good way to find out.

Step 4 - Care for You

When you live with a compulsive gambler, you can get caught up in his addiction, worrying about where he is and what he might be doing.

Angela, a client who struggled with her husband's gambling, found that last straw broken one night just after 3 A.M. when she cried her way through an L.A. blackjack parlor. She begged the manager to turn away her husband when he came in to play. With an infant over one shoulder and a two-year-old in pajamas running behind her, she hit a wall that night and realized her life was broken, that she had hit a bottom of her own and was unwilling to stay stuck in her present situation.

Begging a gambling joint manager to keep her husband out was a start, and when I met her the next week she explained how worn out she was from the lack of sleep over the past two years as her husband fell deeper into a gambling addiction. So while she said her infant was an angel and rarely woke her at night, it didn't matter because most nights she was up anyway, wondering where the man she fell in love with at UCLA years before was spending his time and their money. Angela found she was blaming herself for his behavior, and when we sat and talked about what we could do to begin change, she was embarrassed to tell anyone about what their little family was going through.

Therapy will help you realize that your loved one's gambling isn't your fault and that you aren't alone. Find a therapist who can help you work through these issues. In addition, attend support group meetings, such as Gam-Anon, a 12-step program for spouses, family, or close friends of compulsive gamblers. The group can help you find answers to such questions as What is your role as the spouse (parent, loved one) of a compulsive gambler? How can you be of the greatest help to the person who joins Gamblers Anonymous? If your loved one continues to gamble, how can you live with the problem? Gam-Anon also has a wealth of information to help you cope with the various crises that crop up when someone you love is a problem gambler.

UNTANGLE SOMEONE FROM THE WEB

Professionals disagree about the seriousness of Internet addiction. Some believe it's just a lot of fun, and others argue that it is in the same class as alcoholism. The truth is, it's easy to get hooked on the Web, and it's no joke. Just as drugs or alcohol can cause a physiological reaction, so can the Internet. For people who are gambling, trading stock, or bidding on-line, there's an adrenaline rush that provides a genuine neurochemical kick. I've seen enough Internet addictions to know that it's a real problem, with the potential to ruin relationships.

Signs of Internet addiction are similar to signs of other addictions and include fatigue, declining interest in hobbies, decline in performance at work, use of it to escape from other problems, and withdrawal from friends, potentially caused by an excessive reliance on online "friends." Internet addiction takes on various guises, including:

▶ *Cybersex addiction: addiction to adult chat rooms or online porn*

▶ *Web relationship addiction: online friendships made in chat rooms or Internet porn*

▶ *Web compulsions: compulsive gambling, day trading, or auction shopping*

▶ *Information overload: compulsive Web or database surfing*

▶ *Compulsive game playing*

If you observe any of these behaviors in a loved one, here's what I suggest:

Step 1 - Craft the Circle of Change

If you currently suspect that your partner or your child spends too much time online, craft your circle of change and bring in close family members, friends, and coworkers, if appropriate. In looking for a change plan, realize that there is no standard treatment for Internet addiction, but a typical plan could involve individual counseling, family therapy, a 12-step program, or the treatment of an underlying disorder such as depression. People with an Internet addiction often avoid human contact. A support group provides an opportunity to build offline relationships and improve the addict's social support system. Once everything is in place, schedule your family meeting.

Step 2 - Deliver the Invitation to Change

Before someone can be cured of an Internet addiction, as with other addictions, it will help your effort if they recognize that they're hooked. So as you present your eyewitness accounts, you've got to factually describe what you've seen. Be prepared to present proof of the addiction to counter denial—like actual bills and other documentation. Here is an example of a change message:

Eyewitness account: *Jana, we have been very concerned about you. We've seen you compulsively checking your e-mail, staying awake surfing the Internet past midnight and into the early hours of the morning, and spending lots of money online. Your Internet usage has already cost you three jobs.*

Flash-forward: *If you don't get help, we're worried that this trend will continue and you won't be able to support yourself. We feel you care more about being online than you do about being with your friends. We want to see you get help, and we'll support you in getting help.*

Resolution: *This family loves you, Jana. We love you so much that we're together as friends and family to help you change. We know that a day is coming when you'll be able to enjoy your friends and family more and be able to do well on your job, once this problem is resolved.*

As with any addiction or other problem, you'll want to ask her to begin the change plan immediately.

Step 3 - Champion the Change

The easy accessibility of the Internet makes this compulsion particularly hard to shake. If a gambler stays away from the racetrack, there's less risk of gambling. If an alcoholic doesn't have access to booze, it's easier to stay sober. But if someone uses the computer for work and other things, the temptation is right there staring at him. You can support your loved one in breaking this problem, but you need the right strategy to do it. Here are my recommendations:

Explain in a gentle way that you've set clear time limits on computer usage to trim the amount of online time—say, one hour a day instead of the current eight. Limit time on the Internet for all family members, including yourself. This measure is designed to help control the environment, so that the environment doesn't control her. You may have to schedule those hours in specific time slots and write them on a calendar or weekly planner. Then stick to it. When there are secrets, demands for privacy, and suspicious behavior, check into it.

Internet abuse is a rapidly growing problem in the workplace. Some companies simply forbid employees to use the Internet at work for gambling, searching personal ads, viewing sexual materials, or visiting online chat rooms. If you've got employees who are abusing the Internet, consider asking them to keep time logs of their computer use to improve their accountability when online. Encourage them to get up, walk around the office, stretch, do breathing exercises, meditate—anything to take a short break from their computers. A quick time-out not only helps disrupt unhealthy patterns of online use but can help employees feel more refreshed and better able to tackle their next task.

Work with your loved one to identify triggers for online abuse. A particular chat room, a certain time of day, or a person's mood before going online may all serve to trigger inappropriate conduct and abuse. Help your loved one develop a plan to deal with triggers, such as reading a book, exercising, calling a friend, or working around the house—anything that helps him abstain from problematic online behavior.

Kids are equally at risk of Internet addiction. Checking the temporary Internet files and/or history of your browser can reveal what sites your child has accessed. The history is a list of all the Web sites visited over a certain period of time and can be accessed in the menu of your browser: the button labeled "History" in Internet Explorer, or the "Go" menu in Firefox. Your computer also stores all images, text, and other material from pages accessed during any given surfing period. But your loved one may quickly learn how to delete these records. If you go to the history, or search for the temporary Internet files, and find no records, then you can be sure they are being deleted and that the situation calls for further inquiry.

Place filtering software or other software on your computer that denies access to pornography sites, as well as other questionable places. Software such as NetNanny, CyberPatrol, and SurfControl, typically used by parents to block children from accessing online sexual content, can help clients self-regulate their Internet use. The software can be programmed to automatically block online applications, such as porn sites, chat rooms, or gaming sites, by shutting down a Web browser if the user attempts to access this material. This isn't being manipulative; this is managing the environment to support change.

I like programs like NetNanny, but I encourage you to stay away from installing keystroke-monitoring software, which sends you a log of every site visited and every keystroke entered, unless absolutely necessary. Snooping software puts you in the role of inspector. And, frankly, a lot of what folks discover about the online surfing habits of others can cause very real pain. So restrict computer use with NetNanny, but don't fall into the trap of monitoring every computer keystroke and Web site visit if possible.

Step 4 - Care for You

If you're not careful, you can spend all your waking hours as your family's Internet cop. This can be an energy drain on your well-being. Physically, you can have difficulty sleeping and digesting, have problems with your heart, or suffer from chronic fatigue. Psychologically, you can get depressed or get emotionally numb. Let go and trust in the change plan to do its job in helping your loved one. Make a life for yourself that doesn't involve twenty-four-hour policing of computer usage. Go with family members and friends to the movies, the theater, and other activities, and enjoy your life. Choose to live the life you want.

FREE SOMEONE FROM SEX ADDICTION

Literally millions of men and women—husbands or fathers, wives or mothers, sisters or daughters, brothers or sons—wake up to the realization that someone they love has an obsessive interest in sex that is detrimental to them or to their relationship. It's estimated that between 1 and 6 percent of people have a sex addiction, and men are more likely to become sex addicts than women. That's because men can get sexually aroused pretty quickly from a visual stimulus; but for women, generally speaking, it's about forming a relationship in which sex is only one part.

So what makes a person a sex addict as opposed to someone who's just been caught with their pants down? Three general criteria: First, a sex addict shows a loss of control, whether that's using inappropriate partners or just showing a compulsion to be involved with someone sexually; second, he continues the behavior despite adverse consequences (like being discovered by a girlfriend or wife); and third, he gets withdrawal symptoms when he has to stop it.

Any individual suffering from out-of-control sexual behavior must seek qualified help, or else the behavior will escalate. I remember one client, Stephen Hayes, age forty-seven, who was a sex addict and used the Internet to feed his addiction. In his case, what started out as a small desire from viewing a little pornography online became a compelling urge. Eventually, he began masturbating while he was glued to pornographic images on his computer screen, even at work. Stephen's behavior further escalated. He started visiting sex shops, watched porn movies on his computer, visited massage parlors, and frequented strip joints. Although married, he solicited prostitutes and sought out other sex partners through online personal ads.

There is help for sexual addiction. Although it wasn't easy, his wife of three years, Jane, was brave enough to reach out and ask for it. Though heartbroken and about to draw up divorce papers, she put her hurt feelings aside, mobilized close family members and friends, and delivered the change message. Once Stephen said yes to help, he entered therapy, attended meetings of Sexual Compulsives Anonymous, and joined with his wife in couples therapy, even though their marriage had been dealt a severe blow. It took him several years to learn how to redirect his behavior; but happily, he now experiences a healthy sex life.

Step 1 - Craft the Circle of Change

If you're concerned that your partner may have a sexual addiction, I suggest crafting the circle somewhat smaller—perhaps you and a few friends or family, and a qualified therapist—because the addiction is shrouded in shame, guilt, and embarrassment. Another difficulty for you is to get this person to admit to something he may not see as a problem. All the more reason to include a therapist.

It is essential that sex addicts and those affected by their behavior realize that they cannot recover alone. They must seek help. And help is available through community agencies, professional counselors, and anonymous support groups. In fact, hundreds of safe, confidential, cost-free 12-step support groups are helping folks in pain and their loved ones find relief and freedom from this addiction. Thus, as with any addiction, identify a change plan to present. Some psychiatric medications may be helpful in reducing sexual drive or decreasing sexually intrusive thoughts. These drugs may also allow a person to consider consequences before acting on a sexual urge or impulse. Recovery is possible for those who are willing to take the necessary steps.

Step 2 - Deliver the Invitation to Change

Speak with your partner and discuss your observations and concerns, or have a therapist friend help you if you're feeling too numb with shock. Whatever you decide, it's best to bring the matter out into the open as soon as possible and express to him how you really feel. Some suggestions for dialogue:

Eyewitness account: *Dan, I love you very much and our relationship is important to me. I have caught you cheating on me several times in the very near past and now I've discovered that you're also very much involved in pornography.*

Flash-forward: *I'm very scared that this situation will get worse, that you'll be arrested for a sex-related offense, and our lives will be destroyed, or I'll be exposed to HIV, or other sexually transmitted diseases. Your behavior could kill us!*

Resolution: *Dan, I'm 110 percent behind you and loving you in a warm, open, trustful way. This is a shame-free zone. I maintain hope that things will get better if you agree to change and cure this situation. I love you and there is nothing that I won't do to help you, but one thing I'm not willing to do is stand by and watch you get sicker. I want you to get help, and I want you to get it right away.*

Step 3 - Champion the Change

Living with a sex addict is emotionally painful, isolating, and extremely difficult. It's no different from being emotionally abused. But none of this behavior has to do with you. You should not try to appease an addict by, for instance, losing weight, getting breast implants, or participating in sex acts that violate your values.

If your loved one agrees to get help, please keep in mind that change doesn't become permanent overnight, but it can begin in a moment. Honor his or her desire as well as taking note of your own resilience in deciding that you will walk through this time of renewal, healing, and trust building. To get through this period, set up some ground rules—mainly, to be faithful, to attend therapy together, and to attempt total honesty. Develop an understanding of this addiction. Maintain a healthy emotional atmosphere in your home.

Step 4 - Care for You

Get help for you. This step always sounds easy, but it is difficult to do alone. I suggest that you seek help by attending a support group for partners of sex addicts. You will discover that you aren't alone in living with the effects of someone's sexual addiction, and that there is hope.

The road to recovery is like a poorly maintained country road, full of potholes, bumps, rough spots, and unmarked lanes. Treat recovery like a discovery ride through uncharted territory. You can lessen your burden by maintaining a sense of humor, a sense of purpose, and a sense of community in your own life, while developing a sense of compassion for the addicted.

I do have to add that it is important to think carefully about whether you want to stay with someone who has a sex addiction. By its nature it means he or she may betray you repeatedly. Should change not stick, consult a family law attorney and see what your options are. You deserve to be respected, and your first responsibility is to your children and yourself.

Life brings us all kinds of personal hurts, and dealing with a loved one's sexual addiction is right there at the top of the list. This is why being supportive is tough. It is better under the circumstances to take care of your emotional health, and this is what I recommend to you. When you feel wronged by someone in your life, it can be hard to get past the hurt, and not everyone is willing to try. But people who hang on to anger, grudges, disappointments, and thoughts of revenge pay a high price in their physical health and emotional energy and are at much greater risk of developing chronic diseases, such as heart disease.

Forgiveness is purely something you do for yourself. You are not doing it for the person who has transgressed or wronged you, and you don't even need to express forgiveness to the person in question. This doesn't mean you have to like what he or she did, but you must emotionally release it. When you're ready to do that, mentally rewrite the story of what happened. Instead of seeing yourself as a victim, cast yourself as a strong person who's triumphed over a painful experience. Picturing yourself in a place of victory gives you increased confidence to deal with future disappointments. So don't let the experience drag you down. The consequences of not forgiving and staying stuck are too high.

STOP ANYONE'S OBSESSIVE BEHAVIOR

We all have bothersome worries every now and then. And we all have comforting little rituals. Maybe you like your DVDs stored in alphabetical order or your clothes hung in your closet by color. But that's not necessarily a problem, unless you're so disturbed by an out-of-place DVD or outfit or so consumed by worry that you practically can't function. When worries consume a person and cause extreme anxiety, they are called obsessions. When a person engages in incessant rituals, this is called a compulsion.

A person with obsessions and compulsions is said to have obsessive-compulsive disorder, or OCD. Some common rituals associated with OCD are repetitive hand washing, bathing, or showering. Many sufferers are obsessed with germs and contamination. Some sufferers are hoarders, filling their rooms with decades-old newspapers and odd items for fear that they might throw away something valuable. Others are checkers, waking up dozens of times a night to make certain doors are locked, or even leaving work several times a day to be sure the iron is unplugged. Compulsive hair pulling (known as trichotillomania) is a disorder related to OCD. Like a needle getting stuck on an old record, obsessive-compulsive disorder causes the brain to get stuck on a particular thought or urge.

OCD turns lives upside down. An entire family can be thrown off by a person with OCD. They can never go anyplace, for instance, because the one with OCD has to go through so many rituals before leaving, like bathing for three hours, that everyone is late. OCD disrupts a family's life, so it's imperative that family be the catalyst for change.

Step 1 - Craft the Circle of Change

OCD is a disorder that cannot be fixed alone, and it's not a habit a person can break, like smoking or nail biting. People with OCD lack the objectivity and information to deal with this multifaceted disorder effectively, so change definitely requires the observations and insight of close family members, even coworkers and employers—and definitely a qualified therapist. There are many avenues for treatment, including medication, behavior therapy, or a combination of both, so you'll want to research appropriate treatment plans. Because OCD often causes problems in family life and social adjustment, family therapy is often a good idea. Family therapy promotes understanding of the disorder and can help reduce family conflicts. It can also motivate family members and teach them how to help their loved one.

Step 2 - Deliver the Invitation to Change

A big problem in dealing with this disorder may be that many people know there is something wrong but don't have any idea that it might be OCD.

And although in some cases the disorder can severely disrupt a person's life, many people function normally and hide their compulsiveness out of fear or embarrassment. This is why a family, along with a therapist, must come together in the circle of change and help their loved one see and understand the problem through eyewitness accounts, family maps, and other blockade-busting strategies. Simply knowing the condition is treatable may provide enough motivation to get the person into a therapist's office.

At the family meeting, each person should communicate positively, directly, and clearly. State what you want to happen, rather than criticizing your relative for past behaviors. It's fine to talk about the effect of the behaviors on your life and explain that help and support are available. It is important that everyone in the circle of change speak with genuine care. For example:

Eyewitness account: *Jennie, I love you very much. For a long time now, I've seen you wash your hands constantly and get freaked when someone moves something in your room from its appropriate placement. I've seen you afraid to go out and touch a doorknob in public. I know this situation has cost you friendships, jobs, and position in your church and community.*

Flash-forward: *Everyone is here tonight because we're inviting you in to a process of change that will help you get yourself back to a more functional and happy way of living. We want to help you find a way to get better so that this disorder doesn't take over your whole life.*

Resolution: *Jennie, we support you and we want you to get help right away. In fact, that's one reason why Dr. Shaw is here. She will share with you that yours is a highly treatable condition and there are medications you can take to feel better. With her guidance, there is a way you can get help, and it has been very successful in treating this disorder.*

Negative comments or criticism can make OCD worse, while a calm, supportive environment can help improve the outcome of treatment. Whatever you do, do not tell the person to stop performing rituals. They can't comply, and the pressure to stop will only make the behaviors worse.

Recently, I worked with Brenda, a Sunday-school teacher, who lived alone since her husband of thirty-two years passed away five years ago. Brenda, who has two grown daughters who love her very much, is a compulsive hoarder. Although she has always had a tendency to hold on to things, her behavior became extreme after she lost her husband. Her hoarding got so bad that her entire house was covered with stuff, and there was hardly any space to move. Her family was very worried about her; they involved me and her pastor in a family meeting to convince her to get help. As part of this process, and part of the family support, they told Brenda that she must move out and temporarily live with one of her daughters. Yes, Brenda was literally removed from her own home. The family did not ask Brenda to clean out the clutter. Forced clean-outs don't work, because hoarders are traumatized by them and may even become suicidal.

The best way to help a loved one cope with OCD is to be as kind and patient as possible. Let her know help is available and that you'd like her to pursue the course of action you've researched. The therapist can then fill in the details of what treatment can accomplish. Ideally, a therapy session follows immediately.

Step 3 - Champion the Change

The main form of support is to not participate in your relative's rituals. People with OCD often try to involve family members in compulsive rituals. To keep the peace, family members may play along or help out with behaviors such as hoarding, checking, and washing. If you have helped with rituals in the past, it may take time and practice to change this pattern.

Becoming a cheerleader for the change plan will include not just supporting the ideas and actions you're asking him to do but patting him on the back for the progress he is making. "Dad, I love you and am so proud of the work you are doing to make your house safer. I think the meds you have started have resulted in you being remarkably calmer too! How do you feel?"

Step 4 - Care for You

Understandably, you'll get caught up in concern and caring for the person who has OCD. As a result, you may not take proper care of yourself. You may give up your own activities and become isolated from your friends and colleagues. This may go on for some time before you realize you are emotionally and physically drained. The stress can lead to sleeping problems, exhaustion, and constant irritability. Don't let this happen. Stay in touch with your own support network; do not isolate yourself with this problem. Keep up your interests outside the family. Consider having your own professional support, and take a little time each day just for you.

HELP SOMEONE GO FROM GLUM TO GLAD

When someone you love has those jarring moody moments, it's hard to figure out what to do about it. Does he need a hug? Some chocolate-chip cookies? Deep, meaningful conversation? A kick in the butt? It's a guessing game. If depression begins to overpower a spouse or partner, it's a demanding, even frightening, experience. The first thing to do is establish whether your loved one is, in fact, depressed. Be alert to the symptoms of depression: feelings of sadness, emptiness, worthlessness, helplessness, or excessive guilt; hopelessness; loss of interest in usual activities; decreased energy; difficulty concentrating or making decisions; memory problems; restlessness; sleep disturbances; changes in appetite; and suicidal thoughts.

Step 1 - Craft the Circle of Change

If such symptoms persist, it is time to act. Get the help of close family members, your physician, a trusted clergy person, or someone else outside the family such as a therapist who can validate your concerns at a family meeting. Formulate a plan with your group as to what sort of treatment is best. Depression can be successfully treated with a variety of tools including antidepressants and cognitive behavioral therapy (CBT). CBT is based on the idea that all moods—and their associated disorders—originate in our thoughts. The therapy focuses on adjusting attitudes and beliefs by recognizing and refuting negative thoughts as they occur. For instance, some people react to a mistake or mishap by generalizing to "I'm a failure." A CBT therapist would help the patient get to a more accurate assessment of the event, like "Wait a minute . . . I have a long history of success at doing this." The idea is to counteract errors in thinking.

It's also important to look at diet and exercise and see how they are integrated into your loved one's life. Jeanette, a client we have right now, has a significant history of depression along with compulsive behavior and alcohol dependency. The most effective pieces of her change plan have been the adjustments we helped her make in how and what she eats, along with her getting on a consistent exercise program. So don't overlook these two: what you put in the tank, and how often you take the rig out for a spin. Nutrition and exercise matter.

Step 2 - Deliver the Invitation to Change

Once you believe a problem exists, the next step is to have the family meeting. Mention that he seems unhappy lately. Avoid using words like "sick" or "crazy." People don't need to be labeled; they need to be helped. Let him know that his welfare matters to you. If a therapist is present, have the therapist point out that depression is a medical problem, not a moral weakness, and it can be treated with therapy and/or medication. Advise your loved one to seek help for depression. Present your plan: a visit to the family doctor, a mental health center, a religious adviser, or a therapist. Here is a sample dialogue:

Eyewitness account: *Jason, I love you very much. I've been concerned over the past several weeks because you seem so sad and you don't play basketball anymore with your friends. I've been worried, too, because you're sleeping so much of the time but are still so tired.*

Flash-forward: *I'm really worried, too, that if you're feeling depressed, it will only get worse and you'll sink deeper into unhappiness.*

Resolution: *Jason, your mother suffered from depression; so did your grandmother. These things often run in families, so there's nothing to feel ashamed or guilty about. But unlike in the past, when people didn't know what to do about depression, there's real help available now. I want you to be the person you used to be—happy, energetic, and fun—and with help, I know you can be. All of us here love you and we're committed to supporting you through this, and walking with you to the other side where there's light and wellness.*

If your loved one has never been in therapy and is male, this could be an uphill battle. Men will call a mechanic, but won't call for help with a personal problem. But gender aside, reaffirming your devotion to your loved one could ease him into therapy.

And if he resists? Reiterate your concern; get other family members to reaffirm their own love through expressions of support; and be concrete in pointing out how the gloom of depression is keeping him from the things he normally enjoys—always in nonjudgmental terms. For example, "I know how much you love playing basketball," versus "How come you never play basketball anymore?"

Step 3 - Champion the Change

While your loved one is seeking help for his or her depression, your attitude is paramount. Remain understanding. Be optimistic about treatment. Reassure your loved person that he or she will feel better eventually.

Be there for them. Give them a shoulder to cry on or just listen while they spill out their heart to you. Be patient. Let them know that you care. Try not to offer instant advice or bland reassurance. Ask how you can help. If necessary, accompany your loved one to appointments.

Gently challenge negativity and hopelessness. When you can, in a kind and sympathetic manner, take issue with the depressed person's unrealistic negativity, giving examples of instances where your loved one has been successful. Encourage a positive self-image.

You may have to step in with everyday tasks. Depressed people aren't lazy. They're sick. Household activities like cleaning, paying bills, or feeding the dog may seem overwhelming. You may have to take up the slack for them for a while. Just as if they had the flu, they simply don't feel up to it. Help, but don't encourage helplessness. Try not to do everything for the person, but still be there to support what they were doing for themselves.

Organize daily activities to help your loved one out of the doldrums. When I was a kid and my parents would take us four boys on long road trips, they'd have a bunch of games for us to play in the car. My parents were smart. They knew that by keeping us occupied, we wouldn't misbehave by fighting with one another. Nor would we keep asking, "Are we almost there?" Basically, Mom and Dad were using an effective behavioral tool. Today's cars have DVD players in them, so it's even easier to pacify, but I encourage conversation over DVDs.

If someone you love is depressed, you can help by planning their daily activities. Action is one of the best antidotes to depression, so planning an activity schedule is therapeutic. It gives your loved one a sense of direction and control. It distracts from depression-evoking thoughts, and provides structure to help do positive things throughout the day.

Activities on a schedule might include: get out of bed and get dressed, go grocery shopping, go to the library or museum, exercise, have lunch with a friend, visit friends, attend therapy, go out to dinner, see a nutritionist, see a movie, watch TV or read a book, go to bed.

Finally, offer hope in whatever form they will accept it. This could be their faith in God, their love of their children, or anything else that makes them want to go on living. Find what works best for them and remind them of it whenever they're not sure they can hang on any longer. Love them unconditionally and let them know it's their illness you're frustrated with, not them.

Step 4 - Care for You

Feelings of depression are contagious, so look after yourself. Dealing with a depressed person can be emotionally exhausting and may lead to feelings of burnout. Periodically take some time to step back from the situation and recharge your batteries. Pursue activities that give you pleasure and restore your sense of optimism and well-being. Keep your own lifestyle active and healthy. When someone you love is depressed, it may seem selfish to enjoy your life, but it's healthier for you to remain active.

It's okay to feel upset, angry, frustrated. These feelings are a valid response to a very trying situation. Join a support group. Talk with a close friend, or see a therapist. The important thing is to vent your frustrations rather than allowing them to build up inside.

Remember that you're not responsible for your depressed partner's feelings, actions, or thoughts. You can't make a depressed spouse or friend feel happier, nor did you make her feel depressed in the first place. The depressed person is impaired. She may be withdrawn and shy or sullen and angry. When the depressed person lashes out in anger, it's because she's actually angry with herself and the way she feels. You just happen to be there. And when your spouse or significant other doesn't feel like having sex, don't take it personally. Loss of sex drive is a classic symptom of depression. It doesn't mean she doesn't love you. Relationships can actually weather these challenges and grow stronger for them.

Do not be intimidated by the prospect of changing someone who is dealing with these issues. Expressing your feelings and your hopes for someone's life is a very healthy process—physically, emotionally, and spiritually. What is important is that the process leads not only to a more rewarding, fulfilling life for your loved one but also for everyone involved in his or her life. Inviting the people we love into this process, to freely express their feelings, experience our love, and talk openly is one of the greatest gifts we can give them.

12 Ways to Break Anyone's Most Troublesome Habits

I don't know about you, but I have a mental list I call, "Things I should not have to put up with." My list includes intolerable habits (she won't take out the trash; he uses a fork as a back scratcher); bad manners (he screams at the waiter if the service is slow); offensive behavior (she tells off-color jokes at inappropriate times), or behaving like a crisis junkie (she is a drama queen with a knack for turning the mundane into a three-hankie weeper). If your list sounds anything like mine, these are basically flaws you want repaired, or behaviors you want changed in those you love.

Granted, such habits aren't life-threatening or lawbreaking, but there's absolutely nothing wrong with wanting to break them. In fact, it's better if you do try to break someone's troublesome habits, because you could save a relationship. That's the conclusion of a fascinating study called "Social Allergies in Romantic Relationships," funded by the U.S. government's health research arm and carried out at Louisville University, Kentucky. It charted the end of 160 relationships by looking at the links between nasty habits and relationship success or failure. The researchers found that minor irritations, by building up over time, can make people get so disgusted and resentful that they walk out on the relationship. The study was published in the academic journal *Personal Relationships*.

The study also generated a list of the most annoying habits that can cause a rift between couples and bring them to a breaking point. According to the findings, men disliked the following habits in women: being possessive, critical, and demanding; lateness; talking too much; demands for reassurance about clothing; and taking too much luggage on trips. Women complained of the following: nose picking, burping, sloppy dressing, uncouth behavior, drunkenness, flatulence, and refusal to ask for directions. It defies belief, but all of these can create intense flashpoints in relationships.

I believe that you must step up to bad habits, either directly or diplomatically, or else they can mess up your sanity, ruin your life in a ton of tiny ways, chip away at your peace of mind, and add to the emotional burden of your life. Letting a resentment build creates a time bomb! But the question is, how can you get people to change their ways and do it without their calling you nag, hog, and, well, worse? With a little bit of stealth, strategizing, and an understanding of some timeless psychological tools, you can stop loved ones from getting under your skin and save the relationship. Here's a look at twelve tools that will help. Each of these tools is based on a simple behavioral principle: People are what they do. By changing what they do, you change them.

#1: THE DETACHMENT TECHNIQUE

People go on the defensive if they think you're criticizing them. So never insinuate something is wrong with them, only with their actions. The psychological strategy here is thus to detach the problem from the person; in other words, kick the problem, not the person.

To apply this tool, talk and think about the habit in question as an *IT*—something external to each of you. The *IT* becomes a painful, common enemy that you share and cope with together, rather than a problem one of you creates or something he does to you. Using *IT* keeps an accusatory tone out of the conversation. You'll find yourself being less upset when talking about *IT*, and the detachment helps you distance yourself from and resolve the problem.

Let's suppose that your boyfriend leaves a trail of debris in the apartment you share. There are dishes with a colorful mold pattern stacked in the sink. Old newspapers lie strewn about as if he were housebreaking an elephant. You're forced to spend your leisure hours moving from room to room like a minesweeper, cursing and snarling all the way.

Instead of name-calling, use the detachment technique. Don't scream at him for being a slob; focus on the problem—which is the clutter. Tell him how you feel about *IT*. Use "I" or "we" messages. Ask him how the two of you can work on "the clutter" problem and work on a mutually satisfying way to solve *IT*. Maybe it's taking turns emptying the trash, or rotating chores regularly so no one gets bored or grows to hate a certain task. Once someone sees a problem as *IT* and not *me*, it makes them more likely to do something about the offending behavior. By separating the behavior from the person, you can still love the person but not love the behavior. This is the true foundation of unconditional love, and a potent force for change.

#2: ATTACH CONSEQUENCES TO BEHAVIOR

If you've ever wondered what drives people, you don't have to wonder for long. Just observe the events that follow their behavior and you'll know why they do what they do. The events that follow behavior are called consequences. Behavior is strengthened or weakened by its consequences. A powerful way to reinforce desirable behavior is to give positive consequences.

Positive consequences may be as simple as a sincere expression of appreciation, a smile, gifts, thank-you notes, or compliments. The simplest examples are these: To encourage judicious budgeting in your spouse, wait until she makes a good decision (such as not impulsively buying something that she really wants), and then compliment her on her wisdom and strength in making the decision. Or when you see your child putting his toys away, say, "I really like the way you put your blocks away." Praising your children creates a strong self-image and increases the likelihood that the child will behave in sync with that positive self-image.

These gentle exchanges tell the people in our lives how much we love them. So, whenever your loved one gets it right, tell them in a sincere and respectful way that you really appreciate what they did. They'll then be more likely to do it again, or repeat the conduct more often.

Be careful not to criticize your loved one, or qualify their behavior. Focus on the positive, not the lack of perfection. Saying something like "Thanks for the coffee, but you forgot to add the cream" won't get you anything but resentment.

The ability to express appreciation and give encouragement is a key part of changing someone you love. Everyone wants to feel appreciated. Everyone wants to be encouraged. These things feel good. I know I love to hear appreciation and get encouragement.

Have you given some appreciation and encouragement today?

#3: EXTINCTION

Everything we do is maintained by reinforcement, or payoffs. When we do something, we have to feel like it's worth it. It has to pay off. When the reinforcers for maintaining a behavior are no longer given, we will eventually stop performing the behavior. The process of eliminating (withdrawing or withholding) reinforcers is called extinction.

A classic example is when a toddler has a tantrum at bedtime. When mom and dad put the child to bed and leave the room, he screams and cries. The parents respond by staying in the room until the child falls asleep, maybe for two or three hours. Of course, the child wins in this situation—he gets his parents' attention. By practicing extinction, the parents can gain the upper hand and eliminate the tantrums. All they have to do is leave the room and not return even after the child cries. Eventually, the child will cry less and even start going to sleep after the parents leave the room. The parents removed the reinforcer—in this case, attention—and the tantrums ceased.

Extinction is a great tool to use when the reinforcer is attention. Think about some of the people you know. Do they say obnoxious or outrageous stuff to show off? Do they blab too loudly about their personal lives? Do they use racial slurs? Lots of people have an intense and unhealthy need for attention and affirmation. If their behavior gets on your nerves, practice extinction by simply ignoring them or tactfully excusing yourself from their presence. This sends an unmistakable signal. Do this often enough and watch the behavior gradually dissipate (become extinct), at least around you. Extinction has to be used carefully. It's not the best way to change risky situations in which someone abuses alcohol, drugs, or food to get attention.

#4: MORE OF THIS, LESS OF THAT

Often, we'd like our loved ones to do more of one behavior and less of another. Say, for example, your husband is highly critical of you (or others), always finding fault with your cooking or housekeeping, and you'd like him to be less critical. You can change his behavior by getting him to give a *competing response*, such as complimenting—something that makes it tough for him to be critical at the same time. A compliment competes with a criticism. So when you hear him being critical, you might say, "Well, what do you like about . . . ?" The more he compliments, the less he criticizes. For a competing response to work, it has to be difficult to do at the same time as the undesirable behavior—such as complimenting and criticizing.

#5: HABIT AWARENESS

Maybe someone in your family has the unfortunate habit of biting his nails or picking his nose, and you're sick of it. There is a four-part habit-breaking process that will nip this in the bud pretty fast. Here's how it works:

1. Making him aware of his habit. Have him look in a mirror while performing the habit on purpose every day. Help him become aware of how his body moves and what muscles are being used when he does the habit.

2. Showing him how to develop competing responses. One of the keys to eliminating a poor habit is to substitute it with a better one—which is why competing responses are so powerful. As I described above, a competing response is a behavior that is incompatible with the habit. To qualify as "competing," the response should be performed with the same muscles or body part as the bad habit. With nail biting, for example, competing responses would be to hold a pencil in hand, clench both fists, or put his hands in his pocket until the urge to bite his nails is gone. If he learns to do this more often, he will eventually stop the bad habit. By making the new habit incompatible with the old one, the bad one will naturally decrease in strength, since the two cannot coexist.

3. Relaxation training. Stress goes hand in hand with daily life. Many habits develop out of a need to deal with stress, relieve nervousness, or resolve inner tension. Deep breathing is a good way to ease the stress and anxiety that trigger nervous habits. When your loved one begins to feel overwhelmed or anxious, help her stop for a few minutes and take some slow, deep breaths. This will calm her down, clear her mind of unnecessary clutter, and give her more of a sense of control.

4. Reinforcement. People are generally like Pavlov's dogs. As I explained above, when they do something positive, give them positive reinforcement with praise and they'll be more likely to repeat the behavior. As she works on breaking her bad habit, praise her efforts, and you'll help her stop the habit altogether.

#6: FOLLOW THE DEAD-PERSON RULE

When we want someone to do something, we usually begin our request with "Don't," in effect telling them what not to do. This is a violation of the "dead-person rule." This rule simply states: Never ask someone to do something a dead person can do. Only dead people are capable of not acting or behaving.

A better approach is to couch your requests positively. Consider a typical scene at home. Your husband repeatedly leaves his dirty coffee cup in the sink, never in the dishwasher. If you say, "Don't put your dirty coffee cup in the sink," all your husband knows is that he's not supposed to put his dirty coffee cup in the sink. He could obey you by putting the dirty coffee cup on the kitchen counter, but that still wouldn't satisfy you. It would be better if you said, "Please put your coffee cup in the dishwasher," the behavior you really want to elicit. So, only ask someone to do things that only a live person can do, and you'll get better results.

Using the dead-person rule works well with kids too. Your child may think that everything that he or she does is wrong if all he hears from you is "Don't do this" or "Stop doing that." When children continually hear "no," "don't," and "stop it," the words lose their impact and they simply tune you out. Instead of saying "Don't drop the milk," say "Carry the milk in both hands, like this." Tell your kids what they can do instead of what they can't do, and you'll get better results.

#7: PROMPTS

Are you sick of cajoling or constantly repeating yourself? If so, use prompts more often. They're reminders, or cues, to do something. We rely on prompts every day, such as when we stop at a stop sign or check our appointment calendars. Prompts are useful when you want someone to do something and you don't want to nag. Example: You want your wife to take her medication or, if she has diabetes, you want her to self-monitor her blood sugar levels. Use prompts. Adhesive notes, for example, make the point nicely and avoid a confrontation. Try placing one in the middle of the bathroom mirror or on her computer screen. Or simply give a gentle reminder that it's time to take her pills or check her blood sugar.

For prompts to work best, pair them with a benefit. For example: "Taking your medication will make you feel better." This reminds the person of the positive payoff. When the payoff is positive, she's more likely to do what you want. Also, when your loved one does the right thing after being prompted, praise her. The desired behavior will eventually become second nature, and you won't have to use prompts as often.

A prompt that was a challenge for me to wrap my head around at first has become a staple I use frequently in my life today: a God Box.

A God Box is a vessel (a box, a jar, a something or other that you make—get creative and make a collage over a bottle, even!) that has a slot or opening at the top so that you can stick something into it. My very first God Box was an old glass milk bottle, and I slipped into it pieces of paper on which I had written something to "turn over" to my God. In this way, I gave something to God, and then I would accept my God's direction, or prompt.

Tricky, right? But not really. Writing down how we feel, what we intend to do, and thoughts of how to get there are helpful tools in making the change plan less invisible. I WANT TO GET BETTER is all well and good as an idea, but some bones to a plan coupled with action are better at making hope turn from an idea into a reality.

A God Box can be a great tool to prompt one into a conversation with God. And conversations go both ways. Get it? Got it? Good.

#8: MODELING

If you want someone to behave differently, let them learn from you. This is called modeling, and I've talked about it a lot. We learn language, attitudes, beliefs, manners, mannerisms, habits, emotional responses, and countless other behaviors by watching others. We get many of our habits, such as verbal expressions and body language, from others with whom we identify, such as parents, partners, or siblings.

Here's an example. Maybe there's someone in your life who is a cheapskate, or otherwise exhibits tightwad tendencies. He brags about paying less for something, and makes fun of those who pay more. When the check comes, he leaves the waiter a meager tip. Sure, many people pride themselves on being frugal, believing that thriftiness is a money-management skill. But there's a big difference between possessing the ability to save a few bucks and insisting on it at every turn.

If you're living with a cheapskate and it bothers you, let him see you exhibiting generous acts. Making a financial donation to a worthy cause will make an impression, for example. When you perform an act of charity, tell him what you're doing and why: "I'm donating two hundred dollars to a children's charity this Christmas to help the organization buy gifts for less fortunate kids." Find causes that allow him to participate. Take him to the local food bank or soup kitchen some weekend. Or start a family charity bank and ask everyone to contribute each week. At the end of the month, decide where the money will go. These things will help him make the connection that it is in the act of giving to others that we are able to live our best life.

Modeling also happens to be one of the best ways to instill moral behavior in kids. Almost all children make the occasional social misstep. But when your child acts rude, selfish, or insensitive toward playmates, you worry, Why is he so unkind? Why must she be so aggressive? Why can't she let someone else speak? Children don't come into this world with social graces. They have to learn them, and the way kids learn to behave morally or immorally is through modeling.

In his classic "Bobo doll" study in the sixties, psychologist Albert Bandura had preschoolers watch adults punch and kick an inflatable Bobo doll. Bobo dolls are those plastic figures with weighted bottoms that bounce back when you hit or kick them. Later, when left alone with the Bobo doll, the children turned into pint-sized prizefighters. They pummeled the dolls, just as the adults had done.

This experiment and many others like it showed that we learn by watching. Our behavior and our personalities are products of our observations. It's true, we're all a bunch of copycats. Seriously though, if your kids see mom and dad being obnoxious, rude, or using physical violence against each other, chances are the children will resolve conflict with similar techniques. But if you behave in appropriate and loving ways, your kids will notice and learn from that too. Show by example the type of behavior you wish your child to learn. This applies to all sorts of behavior, from practicing honesty to refraining from violence, smoking, and doing drugs.

#9: THOUGHT STOPPING

Many bad habits are triggered by unhelpful thoughts and ruminations. The longer such thoughts hang around in one's head, the more they make themselves at home and sabotage someone's actions. To help people deal with their anxious thoughts, therapists often teach a technique called thought stopping. The minute a negative thought arises, a person tells himself, either out loud or silently, "Stop it!" Then they relax for a few seconds and switch to a more helpful thought. Some people are advised to wear a rubber band on their wrist that they snap whenever the negative thought comes to mind. The objective is to stop destructive thoughts before they get out of control. Before that one thought spins itself into a twister! Suggest this technique to your loved one as a way to halt negative thinking.

Example: Someone in your life is a shopaholic. She buys things to momentarily forget her troubles. Pretty soon, she's run into debt, so she shops some more, but gets deeper into debt. She's not obsessed with material things. She's hooked on the adrenaline rush it gives her to buy or acquire them. This vicious cycle is threatening her livelihood and personal peace. As a friend or loved one, you can help put an end to this ugly spiral by teaching her how to interrupt her behavior.

Usually, what triggers a shopping spree in compulsive shoppers is a thought such as "I need to go to the store." Point out to this person that a thought like this is unhealthy, and that she must stop herself from acting on it. Mention, too, that urges rarely last longer than thirty minutes if there's no opportunity to cave in. Get her to do something else that will make her feel good besides putting herself in the mall with her credit cards—like going for a walk, calling a friend, being of service to someone or something, or anything that will keep her from fixating on the compulsive taboo. Work together with your loved one to figure out less destructive conduct.

#10: IF . . . THEN

Does your four-year-old have a meltdown every time you leave him with the babysitter? Does your twelve-year-old rebel when you ask her to tackle her homework? Does your teenager drag his feet about cleaning his room? It's challenging to rear responsible, loving human beings—just ask your own parents. But you can be successful by trying a technique called If . . . then.

The technique is based on the psychological premise that more pleasant behaviors will offset less pleasant behaviors. In other words, one activity can act as a reward for another activity. Your parents and grandparents used this all time when they said, "Eat your peas and then you can have dessert."

For example, your son likes to play video games but does not like to do his homework. You, the parent, want the homework done and you also want your son to spend less time playing video games. One behavior (playing the video game) happens often and reliably because your son enjoys it; the other (doing homework) happens less often and completely unreliably. So offer video-game time when your son finishes his homework. One behavior acts as a reward for the other. Not difficult, is it? Simply look for pleasant tasks that can be used as a reward for doing unpleasant tasks, and you'll usually get cooperation.

#11: RULE SETTING

Another tool that comes in handy with parenting is rule setting. As parents, you already know that setting and enforcing rules are an essential part of your job description. Making rules is a no-brainer. Sticking to them is altogether different. It can be a power struggle—one that some parents frequently lose, especially when faced with whining, pouting, and tantrums. But paradoxically, not having rules has been proven to make children more defiant and rebellious. Research since the 1960s has found that a child whose mom and dad are permissive is more likely to have problems in school and abuse drugs and alcohol as teenagers. If rules are wobbly or nonexistent, kids don't feel safe. They can't concentrate as well, think as well, or learn as well.

So set some rules—and be clear and calm about setting them. "There's no hitting in our house," said in a calm way, is more effective than screaming, "I said no fighting!" State the rule, briefly explain the reason for the rule and the expected consequence for its infraction: "We don't throw toys. Someone could get hurt or the toy could break." If the child continues: "I'm going to take that away from you and keep it safe until tomorrow." When you make rules, make sure you enforce them with consistency.

#12: BECOME AN UNDERREACTOR

Don't let people push your buttons. I recommend taking ten seconds to twenty-four hours before responding to any situation you are emotional about. People who overreact to situations often cause much of their own stress. If someone is short-tempered with you, don't react to it. Stubbornly refuse to let yourself become upset. This is hard to do, but you choose your thoughts. When you stay calm, the situation defuses, solutions appear, and stress dissipates. Someone's bad habits won't bother you as much.

When our dog Bandit barks and he's alone, he makes a bit of noise but then simmers down. When Bandit barks, and then Oliver returns a refrain, they feed off one another and really get going! Before you know it, our other dog Harriet has arrived to see what all the noise is about and begins barking like crazy too. They feed off one another and their barking escalates. Their throats must get tired! But on they go, back and forth and bigger and louder. We're not so different than the pooches in these situations. We hear a bark. We bark back. Or not.

If you find yourself in a difficult interaction, don't get emotionally hijacked by the other person. Teach yourself to notice when you're being hijacked, by paying attention to bodily cues like your heart pounding or your palms getting sweaty. Then pause, take a deep breath or two, and start thinking (as opposed to feeling).

Another way to underreact is to stop labeling people's behavior so harshly. Sometimes we get so upset by someone's behavior that we call them names in our minds. This only worsens the situation. The trick is to relabel your loved one's behavior. Instead of calling someone "moody," start thinking of them as "thoughtful"; let "picky" become "careful"; "unpredictable" as "spontaneous"; "quick to anger" as "passionate." You'll be more accepting of a person's habits, and they won't drive you around the bend as much.

Let me add that we all have to deal with annoying people and annoying habits every day. Whatever is bugging you, it's also appropriate to say how the person's behavior makes you feel, and express what you want to happen— without jeopardizing your employment or your relationship. If one person is causing you frustration, approach that person on a friendly level to discuss the situation without causing a confrontation. Try to work out solutions that are mutually beneficial.

There is a great deal more to the successful application of these tools than just simple behavioral techniques. These tools, and indeed the entire change process, must be infused with love. As I've said throughout this book, the greatest power we possess in influencing change is our ability to make people feel loved, yet it is the tool we use the least. The great American psychiatrist Karl A. Menninger once said, "Love cures people—both the ones who give it and the ones who receive it."

Nothing else breathes life into us like love. This explains why people who are loveless and alone tend to experience more anxiety, drink and smoke more, eat junk food, and engage in other behaviors that breed disease. Just knowing that love is alive can help recovery.

Love is an action that strengthens self-esteem and self-worth by helping others see and know their strengths. Love focuses on assets instead of liabilities. Love offers more joy than any material possession could provide. Love shines!

Love is how much we give of ourselves, how much we share with others, and ultimately, how we measure our lives. Ask yourself what it would take to make those in your life feel more loved. Answer this question, act on your answer, and you will find that love is the most powerful force you have for change.

Develop a Sense of Urgency

No matter what you're dealing with, it can go one of three ways. It can get worse, it can stay the same, or it can get better. Odds are that if you do nothing, your loved one's behavior will continue to get worse, or at best stay static. It's known for a fact, however, that many conditions are progressive. They *will* get worse. Most addictions, for example, are primary, chronic, progressive, and often fatal health problems. Behaviors like domestic abuse get progressively worse too. They will escalate until the abuser gets caught by authorities or his victim decides to leave. A tragic picture of how domestic abuse can escalate is when it ends in murder.

Although we care deeply about a loved one who is hurting or in the midst of chaos brought about by some behavior, we think we can do little to help them change. And so we drag our feet, think it will get better (it probably won't), or just live with chaos like it's normal. In the realm of addiction research, an often-cited study of families who have an addicted loved one in their midst tells us that, on average, it will take nine years for loved ones to speak up and try to usher in help. Nine years. Sheesh! Some stretch—3,285 days and nights before we kick ourselves in the butt and do something, or tragedy strikes.

Our reluctance to act reminds me of the story of the frog in the saucepan. If you drop a live frog into a pot of cool water, it will stay right in the pot as long as the water is comfortable. However, if you place a frog in a pan of cool water, set it on the stove, then turn the heat up just a few degrees at a time, the frog will sit there and allow himself to be boiled. The poor creature simply accommodates to his gradually changing environment and fails to realize that he's in dangerously hot water.

This is surely a distressing situation for the frog. But you'll worry less about him when you consider the fact that this happens to us in much the same way. It is a seemingly harmless pattern at first. But bit by bit, we accept greater and greater compromises until it becomes the easy way, the natural way, to live. We lull ourselves into thinking: He's okay. It's better the past three days. She made it to work every day last month. He told me his doctor prescribed it, and he's taking it as prescribed. She didn't really mean it.

If we're lucky enough to be jarred awake, we realize, "Gosh, it's getting warm in here!" And, indeed, when we take a good look, and listen, we find that we are in uncomfortably hot water up to our chins. Our chins!

Unfortunately, you can't simply drift out of this predicament the same way you drifted into it. You've got to row hard, or better yet, rev up the motor. Change requires action and determination. So decide to act now. Use the program in this book. Do something about your predicament, no matter where you are, no matter how immobilized you feel. Just don't languish. Let this book help you get unstuck right here and now.

If you aren't yet convinced, catch a frog and carry out that simple experiment. Better yet, you might periodically check the water in your own pot.

Feel the heat?

Jump!

Appendix I: Resources

Treatment Centers

Help for what hurts is available at all different costs, geographical locations, and treatment approaches. Here is a sampling of treatment centers I often refer to in my practice when working with a family. While a book can become out of date, you can find more and always current information online, at www.BradLamm.com. On this Web site, many more are listed by state so that you can find what you need right in your own backyard.

None of those listed has paid to be included, nor do we have a financial relationship with any treatment center with whom we work or to which we refer clients. We do not receive fees to "place" people into treatment.

SEABROOK HOUSE TREATMENT CENTERS
Alcohol and chemical dependency treatment
Cumberland County, New Jersey, and Tioga County, Pennsylvania
Phone: 800-761-7575
www.SeabrookHouse.org or www.SeabrookWest.org
Intensive inpatient and extended-care treatment—30-, 60-, 40-, and
    120-day programs
Over-18 coed treatment, with single-sex accommodations
Young adult track and a purposeful "Women with Children" track
Semiprivate and private accommodations available
On-site detox in full medical unit
Most insurance accepted (average out-of-pocket cost $12,875)
Family therapy program included in program costs
Partial scholarships available

I love Seabrook House, and the work it does. It's a place for healing and one of the few A-list treatment centers that still accepts insurance for truly quality care. Founded by Jerry and Peg Diehl in 1974 as a nonprofit agency, Seabrook House has gained international recognition as one of the country's premier programs. Today, it is operated by son Ed, though eighty-three-year-old Peg is "the angel on duty," as I like to call her.

Offering three distinct facilities, Seabrook House is licensed and accredited for a total of 157 beds. I gave Seabrook House my grand piano last year to use as it saw fit, and I am involved in its foundation work. Lives are being rebooted here, and some beautiful music is being made.

NEW DIRECTIONS FOR WOMEN
Alcohol and chemical dependency treatment for women 18 and older
Newport Beach, California
Phone: 800-939-6636
www.NewDirectionsForWomen.org
90-day average length of stay
Vibrant "Women with Children" Track
Off-site detox available
Extended-care treatment, including sober living
Limited insurance accepted (90 days cost approximately $22,000)
Partial scholarships available

New Directions for Women (NDFW) was cofounded in 1977 by one of the women who had a hand in my recovery, Muriel Zink. I love its programs and the passion with which it meet folks and families where they are right now. NDFW has a mother-and-children track where a single mom can come during pregnancy or with children in tow, and begin the task of getting better by first getting clean and sober. New Directions is women only, as the name suggests, and this gender-specific treatment protocol is a powerful tool for many in breaking through to lasting change.

Caron Foundation and Caron Renaissance
Alcohol and chemical dependency, and dual-diagnosis treatment
Wernersville, Pennsylvania; Palm Beach, Florida
Phone: 800-678-2332
www.Caron.org
Gender-specific treatment
Adolescent track
Semiprivate and private rooms available
On-site medical detox
Intensive inpatient, outpatient, and extended-care treatment
Family-group participation included in treatment cost
Self-pay & limited insurance (approximately 30 days at $26,000)
Partial scholarships available

Caron has a legitimate track for dual-diagnosis treatment, and its staff-to-client ratio is among the highest in the field. "Limited insurance" means that it generally treats with cash payment upfront, then issues a "superbill" for the client to submit to his or her insurance company.

Caron's Family Program and spiritual piece is terrific. Father Bill has been with Caron since the beginning of time (or soon after) and has walked thousands through the spiritual components of recovery. The property's rolling landscape and physical plant are wonderful. The young adult and adolescent programs are standouts, as are their five-day assessment and evaluation service, for a loved one who is not sure he or she is addicted. On the upper end of cost, Caron is terrific across the board.

Willingway Hospital Recovery Center
Alcohol and chemical dependency treatment
Statesboro, Georgia
Phone: 800-242-9455
www.Willingway.com
Acute inpatient and extended-care treatment
Strong family program
All private rooms
On-site medical detox

Family owned and operated
Insurance accepted (inpatient fixed price of $23,000)

Willingway is family owned and operated. Medical director Dr. Robert Moodey is the son of the founders, John and Dot, both of whom were in recovery. What started in the 1950s in the family living room has grown to become one of the nation's strongest treatment centers for acute alcohol and chemical dependency. Willingway has one of the strongest medical detox units in the country in my estimation.

SHADES OF HOPE
Disordered-eating treatment
Buffalo Gap, Texas
Phone: 800-588-4673
www.ShadesOfHope.com
Mandatory family program
Inpatient program and week-long intensive programs throughout year
Co-occuring disorders including drugs & alcohol
Semiprivate rooms
Family owned and operated
Limited insurance accepted (42-day primary inpatient at $25,200)
Partial scholarships available

Founded by Tennie McCarty, Shades of Hope is the best, bar none, treatment for those struggling with disordered eating, including:

▶ *Bulimia*
▶ *Exercise and laxative bulimia*
▶ *Anorexia*
▶ *Body dysmorphia syndrome*
▶ *Compulsive overeating*
▶ *Obesity*

I love the work being done at Shades of Hope, and have seen real miracles happen there. Disordered-eating treatment (not dieting) is an area of the treatment universe in which a few overpriced luxury spots have done a disservice to the vital work being done at places like Shades. About fifteen minutes outside Abilene, Texas, Shades is a sweet setting for getting better. Its clients are 90 percent women.

ROSECRANCE ADOLESCENT TREATMENT CENTER
Adolescent alcohol and chemical dependency treatment
Rockford, Illinois
Phone: 815-391-1000
www.Rosecrance.org/programs/adolescents.asp
Primary addiction treatment for adolescents
Insurance accepted (40 days approximately $25,000)
Limited scholarships available

Rosecrance provides acute treatment programs for teens, ages twelve to nineteen, who are struggling with addiction. It is gender-specific treatment in a peer-led program. I really love this program. Its sister program is the Monarch Recovery Program, where young women stay longer term.

PRIDE INSTITUTE
Intensive inpatient and extended-care treatment
Minneapolis, Minnesota
Phone: 800-547-7433
www.Pride-Institute.com
Over-18 coed primary addiction treatment
Specializing in the gay, lesbian, bisexual, and transgender (GLBT)
   community
Strong sexual-addiction co-occurring track
Family therapy program included
Outpatient adolescent addiction treatment
On-site medical detox
Insurance accepted (28 days at $19,600)

PRIDE Institute is a top pick for treatment for gay and lesbian folks. Its programs address a variety of addictions through small group sessions, one-on-one counseling, and group education. A staff member of mine found a solid foundation for recovery at PRIDE many years ago. PRIDE participates in many insurance carriers' in-network treatment plans, and is located just outside Minneapolis, in Eden Prairie, Minnesota. For the LGBT community PRIDE is a strong resource.

MOUNTAINSIDE ADDICTION TREATMENT CENTER
Alcohol and chemical dependency treatment
Canaan, Connecticut
Phone: 800-762-5433
www.Mountainside.org
Intensive inpatient treatment
Over-18 longer-term treatment with single-sex accommodations
Semiprivate rooms
Off-site detox
Self-pay ($7,500 per month approximately)

Mountainside is another center that is doing impressive work. In fact, a vibrant recovering community has sprung up around Mountainside in Canaan as a result of the center's successful work. Mountainside operates a coffee shop nearby for those in the extended-care program. The center incorporates elements of an adventure-based program and is situated in a comfortable (but not fancy) mountainside lodge.

There is not a detox program here, however. Nor is there treatment for people with dual diagnosis, since Mountainside does not have the medical staff to manage medication needs. But at this price level, few treatment centers are doing better work than Mountainside for traditional alcohol and chemical dependency.

ST. CHRISTOPHER'S INN FOR MEN
Alcohol and chemical dependency treatment
Garrison, New York
Phone: 800-457-0027

www.StChristophersInn-graymoor.org
Over-18 longer-term treatment with single-sex accommodations
Large dorm-style setting
Ambulatory on-site detox (limited)
Intensive inpatient—average stay 60+ days
Insurance accepted, including New York State Medicaid
If uninsured and a New York State resident: All room & board provided
   at no cost

Operated for one hundred years by the Franciscan Friars of the Atonement, St. Christopher's Inn does outstanding work without regard to a person's ability to pay. I'm a big fan of SCI, and the folks who run it do so as a true labor of love. If a person is willing to accept help, they can find it at St. Christopher's Inn. The physical plant is quite nice, while the accommodations are more like dorm-style lodging and food service—not fancy but fine.

HANLEY CENTER
Alcohol and chemical dependency treatment
West Palm Beach, Florida
Phone: 866-442-6539
www.HanleyCenter.org
Home to the nation's premier senior recovery program
Over-18 coed treatment with single-sex accommodations
Semiprivate and private rooms available
On-site detox
Intensive inpatient and extended-care treatment
Family program—one person at no charge
Self-pay (30 days at $24,500)

Hanley's Florida location makes it a pleasant place for rehabilitation during the winter months. I have received very positive responses from clients who have participated in Hanley's programs. Its Center for Older Adult Recovery is its most well-known feature, but the program built its reputation years ago on nuts-and-bolts alcohol and drug treatment. Once part of Hazelden's network of treatment centers, Hanley returned as a solo provider a few years back. Hanley offers both age- and gender-specific treatment services for alcoholism and substance abuse that are designed to meet the needs of men, women, and older adults. I embrace its work and mission.

GOSNOLD TREATMENT CENTER
Alcohol and chemical dependency treatment
Falmouth, Massachusetts
Phone: 800-444-1554
www.Gosnold.org
Over-18 coed treatment with single-sex accommodations
Semiprivate and private rooms available
On-site detox
Intensive inpatient and extended-care treatment
Family program available
Insurance accepted (30 days at $13,700)

Gosnold is a lower-cost treatment provider that accepts many participating insurance carriers. Nicely situated on Cape Cod, Gosnold has a rich history of doing what it does best, namely, solid treatment for straight alcohol and chemical dependency. A large portion of its clientele is opiate addicted, and its work in this realm is top-notch. Gosnold's extended-stay programs are terrific too, and at the price level, no one is doing it better for the cost. I've used Gosnold for years, and it remains a reliable regional provider.

HAZELDEN TREATMENT CENTERS
Alcohol and chemical dependency treatment
Center City, Minnesota, and Newberg, Oregon
Phone: 800-257-7810
www.Hazelden.org
Adolescent and adult treatment
28-day inpatient program $27,000
Family program additional fee

Most insurance accepted
Some financial aid available

One of the nation's best-known treatment providers for substance-abuse recovery, Hazelden has been helping people since 1949. It was at Hazelden that the 12-step model of recovery became rooted in a residential environment. Its Springbrook program, in Newberg, Oregon, is best known for its treatment of health-care professionals—doctors, nurses, pharmacists, and so forth.

BETTY FORD CENTER
Alcohol and chemical dependency treatment
Rancho Mirage, California
Phone: 877-449-5205
www.BettyFordCenter.org
Intensive inpatient, outpatient, and extended-care treatment
Over-18 gender-specific treatment with single-sex accommodations
Semiprivate rooms
On-site detox
30-day program at $24,000 / 90-day extended program at $42,000
Family-group participation included in treatment cost
No insurance / Self-pay
Partial scholarships available

From its earliest days, the Betty Ford Center has treated women and men suffering from chemical dependency. The Center has always saved 50 percent of its space for women and 50 percent for men. Treatment is gender-specific; women and men reside in separate halls. Today the Betty Ford Center offers programs for the entire family system affected by addiction. Their Family Program sets the industry standard. Top-notch!

Web Sites

We host many free regularly scheduled support groups each week through my online Cisco-powered Change Institute. Video and audio, it's the next best thing to actually being in a room with other folks, and support matters, even if you cannot leave the house or work to get it.

Tapping into these online meetings will help you remain hopeful, connected, and moving, no matter what your circumstances. Find these meetings and links to other available support regionally and nationally at www.BradLamm.com.

AL-ANON/ALATEEN
www.Al-Anon.org

This is the home base for the support group for the loved ones of those who are addicted. There is a wealth of information here for supporting a loved one through change and recovery.

ALCOHOLICS ANONYMOUS
www.AA.org

Alcoholics Anonymous is a fellowship of men and women who share their experience, strength, and hope with each other that they may solve their common problem and help others to recover from alcoholism. The only requirement for membership is a desire to stop drinking. There are no dues or fees for AA membership; they are self-supporting through contributions. AA is not allied with any sect, denomination, politics, organization, or institution. Its primary purpose is to stay sober and help other alcoholics to achieve sobriety. The Web site is a wonderful information resource and helps people locate meetings in their area.

ASSOCIATION FOR MARRIAGE AND FAMILY THERAPY
www.TherapistLocator.net

This resource will assist you in locating a marriage and family therapist in your area. The listed therapists are Clinical Members of the American Association for Marriage and Family Therapy. The directory provides information on the therapists' office locations and availability, practice description, education, professional licenses, health-plan participation, achievements and awards, and languages spoken. Once you have obtained a list of therapists in your local area, call and interview several over the phone to determine which one is the best match for you.

CELEBRATE RECOVERY AND FRIENDS IN RECOVERY

www.celebraterecovery.com

www.FriendsInRecovery.net

Celebrate Recovery and Friends in Recovery are biblical and church-based addictions-recovery programs. They are built on principles taken from scripture. The Web sites will help you locate a group near you.

DEBTORS ANONYMOUS

www.DebtorsAnonymous.org

Debtors Anonymous offers people in financial trouble recovery from compulsive debting and hope for a healthier, happier, more prosperous life. The group's basic text, *The Currency of Hope*, is a must-read.

GAMBLERS ANONYMOUS

www.GamblersAnonymous.org

Gamblers Anonymous is a fellowship of men and women who help themselves and others to recover from a gambling problem. The only requirement for membership is a desire to stop gambling. The Web site has a meeting directory to help you locate meetings in your area.

GREYSHEETERS ANONYMOUS (GSA)

www.GreySheet.org

GreySheeters Anonymous is a group of folks working to recover from compulsive overeating. It is more rigid than OA and I love what they do. There are no dues or fees for membership. GSA's primary purpose is to eat three weighed and measured meals a day and help other compulsive overeaters to achieve this goal.

NARCOTICS ANONYMOUS

www.NA.org

NA is an international, community-based association of recovering drug addicts with more than 43,900 weekly meetings in over 127 countries worldwide. Its Web site contains resources and information on how to locate meetings in your area.

NATIONAL ALLIANCE ON MENTAL ILLNESS (NAMI)

www.NAMI.org

NAMI is the nation's largest grassroots organization for people with mental illness and their families. Founded in 1979, NAMI has affiliates in every state and in more than 1,100 local communities across the country. Its Web site is a rich resource for information and support for people who are struggling with mental illness.

NATIONAL ASSOCIATION FOR CHILDREN OF ALCOHOLICS

www.NACOA.net

You'll find helpful information here for kids and adults alike. I love their book *An Elephant in the Living Room* by Jill M. Hastings and Marion H. Typpo to help families with children assess, address, and open up with gentleness the topic of addiction and mental illness.

NATIONAL COUNCIL ON ALCOHOLISM AND DRUG DEPENDENCE

www.NCADD.org

Marty Mann (1904-1980) founded NCADD and dedicated her life to teaching the public that alcoholism is a preventable and treatable disease, not a moral failing. She was living proof that alcoholics are capable of recovery. The council's mission is to knock out the stigma and the disease of alcoholism and other drug addictions.

NATIONAL INHALANT PREVENTION COALITION

www.Inhalants.org

You'll find information on inhalants on this Web site, with tips on breaking the cycle.

NATIONAL INSTITUTE ON ALCOHOL ABUSE AND ALCOHOLISM (NIAAA)

www.NIAAA.NIH.gov

The NIAAA provides leadership in the national effort to reduce alcohol-related problems. Its site is packed full of information and educational pieces.

OVEREATERS ANONYMOUS

www.OA.org

Overeaters Anonymous offers a program of recovery from compulsive eating using the Twelve Steps and Twelve Traditions of OA. Worldwide meetings and other tools provide a fellowship of experience, strength, and hope where members respect one another's anonymity. OA charges no dues or fees; it is self-supporting through member contributions. OA is not just about weight loss, gain or maintenance; or obesity or diets. It addresses physical, emotional, and spiritual well-being. It is not a religious organization and does not promote any particular diet. If you want someone you love to stop compulsive overeating, this is a great place to start and to find meetings in your area.

SUBSTANCE ABUSE & MENTAL HEALTH SERVICES ADMINISTRATION

www.SAMHSA.gov

SAMHSA's vision is: a life in the community for everyone. To realize this vision, the agency has sharply focused its mission on building resilience and facilitating recovery for people with or at risk for mental or substance-use disorders. You'll find plenty of helpful information here, and many resources to sift through.

XA SPEAKERS

www.XA-Speakers.org

This is a rich online resource for audio recordings of support groups online, from Al-Anon to Narcotics Anonymous to Overeaters Anonymous and others.

Appendix II: Some Helpful Forms

1. HIPAA Disclosure Authorization Form (blank)
2. HIPAA Disclosure Authorization Form (example)
3. What to Pack
4. Meeting Sign-in Sheet

HIPAA DISCLOSURE AUTHORIZATION FORM

Full Name _____

I hereby authorize _____ to use or disclose my
                                        (Discloser)

protected health information related to _____
                                           (Type of Information)

to _____ for the following purpose:
                           (Recipient)

_____

_____

- I understand that I may inspect or copy the protected health information described by this authorization.

- I understand that, at any time, this authorization may be revoked, when the office that receives this authorization receives a written revocation, although that revocation will not be effective as to the disclosure of records whose release I have previously authorized, or where other action has been taken in reliance on an authorization I have signed. I understand that my health care and the payment for my health care will not be affected if I refuse to sign this form.

- I understand that information used or disclosed, pursuant to this authorization, could be subject to redisclosure by the recipient and, if so, may not be subject to federal or state law protecting its confidentiality.

_____   _____
        Date   Signature of Individual or Representative

                            _____
                      Authority or Relationship to Individual, if Representative

EXPIRATION DATE: This authorization will expire on _____

If no date or event is stated, the expiration date will be six years from the date of this authorization.

COPY PROVIDED: The subject of this authorization shall receive a copy of this authorization, when signed.

HIPAA DISCLOSURE AUTHORIZATION FORM

Full Name Connie Cottauge _____

I hereby authorize Seabrook House Treatment Center _____ to use or disclose my
                                         (Discloser)

protected health information related to Healthcare and Mental Health _____
                                                     (Type of Information)

to Brad Lamm _____ for the following purpose:
                     (Recipient)

 to help coordinate insurance involvement and family education work _____

_____

- I understand that I may inspect or copy the protected health information described by this authorization.

- I understand that, at any time, this authorization may be revoked, when the office that receives this authorization receives a written revocation, although that revocation will not be effective as to the disclosure of records whose release I have previously authorized, or where other action has been taken in reliance on an authorization I have signed. I understand that my health care and the payment for my health care will not be affected if I refuse to sign this form.

- I understand that information used or disclosed, pursuant to this authorization, could be subject to redisclosure by the recipient and, if so, may not be subject to federal or state law protecting its confidentiality.

_____   _____
      Date   Signature of Individual or Representative

                    _____
                    Authority or Relationship to Individual, if Representative

EXPIRATION DATE: This authorization will expire on _____
If no date or event is stated, the expiration date will be six years from the date of this authorization.

COPY PROVIDED: The subject of this authorization shall receive a copy of this authorization, when signed.

What to Pack

Clients should pack seven to ten days of comfortable, casual clothing. Your clothing should reflect a healthy attitude toward recovery. No alcohol or drug images on clothing.

Workout clothing for exercise as you desire.

Health Insurance ID card and/or prescription card for medications. Driver's license for ID

All toiletries, e.g., toothbrush, toothpaste, shaving cream, deodorant. Also, don't forget sunblock. No toiletries with alcohol are allowed.

Sealed packs of cigarettes as needed; no cigarettes are sold on-site. Individually wrapped cigars only.

Small clock radio for nightstand.

Pillow if you prefer the comfort of sleeping with your own.

Slippers and/or flip-flops and bathrobes and shower shoes.

Belts as needed.

Umbrella, jacket, or sweater (some campuses are large and consist of many buildings).

No more than $200.00 spending money.

No computer, cell phone, or PDA.

Use of books varies by treatment center. Generally only recovery-related books are allowed. Generally no magazines are allowed. Use of music players varies.

Anything you forget can most likely be found nearby.

PHONE CALLS

Policy regarding outgoing phone calls, especially during the first week or so, varies by treatment center. There are no incoming calls due to federal confidentiality laws.

Meeting Sign-In Sheet

MEETING NAME	DAY	DATE	TYPE	TIME	INITIALS
Ex: SOBER, SANE	MONDAY	6/1/09	AA	6pm	BL

Selected References

Bandura, A., Ross, D., et al. 1961. Transmission of aggressions through imitation of aggressive models. *Journal of Abnormal and Social Psychology* 63:575–582.

Bookwala, J. 2005. The role of marital quality in physical health during the mature years. *Journal of Aging and Health* 17:85–104.

Centers for Disease Control and Prevention. 2009. National Center for Health Statistics. www.cdc.gov/nchs.

Christakis, N. A., and Fowler, J. H. 2007. The spread of obesity in a large social network over 32 years. *New England Journal of Medicine* 357:370–379.

————. 2008. Dynamic spread of happiness in a large social network: Longitudinal analysis over 20 years in the Framingham Heart Study. *British Journal of Medicine* 337:a2338.

Cunningham, M. R., Shamblen, S. R., et al. 2005. Social allergies in romantic relationships: Behavioral repetition, emotional sensitization, and dissatisfaction in dating couples. *Personal Relationships* 12:273–295.

De Vogli, R., Chandola, T., and Marmot, M. G. 2007. Negative aspects of close relationships and heart disease. *Archives of Internal Medicine* 167:1951–1957.

DiClemente, C. C., Prochaska, J. O. 1982. Self-change and therapy change of smoking behavior: A comparison of processes of change in cessation and maintenance. *Addictive Behaviors* 7:133–142.

Garrett, J., Landau J., et al. 1998. The ARISE Intervention. Using family and network links to engage addicted persons in treatment. *Journal of Substance Abuse Treatment* 15:333–343.

Huslin, A. 2007. Are you really ready to clean up your act? Maybe you need to understand your bad habits. *Washington Post*, January 2, online at www .washingtonpost.com. Accessed February 2008.

Kottke, T. E., Battista, R. N., et al. 1988. Attributes of successful smoking cessation interventions in medical practice: A meta-analysis of 39 controlled trials. *Journal of the American Medical Association* 259:2883–2889.

Landau, J., and Garrett, J. 2008. Invitational intervention: The ARISE model. *Alcoholism Treatment Quarterly* 26:12.

Landau, J., Garrett J., et al. 2000. Strength in numbers: The ARISE method for mobilizing family and network to engage substance abusers in treatment. A Relational Intervention Sequence for Engagement. *The American Journal of Drug and Alcohol Abuse* 26:379–398.

Walker, M. S., Larsen, R. J., et al. 2004. Smoking urges and relapse among lung cancer patients: Findings from a preliminary retrospective study. *Preventive Medicine* 39:449–457.